THE LIBERTY CRISIS

THE LIBERTY CRISIS

Bruce G. Siminoff

Glenbridge Publishing Ltd.

Copyright © 1995 by Bruce G. Siminoff

All rights reserved. Except for brief quotations in critical articles or reviews, this book or parts thereof must not be reproduced in any form without permission in writing from the publisher. For further information contact Glenbridge Publishing Ltd., Lakewood, CO 80232.

Library of Congress Catalog Card Number: LC 94-76347

International Standard Book Number: 0-944435-27-0

Printed in the U.S.A.

To my children, so that
they may grow up with
freedom at their sides

One day through the primeval wood,
  A calf walked home, as all calves should;
But made a trail all bent askew,
  A crooked trail, as all calves do.
Since then three hundred years have fled,
  And I infer the calf is dead.
But still he left behind his trail,
  And thereby hangs my moral tale.

  The Calf Path
  Sam Walter Foss (1858-1911)

Contents

Introduction

1. Our Regulatory Nightmare	1
2. The Bill of Rights and Freedom	48
3. How Regulation Affects Our Lives	56
4. Freedom's Worst Enemy—Environmental Hysteria	70
5. Freedom and the Economy	108
6. The Sheriff of Nottingham	130
7. Big Brother is Watching You	154
8. We Are Not Being Heard	178
9. Helping Others	198
10. The Liberty Index	216
11. Conclusion	229

Appendices:

I. Glossary of Superfund Terms	259
II. Regulation and the Price Per Life	262
III. Cancer Risk Assessment May Harm Health	263

Notes   266

Acknowledgments

My thanks are extended to my sons, John A. and James W., for guidance and proofreading, and to my wife, Anne Elizabeth, who helped editorially and was most supportive during the project.

Special appreciation goes to JoAnn Chaplin for typing; James A. Keene, Mark Lipton and John Galandak for editing and suggestions.

I wish to thank the following who granted permission to quote from articles appearing therein:

> Dr. Bruce N. Ames, University of California
> Competitive Enterprise Institute
> Fairness to Land Owners Committee
> *Forbes Magazine*
> Heartland Institute
> *Investors Business Daily*
> *Jems Magazine*
> Machine Design
> National Paint and Coatings Association
> *Nations Business*
> *The New York Times*
> *The Observer Tribune*
> Ohio University Press
> Phillip Morris Corporation
> *The Pocono Record*
> Shanley & Fisher
> *The Star Ledger*
> *The Wall Street Journal*
> *Washington Times*
> Wolff & Samson

Introduction

Nothing is more precious than liberty. Without freedom human beings would be doomed to lives of abject weariness. Our forefathers felt oppressed and fled their homelands. Not finding sufficient liberty in the colonies, they revolted and began their own independent nation. It was a nation conceived in pain, and only a very small percentage of the colonists actively supported the goals and aspirations of the rebels. When Thomas Paine, the pamphleteer of the American Revolution, died on June 8, 1809, only six people attended his funeral service in New York. He had helped to give voice to the revolution, but was soon forgotten by those he had helped.

Once the yoke of an oppressive sovereign was unhitched, the colonists set about establishing a contract between the new government and its citizenry. But the Articles of the Confederation did not work, and a constitutional convention followed. That agreement, setting out the details of how to live with one another, was written in the form of our Constitution, with its subsequent addition of the Bill of Rights.

The arguments, compromises, and subsequent agreements worked out at the constitutional convention should be studied and reviewed by all Americans. The founders hoped that the Constitution, that complexly-forged agreement, would serve to protect the newly-freed citizens from tyranny, oppression, and the excessive intrusion of government into the personal affairs of its citizens. Tyranny can take many forms, and our forefathers were well-aware of its numerous disguises; hence they formulated written guarantees as a Bill of Rights. These early Americans learned of these transgressions from personal experience, not merely the specter of it.

They feared a future tyrannical government. So, the Second Amendment to the Constitution permitted the bearing of arms by a well-regulated militia of citizens. The second amendment was specifically created as a warning to future governments that armed citizens, separately or together as a militia, could deter future attempts at despotism. The right to indictment by a grand jury and trial by a jury of one's peers was viewed as security against government's attempt to use unjust prosecution as a way to stifle dissent or coerce behavior.

Unfortunately, while the words of our founding fathers still remain, many of their insightful and hard-won protections have slowly, yet continually been eroded through the pressures of special interest groups, the ignorance or indifference of our elected officials, the federal courts, and the fifth estate, our unelected bureaucracy. The excessive zeal of lawmakers and unfettered bureaucracies have jeopardized our cherished freedoms. In many ways we have circled back nearly two hundred and twenty years to the point of inspiration of the American Revolution. Some of the same issues are haunting us once again. Here are just a few examples.

Under environmental regulations an individual can be held responsible for crimes that he didn't commit and imprisoned if his business runs short of money (Chapter 4). The prohibition against ex post facto laws has been voided by many environmental as well as tax statutes (Chapter 4). The right against self- incrimination has been trampled by various government regulations. Private property is no longer as private as it once was, and even farmers can be accused of various misdeeds for the mere usage of water in their normal agricultural operations (Chapter 6).

What the founders never foresaw was a tyranny engendered by overwhelming paperwork, fanatical bureaucrats, and a vast web

Introduction xiii

of regulations, creating a stranglehold on many normal human endeavors. As you will see, this modern-day oppression has infected our culture and diminished the rights of all Americans. Why have Americans permitted this to happen? The answer remains somewhat of a mystery, although it is explored herein.

This book belongs to no political spectrum. It is not a book written for Democrats, Republicans, Libertarians, or Perot supporters. Rather, the problems cut across party lines and touch all of us. No one, regardless of his or her political viewpoint, can be immune from the unfairness of the changes that have occurred.

From the 1770s to the 1950s, America achieved an admittedly imperfect balance between unfettered individualism and reasonable regulation for the public good. In the late 1950s and early 1960s this balance began to shift. Rules, regulations, and bureaucratic growth began to emerge as a new dynamic force in American life.

During this time the goal of the people and their government was to create a "perfect" society with a minimum of unhappiness and a responsible concern for injustice. Since the goals were viewed as positives, the means to achieve them were not critically examined. Bureaucracy grew and took on a life of its own. In a relatively few years, Congressional employment grew to over ten thousand persons. Bureaus began to micromanage all aspects of American life, and then created rules to protect their turf. The rule makers insulated themselves and became distanced from the general population.

Bureaucratic growth was not invented by Americans in the 1960s. The kings in medieval Europe required castles and moats. Then came the lords, then the castle, then the moat. Then taxes were needed to maintain the castle, and soldiers were needed to protect the moat. The castle was needed to protect the lords and also served to distance them from the people.

In the United States from the middle of this century, rules and regulations grew so fast that they produced a topsy-turvy effect. In the 1980s, laws to protect the environment seemed to be a needed societal requirement. In answer to the issue, the bureaucrats expanded that need to include collateral issues only vaguely related to the original need. For example, heavy fines are now administered for late paperwork, missed deadlines, or minor infractions (Chapter 4). These minor paperwork misdeeds do not pollute the environment. The original goal was to protect the environment, but during the process, the goal appeared to be to protect and enlarge the bureaucracy.

During the same period our society has developed a "nasty syndrome." We in America treat each other badly. This change seems to be traceable to the Vietnam War era. The "nasty syndrome" can be exemplified in both normal and in most unusual circumstances. In California a state exam is required to become certified as a Paramedic (Chapter 9). However, all fifty counties have established their own, individual licensing procedures. A paramedic has to take a test and *pay a fee in each county* in which he practices, after the state test. That annoying bureaucratic extension of insanity effectively limits the state's licensing procedure and twists the intent from societal protection to revenue raising and bureau building. The question to be asked about California Paramedic licensing is, "Are we protecting public health, or simply creating a public nuisance?" Here, the duplication spawns paperwork, creates more fees, but in the end, shortchanges the people needing medical care. Or perhaps the end result is designed just to protect a bureaucracy!

Unfortunately, rules, regulations, and bureaucrats have gone far beyond intelligent limits, exceeding rationality in many areas. The growth of nonproductive bureaucracies have sapped our economy, contributed to the loss of jobs, and caused business to move out of the United States. It has created a climate where government views those in the regulated community as the "enemy."

More importantly, we, the citizens of America, have ceded, without a fight, many of our freedoms to unelected rule makers.

With the indifference or cowardice of our elected leaders, the bureaucrats have created their own protected enclaves. They have continued to spew out rules and regulations that have materially eroded basic freedoms and have altered our personal and family lives. Our elected representatives appear to be insensitive to this growing menace.

The Liberty Crisis shows the depth of the problem and offers solutions. If left unchecked, an errant bureaucracy can erode our rights as individuals. Should you believe that protection will come from our existing laws, lawmakers, or courts, one thought is necessary. The courts have generally accepted an agency's explanation as expert testimony. With this precedent, the plaintiff, or person trying to seek justice, must convince the court that *the expert is wrong*. A petitioner thus begins his travail with two strikes against him, not to mention the cost of the court action itself.

Only you and I can solve these problems. If, together, we fail — there is no one else.

Chapter 1

Our Regulatory Nightmare

"If laws could speak for themselves, they would first complain of the lawyers who wrote them."

Lord Halifax

On Sunday, September 6, 1992, the New York Giants were playing the opening game of their football season against the San Francisco Forty-Niners. It was a cheerless day, misty, cold, and drizzling.

Early in the game San Francisco had taken the lead; the score was then seventeen to seven. The Giants were driving for a touchdown in an attempt to narrow the gap to three points. They had maneuvered downfield and went into a passing formation. Phil Simms, the quarterback, faded back, looked for a receiver, but couldn't find one open. He moved to his left and met a huge Forty-Niner, who sacked him with a bone crushing tackle and an inglorious ten yard loss.

The lineman, seeing the near mortal blow he had dealt to the Giants' chances, spontaneously commenced a short animated dance in celebration of the event. Just as quickly, two yellow flags went down, thrown by two different officials. The stands grew silent since the crowd sensed that the infraction could be another turning point. Was the penalty to be holding, face masking, roughing the quarterback, or? The answer was none of the above. The penalty had been assessed for an "illegal demonstration." Players, under NFL rules, are prohibited from dancing, waving their arms, or actively demonstrating following a successful sacking of the quarterback or any other such triumph. They are expected to remain unexcited about their individual efforts.

John Madden, announcing for CBS-TV, saw it differently and mused, "That guy was penalized for being too happy. . .They shouldn't have rules like that." Madden's comment was quite incisive.

The above incident clearly shows what a little overzealous rule making can bring about. But like the N.F.L. rule against "being happy," such strange rule making has been tacitly accepted by many Americans. We have accepted rules that not only limit our "being happy," but also diminish our inherited rights and privileges won by our ancestors at great personal cost.

It is axiomatic that rules are part of life. As small children, we are taught that we can't play with fire, can't run into the street, and shouldn't put our heads into a hot oven. No baseball or football game would be playable without rules or be manageable without umpires to enforce them. This is not a book proposing anarchy. It is a book about over-zealous rule making, bureaucratic excesses, and the resulting erosion of our liberty.

So, where, when, and how did these problems begin? How did we lose our liberty simply by agreeing to what we believe are the rules of the game? Obviously, the greatest risks occur when laws or regulations start off as sensible and then become overbearing, arbitrary, or capricious. Few start out with evil intent. Rules generally have their roots in the public good.

Much of the mischief is reinforced when politicians, congressional committees, and the courts take sides with the professional regulators, because "they are the experts." Combine freedom with a protected bureaucrat and you have a potentially explosive mixture. When you add into this compound the costs of defending oneself or fighting errant regulators, the mixture becomes

Our Regulatory Nightmare 3

increasingly dangerous. If rule making exceeds its initial boundaries, then freedom is threatened.

Government began its excess of regulatory zeal in the 1960s. It has since intruded and dominated our very lives. Many unfortunate regulations can be unmasked by the single question: "How overzealous is it?" Let us examine a few documented cases in which citizens were adversely affected by aberrant rule making.

On a warm weekend in the Spring of 1992 a neighborhood group put a plan into motion to defend their children against violence and their community against crime. The idea evolved from a true sense of collective citizen involvement. Our forefathers would have been proud of this neighborhood's spirit, goals, and action plan.

It was in the Bronx, a borough of New York City, that a group of citizens had been galvanized to clean up the hazards of an abandoned lot. The property had become dangerous to children, passersby, and the community at large. On this abandoned street corner, people had dumped garbage, syringes, drug paraphernalia, dead animals, and the like. The parcel, which was a corner lot, had been used by neighborhood school children as a path or a short cut to school and play. Perceiving a clear and present danger to their kids, a group of local parents were moved into action.

In addition to the obviousness of strewn debris were natural hiding places created by dumped refrigerators, old television sets, and kitchen appliances. Drug abusers, muggers, and other human hazards populated the lot at night causing fear and distress in the neighborhood. The police had logged numerous complaints, but nothing had been done.

Finally, a community leader stepped forward. He galvanized the local citizens, church groups, the local fire station, and nearby businessmen into action. He urged them to do something about it themselves. Subsequently, an ad hoc group was organized, planned a strategy, picked a weekend, and set out to attack the problem. They would clean up the lot themselves, without government assistance.

Each constituency contributed its component of strength to resolve the problem. The fire department set up emergency lights, neighbors supplied manpower, and local eateries sent free food and drinks. A motivated contractor supplied two dump trucks, a foreman, and a bucket loader. Hardware stores donated shovels, and a lumber yard gave wheelbarrows. A local parish priest was heard to remark, "It's a miracle."

Execution of the plan was to commence on a Friday afternoon, working eight consecutive six-hour shifts until Sunday night, when cleanup activities were to end. Since the area was totally illuminated, all shifts could be equally effective. With dozens of citizens pitching in, the targeted completion date of Sunday afternoon was achieved, nearly on schedule. The lot had been picked clean. From an eyesore, there evolved a safe, clean site, which doubled as a secure short cut for neighborhood kids and pedestrians. Places to hide were eliminated. Top soil was donated and small shrubs planted. All at once, everyone stood back and felt good about themselves and their community efforts. There was a feeling of civic pride in the Bronx that Sunday.

The leader of the project was interviewed by the press and stated publicly that all of the involved groups should be given "citizenship awards." A local country music radio station praised the group as a model for citizen action in the five boroughs of New York City. Two religious leaders, who had blessed the effort in a convocation, later praised the cooperation of all ethnic groups. The job had melded the neighborhood into one unit. Case closed?

Well, not quite!

What seemed to be a model of community involvement was promptly derailed when the New York City Sanitation Department

Our Regulatory Nightmare   5

found out about the private successful efforts of the action oriented neighbors.

Instead of the delivery of citizen's medals, at approximately 5 P.M. that Sunday, a dozen New York City Sanitation Police officers, brandishing firearms, descended on the site. Car doors opened and the police surrounded the scene. For their community efforts the leaders, as well as the business contributors, were cited for illegal and errant behavior. As the New York City Sanitation Police saw it, this truancy took two forms, (1) the citizens had not filed for a permit to clean the lot, (2) the donated trucks were not licensed to carry garbage or waste materials within New York City. Fines were threatened in the multi-thousand dollar range.

"How could you dare to clean up a lot without permission?" asked one of the sanitation officers.

In the topsy-turvy world of modern day callous America, the transgression of these citizens almost earned them fines and/or imprisonment — not the citizens' medals they deserved.

Yes, the good citizens were technically required to obtain a permit to clean up and transport the waste. But the bad citizens and drug dealers didn't obtain a permit to create the dump. Muggers and rapists don't ask permission to lurk in the shadows either.

When positive citizen action is strangled by government, we all lose. When good is perceived as bad, and bad as acceptable, we all lose twice. Often, our own bureaucrats turn the tables against us, the law-abiding people. Well-meaning citizens are abused while transgressors often get away with their crimes. The pattern has become more prevalent and shines across the broad spectrum of regulation.

Permits, licenses, rules and regulations are a necessary part of a complex society. No one is born with the right to drive a bus load of passengers without demonstrating the ability to do so. No one should be able to fly a plane without being qualified. But if a license is unfairly delayed or its cost raised to unaffordable levels, then it no longer is a license but a barrier.

Rules are required for many human pursuits. It is the practical application of rule making that is the problem. Let us contrast the sport of "bungee jumping" with rules to regulate the growing and distribution of fruit.

Beginning in 1989, a bungee jumping mania swept the United States from West to East. By 1992 it was estimated by sports industry sources that the new craze represented a $70-$80 million business nationwide. Because of its newness, there were few regulatory encumbrances at the outset.

Because of several accidents and a few reported deaths, government agencies, both state and federal, began to examine bungee jumping. In April 1992, the State of Massachusetts halted all bungee jumps from cranes. In August 1992, New Jersey temporarily halted jumps taking place in amusement parks, giving state inspectors a chance to examine the equipment. In New Jersey, the action taken was the result of a woman jumper who suffered a spinal cord injury in July 1992, allegedly due to a (pre-jump) faulty scale.

At about the same time, Pennsylvania began its own inspections of all amusement areas that utilized portable cranes. By September 1992, approximately thirty states had begun to regulate the industry.

Even the North American Bungee Association welcomed some of the proffered rule making. But like all business owners their fears were that the rules would become overly restrictive and, as a result, seriously impact their businesses. While some of the newly suggested rules were aimed at providing safe equipment, others required that liability insurance coverage be at least $1,000,000. Some states, like Maryland, imposed such stringent rules that the viability of bungee jumping as a sport in that state was threatened.

Our Regulatory Nightmare 7

Jim Morkosky, Maryland's Director of the State's Department of Labor and Industry, safety inspection unit, was quoted as saying:

> Since the state began regulating bungee jumping in November (1992), *none of the 60 companies* (who have contacted us) has been able to comply with the new guidelines.[1]

It is not the intent here to generate a spirited discussion on the rights of bungee jumpers versus state regulators. But a zero to sixty ratio indicates a rather harsh oversight, and just not simple rule making. Should people have a right to bungee jump if they wish to do so? While government does have a public safety responsibility, it also has the obligation to regulate fairly and to reasonably oversee the utilized equipment. Safety must be weighed in a delicate balance with individual liberty.

There is no way to make bungee jumping perfectly safe. The goal should be to improve safety consistent with the economic realities of running a viable commercial enterprise, combined with honest disclosure of the dangers. Regulations, which prohibit bungee jumping, violates the rights of those who want to jump and those who wish to provide jumping facilities.

Safety regulations, which permit any business to function in the public interest, is acceptable. Unfortunately, the trend during the past three decades has permitted regulators to set themselves up as the final arbiters of a citizen's free choice, and as seen in Maryland, no one qualified. Do unelected bureaucrats have the right to decide that no one qualifies?

When regulation exceeds that fine balance of public interest, the citizen loses. Regulation then becomes the tool of the regulators, and free choice is denied, often resulting in oppression. The average citizen doesn't much care one way or another about the success or failure of the zany world of bungee jumping. But, as we shall see, the dangerous trend of rule making has moved from safety and protection toward bureaucratic excesses.

Can we contrast the rule making process as applied to bungee jumping with the regulation of fruit? Fruit is not inherently dangerous. Fruit, in its normal state, does not pose a national health hazard, and would not seem to be the proper subject of a book discussing personal liberty or in any logical framework a reasonable contrast to bungee jumping. But this is not the case.

How many Americans know that it is against federal law for fruit growers to sell peaches that are smaller than $2\frac{7}{16}$ inches in diameter? How many Americans know that nectarines smaller than $2\frac{3}{8}$ inches in diameter are likewise prohibited? The United States Department of Agriculture imposes these regulations on California farmers. Should a farmer sell fruit that is smaller than the rules allow, he can be subjected to a substantial fine and/or penalty. These regulations are not simply imposed by faceless bureaucrats from Washington. Rather, they are enacted through a delegated system called "The California Tree Fruit Agreement." These regulations are voted on by the fruit growers themselves and then imposed with the force of law. Sixty-six percent of the growers can impose economic hardships on the other thirty-three percent by arbitrarily determining an acceptable fruit size. Many farmers contend that this type of rule making is simply a way for the larger growers to force the smaller growers out of the fruit business.

Our nation was founded on principles intended to protect the minority from the tyranny of the majority. Majorities were not supposed to impose their will on minorities by subverting the law to advance their special interests. On the economic side regulating the size of fruit allows the growers to control the consumer market place. Whereas bungee jumping is a sport that is a legitimate target of government safety supervision, the regulation of the size of fruit is hardly a societal need. Please understand, we are talking about the size of fruit — not health hazards posed by spoiled fruit. In the former, overregulation just provides its own justification; there is no logic or rationale. While we the consumers are just having the wool pulled over our eyes, the minority farmers can lose their farms.

Where can overregulation lead? In his famous book, *1984*, George Orwell predicted that surveillance devices would be tracking the average citizen. The amazing Mr. Orwell was only a few years off on his prediction.

During the late 1980s in Texas, cameras were installed along the road to record and photograph speeders. These devices were intended to introduce a kind of automated "Robo-Cop" system to the Texas highways. Interestingly, it has been reported that many of these spy camera devices were actually destroyed by ordinary citizens. Texans did not take kindly to being observed and ticketed by remote control. In several other states during 1992 similar proposals were made in state legislatures to install "Photo Radar Computers." Some of these proposals called for the devices to be installed along highways and monitored by the State Police. Like their android brethren in Texas, these machines would photograph cars, ascertain whether they were speeding, and automatically generate a summons by the mail. The citizens so ticketed would lose their right to face an accuser or explain the circumstances to a human being. Likewise, if a car was borrowed or stolen, a citizen would have to prove after the fact that he was not the driver at the time of the incident.

Every citizen has the right to know the charge and confront his accuser. A machine offers no such comfort. George Orwell coined the phrase, "Big Brother is watching you." Photo radar is a good example.

What would be the next step after highway photo machines became law? Perhaps photography in high crime areas? But where would surveillance start and where would it end? Photographic policing power is full of potential abuses. This technique, if widely adopted, would simply increase the citizen's suspicion and contempt for the law. Photo surveillance is a violation of one's right to privacy and has no place in a free society. Fortunately for the citizens of most states where photo surveillance has been proposed, the idea was rejected. The citizens of Texas, a braver lot, acted independently. They trashed the surveillance units.

Perhaps the scariest part of the photo radar scheme was that it was suggested by elected officials, and that a democratically elected legislator would seriously consider it. Modern-day Americans seem to be viewed by their elected government officials as objects or subjects, certainly not as equals. H. Ross Perot's admonishment during his presidential campaign in 1992 was right on target.

> Washington has created a government that comes at us instead of a government that comes *from* us. . . . You are the owners of this country. Nobody else can do the job. Our system has been corrupted because we weren't exercising our responsibilities as owners.[2]

One of the reasons that we are losing our liberties is that we have abdicated our responsibility as the owners of the country. We have permitted elected officials to assume a privileged lifestyle upon taking office. What we have is what we as a people have allowed politicians to give us, after keeping their share of our money.

Our Regulatory Nightmare

J. P. Morgan once described the banking business. His response is also applicable to the current government attitude regarding the citizenry. "The banking business is the only business on earth where the bankers take the money that you give them, and then believe it to be theirs."

When you combine surveillance with absurd rule making, real mischief results. The mental process seems to start with, (1) a regulatory lie (2) ignoring legal protections (3) tell another lie (4) believe the lie (5) enforce the lie (6) finally, fine you for violating the lie! If you cloak your actions in socially acceptable slogans, then the results are not challenged.

In Chester, New Jersey, during the fall of 1989, two men in a boat were engaged in photographing the property of Mrs. Cynthia Strelec. They later identified themselves as New Jersey State Policemen. They inquired about the ownership of the property and subsequently determined that it was owned by Mr. and Mrs. Strelec. Soon after, they informed the homeowners that they would be given a summons for "placing debris in and/or adjacent to a waterway."[3] The fine would be $100 plus $15.00 for court costs.

The homeowner's offense was based on absurd and unnecessary environmental regulations. The problem was falling leaves! Mrs. Strelec had raked the leaves in her yard and piled them in a mound at the rear of her property. The Black River Wildlife Management Area (B.R.W.M.A.) abutted the rear of her home. When a wind blew, the leaves were lifted into the air as they often are in the fall. The wind carried them to a hillside area near Lake Lillian, which was under BRWMA's management. As specified in their summons this everyday happening was considered to be "polluting" by the State Police.

This power was engendered under various regulations of the New Jersey Department of Environmental Protection, which has become infamous for absurd rule making. The Department has seen fit to cast its power over leaves, grass clippings, and other normally occurring events of nature. Although this may be viewed by some as an amusing example of bureaucratic excess, it was not humorous to the property owner. Actions of this type by bureaucrats not only offend one's sense of fair play, but they light the path to deeper erosions of individual liberty.

Here is a midwestern nightmare to contemplate: Property owners in Iowa and the Midwest have wetland regulation problems that are different from those in the east or south. Here, the "voluntary" compliance controls in the farm bill, commonly called swampbuster regulations, are important. But Iowa farmers are also subject to the United States Army Corps of Engineers (The Corps) and the United States Environmental Protection Agency (EPA) jurisdiction. The Corps, however, generally allows the United States Department of Agriculture (USDA) Soil Conservation Service (SCS) to do the day-to-day enforcement, allowing Corps personnel to focus their attention on those property owners who do not participate in the government's farm programs.

One such property owner is Mahaska County farmer, Mark Groenendyk. In April, 1989 Mark purchased a poorly-maintained 284-acre farm located in the flood plain of the South Skunk River. Levees, diversions, and drainage ditch improvements, already on the farm, had fallen into disrepair, and parts of the crop land had been abandoned. There was also a stand of timber, reducing crop productivity.

More than 70 years ago the South Skunk River had been channelized. For miles both upstream and down from Mark, the flood plain had been cleared and converted to highly-productive grain farms. Mark was determined to make his farm as productive as his neighbors. He wanted to clear his trees to till more land and rebuild and extend his levees.

The SCS told him there was no problem since he was not in any farm program, and verifying with the Iowa Department of Natural Resources (DNR) that he only needed a flood plain permit for a new levee, Mark hired an engineering firm to prepare his permit application. Mark and his father then set out to log his timber and to improve his property for crop production.

On October 30, 1989, biologists from the Corps visited Mark's farm and informed him that he had filled wetlands. A letter followed from the Corps directing him to apply for an after-the-fact permit or be exposed to a fine of up to $25,000 per day. They also ordered Mark to "cease and desist all unauthorized activities." Shortly thereafter biologists from the United States Fish & Wildlife Service came to the farm and charged that Mark had impacted more than 100-acres of wetlands.

With a water table normally five feet or more below the surface, Mark rejected the Park's jurisdiction — which would have resulted if he filed a permit application. Instead, Mark did agree to allow the Corps to do a wetland delineation on his farm.

A platoon of Corps personnel from as far away as Vicksburg, Mississippi, descended upon Mark's farm for two days in September, 1990. They used a methodology in the now-discredited 1989 "wetland manual." At no time did they find water within four feet of the ground surface. In a strained assumption they concluded that Mark's farm just barely managed to satisfy the seven day flooding criteria for wetland hydrology. Thus they declared 95 percent of the farm to be wetland. The presence of hydric soils confirmed the "experts" hydrology assumption. The possibility that the hydric soils (soil requiring an abundance of moisture) could be relics of conditions existing prior to the river channelization and that there were no wetlands on adjacent cropland of the same soil type and elevation were ignored.

In a March 5, 1991, letter the Corps ordered Mark to fill in his ditches, to commence reforestation of his property, and to submit a plan for mitigating damages to "waters of the United States." If this were not done by July 1, 1991, his file would be turned over to the United States Justice Department for prosecution.

Unbeknownst to Mark, he had been selected as a target of the Corps and EPA plan — labeled "Wetland Enforcement Initiative." Each region was to file legal actions against several "high-profile" violators on the same day. Simultaneous press conferences would be used to gain maximum public exposure, and all "targets" would be prosecuted as warnings to the rest of us. These cases were to be filed on Earth Day, April 20, 1991, and again in September, 1991.

Upon learning of this initiative the White House stopped it, but that did not deter the Corps pursuit of Mark. On March 2, 1992, legal counsel to the Corps advised Mark to comply with its directive or face prosecution.

At great expense, Mark hired an attorney, an engineer, and a biologist to assist him in his defense. Since they sought a determination from the SCS, they believed that agency would be more reasonable. But the Corps immediately began pressuring the SCS to be in lock step with them. A Corps official was heard to say, "We are going after Groenendyk and we don't want you to buckle. It will hurt our case."

In May 1992 Mark endured a sham of an appeal hearing at the SCS area office level. Mark submitted an extensive engineering study showing that of the 111 floods that had been recorded over the previous forty-seven years, normal floods had not inundated his farm for the required seven days. Evidence from twenty-three monitoring holes drilled on the farm also showed that the water depth was normally four to five feet below ground levels.

Rather than do a proper analysis, the SCS ignored Mark's documents and refused to believe that the drainage ditches on his farm were there prior to his purchasing it. They ruled that 150 acres of Mark's farm were jurisdictional wetlands.

Mark immediately appealed to the SCS state office, which took over 150 days to respond, ignoring the fifteen day response requirement. Claiming they did not have enough information, the SCS wanted to do another four-day survey on his farm. Mark respectfully declined to allow the inspection. He now awaits their decision. If it is adverse, he will appeal to the national office and possibly thereafter to the courts.

Mark had allowed numerous government officials on his farm on seven different occasions over a two year period, had bent over backwards to furnish the information they demanded, and had spent thousands of dollars defending his right to the economic use of his property. The regulators have spent thousands more of our tax dollars to force his submission.

But what of the Corps' threats to prosecute? In November, 1992 a government car was seen parked by Mark's farm with two men watching Mark work in his field. Suspicious neighbors followed the car. The two were identified as Corps and Justice officials.

Mark could have solved his problem by giving the government his farm!

Mark is 25-years old. On January 3, 1993, his wife, Tammy, gave birth to the couple's first child, Bryant. You will not find a more decent, moral and honest man than Mark. This young farmer should be the pride of his country, not its target for incarceration.[4]

As the twentieth century begins to ebb, its last decade will cast an ominous shadow on individual liberty and property rights by the use of a relatively new word "wetlands."

Property owners, whether businessmen or not, are having their assets and dreams impinged by an innocuous sounding federal rule book entitled: "Wetlands Regulations." But unlike leaves and grass, water-related problems can get serious. As the above story shows, if the United States Army Corps of Engineers or the EPA were to make a determination that your property runs afoul of a *purported wetlands site,* it is up to you to prove you are not abusing the regulations. The mere charge can place you in the position of proving that an unfounded assertion is false. Such proof can be financially ruinous.

Take the case of Melvin Dominique of Lafayette, Louisiana. Mr. Dominique purchased more than thirty acres of refuse-laden land to set up a crawfish farm. He mortgaged his home to secure the necessary capital to clean up the property. "After readying the property, Mr. Dominique constructed new levees and ponds in order to raise his commercial crops of crawfish. Soon after completing this project he was notified by the United States Army Corps of Engineers that he had despoiled an area designated on their maps as wetlands."[5]

Shortly thereafter the Corps ordered Mr. Dominique to destroy the levees, or be charged with *criminal and civil* environmental violations. Mr. Dominique had to comply since he did not have the financial means to fight back. After giving in to the Corps, the property now cannot be used for the intended commercial purposes, hence, its value plummeted. Given a Hobson's Choice, Mr. Dominique was placed in the position of losing his home as well as his land, all because of a *map in an Army engineer's office.* His alleged offense was not that he polluted aquifers, rivers, and lakes, but because he was there. Conversely, Mr. Dominique's efforts were positive to the community. He wanted to turn a junkyard into a commercial enterprise.

How does a property owner whose only crime is to clean up and develop a piece of property defend himself against such powerful allegations? If an average citizen were to persist in his own defense, he would quickly be impoverished by the cost of such a battle against the impressive batteries of federal lawyers. On the other hand, if one simply accedes to the demands, then the value of his property can be depressed. A property has little commercial or economic use once it has been determined to run afoul of wetlands regulations. Unfortunately, the definition of wetlands has been so broadened by the bureaucrats that nearly every piece of property in America might currently qualify as wetlands, at one time or another.

The retired official who once headed the Army Corps of Engineers Regulatory Office, Bernard Goode, publicly agreed that the Corps-inspired wetlands assault on property owners is unfair:

> Even when I was in government the wetlands program seemed wrong, I've come to know just how unfair, outrageous, and abusive to land owners it really is.[6]

Just what is our current national wetlands policy? It is important to look at the guidelines promulgated by the Clinton Administration in 1993, so that the background of this policy is understood. The Clinton Administration:

- **Established a stringent policy that resources use with unclear guidelines.**
  The definition of wetlands is that of the National Academy of Sciences.

- **Codified "no net loss" of wetlands**
  Clinton has taken Bush's campaign promise two steps further. Not only did he issue an executive order mandating "no net loss" but also mandated a long-term goal of *increasing* the quality and quantity of the nation's wetlands.

- **Streamlined permit decisions**
  The policy gave the United States Army Corps of Engineers one year to modify its regulations to set a deadline from sixty days from receipt of a completed application to ninety days from public notice. This should make very little difference since the Corps rarely met its regulatory deadlines and the new policy contains no penalty provisions.

- **Established an appeal process**
  The policy gave the Corps one year to develop an administrative appeal process. Landowners will not be going to an independent party with their grievances. They will appeal to the very bureaucrats who hassled them in the first place. The process allows third parties to participate, and requires the landowner to appeal before initiating judicial action, thereby extending due process.

- **Expanded regulated discharge**
  As desired by the bureaucrats, the policy expanded their regulatory reach from dredged and fill material to excavation, ditching, channelization, landclearing, pilings, etc. Called the Tullock rule (from the North Carolina Wildlife Federation v. Tullock) the policy greatly widened the regulators' purviews.

- **Ignored private property rights**
  The policy states: if a landowner "believes that any government action amounts to a taking, the courts are available to review such claims and to determine whether compensation is due."

The problem is that this sounds fair, but it isn't. It takes years to pursue these cases, and the costs are astronomical. Most citizens cannot afford this kind of justice.

The Clinton Administration wetlands policy did very little to help restore fairness and property rights to homeowners, farmers, and businessmen.

It's one thing to be told to remove levees, but another to go to jail, as Mr. Ocie Mills and his son, Carey, found out. Their crime was that they unclogged a drainage ditch located on their own property located in Florida. This act permitted soil to move "illegally" onto their land. "Both father and son were given a jail term for their actions. As a result of unclogging their drain, the government prevailed in their argument that they had *trespassed* on a section of wetlands which occupied a corner of their property."[7]

Compromising personal liberty is never funny. But some actions taken by mindless regulatory zealots evoke a black humor. In 1983, the central valley of California entered its first year of a five-year drought cycle. By 1988 the area was in a full-fledged drought. As William Lyons and his family found out, federal wetlands regulations respected neither citizens' property rights nor natural drought conditions.

Mr. Lyons had received approval to convert a piece of his property from grazing area to farming. Shortly thereafter a United States Government agency intervened, insisting that the area that Mr. Lyons intended to farm was in reality a disguised wetland. The Government then informed Mr. Lyons that he could be given a jail sentence as well as fines of $5,000 per day if he persisted in attempting to grow crops on that location.

In that geographical section of California rainfall usually averages ten to fifteen inches per year, hence the concept of wetlands, itself, was and is ludicrous. The Lyons family chose to fight the government. The outcome is as yet unknown.

Laws, rules, and regulations must be promulgated with a view to their cause and effect. Individual rights and the economic concerns of those being regulated must also be considered. Think of rule making as a drawing from a pool of water. Each cupful removed from the pool leaves a half pint less in the pool. Eventually, all the water is gone. If done slowly and unobtrusively, the water can disappear before we are aware of it.

We have seen the wholesale appropriation of private property by an expansive interpretation of the word "wetlands" as found in the federal regulations. The definition appears in the Clean Water Act of 1972, which "forbids the discharge of dredged or fill materials without a permit into navigable waters of the U.S.A." However, the definition as promulgated by the EPA defines "navigable waters" to encompass "waters such as intrastate lakes, rivers, streams, mudflats, sandflats, sloughs, prairie potholes, wet meadows, playa lakes, natural ponds," etc.

Although the protection of "wetlands" as contemplated by the original 1972 law is warranted, these expansive regulations have caused havoc to many American property owners. The protection of real wetlands is a worthy cause. Unfortunately, the emotions of the issue have ensnared citizens who farm, use water, or just have dampness on their property.

A builder located in the state of Illinois found out about wetlands the hard way. He attempted to obtain a permit to develop a forty-acre parcel. Located there was a small, clay-lined, slightly recessed area on one part of his property. The section in question only encompassed two percent of the total square footage of the acreage under development.

When it rained, however, this spot filled up with water, since it had old clay underpinnings and little natural absorption. Without rain the area was very dry. To the property owner's dismay the EPA asked the following question. "What would happen if migratory birds used the site as a stopover on their northbound or southbound flights?"⁸ The project would be judged based upon the answer. However, the query was much akin to Henny Youngman's famous question, "How often do you beat your wife?" Since no definitive response was possible, the company, which had already flattened the clay-lined area, was ordered to reverse the process and restore the property to its original condition.

Undaunted by science or logic, the EPA assessed a penalty against the developer. The fine for flattening the depression was set at $100,000. Any delays in compliance with the EPA's "anti-flattening" order would be calculated at $25,000 per day. Most companies or individuals faced with fines of this magnitude are powerless to defend themselves because of the potential economic consequences the fines would engender. The overwhelming power of the agency and the level of their penalties are difficult to fend against. Small business or individuals usually can't fight back due to the sheer weight of the legal costs involved. Justice only exists in cases of this nature if the two competing parties are equal. But that seldom is the case. Few companies can take on the federal government, which is endowed with billions of taxpayer dollars that can be used to beat the challengers into submission. The Illinois developer was denied the use of his property by excessive zeal, overregulation and silliness, each of which had no boundaries.

This story had an unusual ending. The Illinois developer had sufficient financial resources to fight and they won. The absurdity of the EPA's position impressed the federal judge who heard the case. But most of us would not be able to bear the costs of mounting a defense against this out-of-control regulatory juggernaut.

Fortunately, Hoffman Homes stuck it out, and in "Hoffman Homes, Inc. v. EPA," (90-3810, 7th Circuit, 7/19/93) the judge:

> Rejected administrative law judge's finding of EPA jurisdiction over isolated wetland because of potential use of

wetland by migratory birds. While acknowledging that use of wetlands by migratory birds can qualify as connection between interstate commerce thus allowing regulation, in this instance, EPA failed to provide substantial evidence that the area in question was suitable for such use. Court noted that there was no evidence that migratory birds utilized the site and having avoided Area A the migratory birds have thus spoken and submitted their own evidence. We see no reason to argue with them.[9]

The Wall Street Journal observed "in its Wetlands regulation the EPA has wandered far from the language of the statute it enforces, from the Constitution and from traditions of American government."[10]

We have a well-known law on the books entitled, "The Endangered Species Act." The law protects animals but not human beings. Here again the law is misbalanced as John Shuler of Dupuyer, Montana, found out.

Mr. Shuler owns a sheep farm, and one evening in the spring of 1993 he observed a grizzly bear racing for his sheep pens. As it turned out there was not just one bear but several. Mr. Shuler went for his rifle and fired it in the air to scare the bears away.

One of the bears did not scare so easily and headed for the farmer. The farmer perceived a threat to himself, and in self-defense fired three shots into the bear, killing him.

Case closed. Well, not quite closed. Grizzly bears are on the endangered species list. You can't kill one even if your life or property is endangered, as Mr. Shuler found out.

Though the Montana farmer had participated in the government's program to chase the bears away, they had continued to bother his sheep. Mr. Shuler had previously told the Interior

Our Regulatory Nightmare

Department that he had lost over a thousand dollars worth of sheep to the grizzlies. It didn't matter, since his fine of $4,000 for violation of the Endangered Species Act (killing the bear) was levied on him without sympathy.

> Message to farmers everywhere: If your livestock or crops are threatened by an endangered species, you have no alternative but to sit by and let them be decimated, or of course go out of business. . . . most cling to the notion that a man has a right to protect his property as well as his life.[11]

Lest you think you still have the right to defend yourself (or others), think twice. A San Francisco cab driver, who should have received the "citizen of the year award," found himself in deep trouble by performing a public service. He became involved in a situation from which most people would have shied.

When H. Charles Hollom spotted a robbery in progress, he drove in pursuit of a street criminal who had just mugged a Japanese tourist before his very eyes. With the robber still in possession of the tourist's purse, he caught up with the suspect and pinned him to a building with his car. The mugger suffered a broken leg in the process of being captured.

When the police arrived, they arrested the mugger, whose name was McClure, and commended the taxi driver. Mr. McClure was tried and sentenced to jail for ten years for "strong armed robbery." In a normal perception of events it would be reasonable to believe that the story now ended. But it did not.

> The convicted mugger filed a civil damage suit from prison, charging that the taxi driver used excessive force when he subdued McClure. McClure's attorney was quoted as saying "I do not think it is fair to take a 4,000 pound cab and ram someone against a wall.[12]

The hero taxi driver lost. The criminal won. The court ordered Mr. Hollom to pay $24,595 in damages for the use of "excessive force," in subduing the transgressor!

Our system has turned against the good guys; and not just citizens who are willing to get involved. The bureaucrats have also created unreasonable obstacles for those who seek to produce or provide a service. Imagine the District of Columbia government squaring off against the African American owner of a hair braiding salon.

Nationwide there are hundreds of occupations that require licenses. Many are, of course, needed for consumer protection, such as doctors, dentists, chiropractors, and nurses, etc. Unfortunately, in our complex society the bureaucrats license businesses or professions that neither require it nor are worthy of government interference. Some examples are dry cleaners who are licensed in California, computer programmers (proposed in New Jersey), septic tank cleaners, and bee keepers.

The power to license, like the power to tax, if not tightly controlled, can be a way of destroying one's freedom to work.

A hair braiding salon, called Cornrows & Company, had been ordered to cease business because its unlicensed cosmetologists, all ten of them, were performing grooming services on African-American customers.

The owner, Mr. Uqdah, stated that he "only braids hair, and doesn't use chemicals...hence it makes no sense for employees to spend 125 hours learning how to shampoo."[13] The major problem for this Afro-American businessman was that no cosmetology school teaches Afro-American hair braiding. While there are schools that teach a similar trade and would offer a diploma to Mr. Uqdah's ten employees, they are extremely expensive, about $4,000-$5,000 each, or a total of $50,000 if all employees were given the required course. Even after the employees had completed the required course (related but not the same), the skill in question, "hair braiding," would still be formally unlearned. If there is no need for the license, why require it? Has anyone ever been harmed by an uneven haircut?

A *Wall Street Journal* reader, who noted the Cornrows story as I did, offered his own comments in a letter to the editor:

> Recently you chronicled the struggle of Cornrows Inc. in Washington, D.C., to escape excessive and irrelevant Jim Crow-style regulations of that small African-American hair-braiding business. In Massachusetts' Hanover Mall, the Victoria's Secret store had to wall off about one-fourth of its retail space to avoid being forced to install six employee restrooms instead of four. This is based on an arbitrary formula linking the number of square feet to the number of bathrooms. The formula made no allowance for the fact that all the salespeople would have to answer nature's call simultaneously to utilize all that expensive plumbing, and that there is little need for three employee men's rooms in a store that sells women's lingerie.[14]

While the Cornrows example illustrates the power of bureaucrats to needlessly destroy a man's business, New Jersey bureaucrats tried to go one step further in dictating how we are served eggs. In January 1992, the New Jersey State Department of Health adopted regulations requiring "that any eggs served in restaurants, hotels, coffee shops, nursing homes and hospitals be cooked until they are firm."[15] The regulations were promulgated as a response to the department's fear of potential salmonella poisoning. Violators were to be subjected to a $25 to $100 fine per transgression.

The health department, in an explanatory statement, stated that the white part of every cooked egg should be firm to the touch. The yellow portion or the yolk should be beginning to thicken. These requirements would have to be followed for an egg to be legally cooked. A preparation temperature of 140° F. was made part of the regulations in a technical bulletin that accompanied the rule.

Under the proposed Health Department regulations, scrambled eggs would be permitted, but only if thoroughly cooked. Loosely scrambled eggs were to be banned from all of the restaurants doing business in New Jersey. In addition, food preparations made with raw eggs would be likewise prohibited. The banned dishes would include homemade mayonnaise, mousses, meringues, caesar salad, and hollandaise sauce, just to name a few of the targeted delicacies.

Fortunately the "runny egg" regulations, as they came to be known, were subjected to funny salutes by citizens, tirades from restauranteurs, and hundreds of letters to the editors of various newspapers. Even Johnny Carson on the Tonight Show lampooned the whole affair and actually helped bring the inane episode to a close. The Health Department, subjected to such deep and intense ridicule, withdrew the regulation. The whole affair went quietly into history.

The point of the story is that we must ask ourselves a simple overriding question. How did the balance of personal freedom shift so sharply that Health Department officials *could believe they were endowed with such royal prerogatives*? While Americans have naively permitted agencies to chip away at their freedoms, how far will they allow the chipping process to go? Are we willing to permit a new layer of food bureaucrats to mandate what we are to eat?

A public health claim could be made against any food or drink. If we don't wash our carrots, lettuce, or potatoes, for example, then we could be eating dirt or germs. Regulations could be passed almost without letup.

Did you know that ordinary, "healthful" food contains carcinogens? Many foods have concentrations of rodent carcinogens (the measurement is called "Natural Pesticides"), which are normally processed by the human body. Some examples are:

Food	Carcinogen Concentration (PPM)
Parsley	14
Orange Juice	31
Basil	82
Coffee	100
Apples	50[16]

The above chart is simple, and yet thought provoking. Some bureaucrats and ardent environmentalists would have us believe that we are to remove all cancer causing agents from our air, water, and surroundings. They have launched a nationwide effort to enact a one-in-a-million cancer risk for pollution cleanup standards. This standard is unsupported by scientific data but plays well to the fears of a public mislead by the environmental community. The fact is that nature, itself, comes complete with carcinogens, and the body has learned to deal with it over centuries of exposure.

Since the body has its own defense systems that permit us to consume naturally occurring chemical rodent carcinogens in our normal diet, it would appear that nature is out of sync with the "one-in-a-million" environmentalists. Further, our body's own defense system, along with its naturally occurring enzymes, equally ward off synthetic as well as natural assailants, as long as moderation is followed.

Dr. Bruce Ames, of the Division of Biochemistry and Molecular Biology of the University of California, has done substantial work in this area. A speech given by Dr. Ames to the Center for Scientific Ecology on this very subject is reprinted as Appendix III. Please review that appendix to gain an understanding as why scientific truth is more important than unscientific rules and regulations that exaggerate the risks.

Rachel Carson's *Silent Spring* (1962) became the inspiration for the environmental movement. Its elegant prose expressed passionate outrage at the ravaging of beautiful, unspoiled nature by man. Its frightening message was that we are all being injured by deadly poisons (DDT and other pesticides) put out by a callous chemical industry. This message was snapped up by intellectuals and the book sold over a million copies. Many organizations have sprung up to spread Carson's message.

The powder was DDT, which actually saved tens of millions of lives, more than any substance in history with the possible exception of antibiotics. The benefits of DDT were omitted from the book. *Silent Spring* said the American robin was "on the verge of extinction," yet Roger Tory Peterson said it was the most numerous bird on the continent. DDT was highly toxic to mosquitoes, but of very low toxicity to honey bees and higher animals. In the third world, DDT saved millions of lives of children who were exposed to malaria and other insect-borne diseases.

DDT displaced the more toxic and persistent arsenate. DDT was the first of a series of synthetic agricultural chemicals that have advanced public health by increasing the supply and reducing the price of fruits and vegetables. People who eat few fruits and vegetables, compared to those who eat about 4 or 5 portions a day, have about double the cancer rate for most types of cancer and have increased heart disease and cataracts as well. Thus, pesticides lead to lower cancer rates and improved health. Life expectancy has steadily increased in our era of pesticides. Pesticide residues in food are trivial in terms of cancer causation or toxicity. There has never been any convincing evidence that DDT (or pesticide residues in food) has ever caused cancer in man or that DDT had a significant impact on the population of our eagles or other birds.

Carson's fundamental misconception was: "For the first time in the history of the world, every human being is now subjected to contact with dangerous chemicals, from the moment of conception until death." This is nonsense: every chemical is dangerous if the concentration is too high. Moreover, 99.9% of the chemicals humans ingest are natural. For example, 99.99% of the pesticides humans eat are natural pesticides produced by plants to kill off predators. About half of all natural chemicals tested at high dose, including natural pesticides, cause cancer in rodents. People determined to rid the world of synthetic chemicals refuse to face these facts. Risk assessment methods build in huge safety factors for synthetic chemicals while natural chemicals are ignored. Current policy diverts enormous resources from important to unimportant risks.[17]

The one-in-a-million standard, when defined, means that a pollutant should not be permitted to cause one additional cancer death per million persons. This exposure is calculated as one to a million for the duration of a seventy year period. If a cleanup does not meet or exceed this standard, it might not receive approval from the Federal EPA.

In many instances, however, this means that a cleanup must exceed the parameters of natural backgrounds. Yet, "most cleanups under Superfund and other federal programs are done under the one-in-a-million standard."[18]

Why do we accept emotional answers to common sense questions? Could it be that it is simply easier to let someone else do the fighting?

As Americans we have ceded much of our precious freedom by accepting many of the unnecessary limitations on our freedom ordained by the regulatory community. Instead of drawing a line in the sand, we have permitted the expansion of bureaucratic fiat so that almost any law or regulation, even if absurd, wasteful, or costly, can be promulgated. The "runny egg" fiasco ended only because it became the butt of jokes, not because it intruded on our liberty! The officials who wrote that regulation only retreated because of public embarrassment. Their attack on our rights wasn't halted; it was simply placed in suspended animation for a short while. The same miscreants are poised for a new assault since we have become such easy prey to their onslaughts.

If you think the "Runny Eggs" fiasco is the zenith of bureaucratic bungling, try to understand the rationale behind the sale of baked goods to our military forces. First, a vendor must be prepared to read nearly fifteen pages of single-spaced regulations in order to understand the purchasing specifications relating solely to the sale of fruitcake. One section states that, "the presence of vanilla flavoring shall be organoleptically detected."[19] I had never heard of the word "organoleptic." I dashed for the dictionary to find its definition. According to *Websters New Collegiate Dictionary*, organoleptic means: "1. affecting or employing one or more organs of special sense. 2. determined by organoleptic examination." Perhaps the government regulation could "test fruitcake to determine if it has an aroma of vanilla."

It is not just the paperwork and rule making that is out of hand, it is our acceptance of its institutionalized existence. We tend to laugh at it. "Oh, that's the Defense Department, again," one might say. Ask yourself what effect excessive rule-making has on your daily routine and your own rights? While excessive Pentagon paperwork may not affect your liberty or mine, its underlying thought process does. Unfortunately, there seems to be no counterbalance to this continual overreaching. Every rule and regulation takes away something from someone.

Another example of this highly illogical thought process occurred in the Brandt Child case. Most people know that our Constitution guarantees the "right of private property" to its citizens. Yet, in the last thirty years this right has been continually diminished by a spate of new laws and corresponding regulations. Rules covering environment, highway access, zoning, property seizure, and wetlands have literally changed the way private property is owned by our citizens. But no constitutional convention was ever held to effect this change. No citizen ever agreed to limit his rights; they were simply eliminated or curtailed for us.

Property can now be taken away without compensation or rendered commercially useless. Under the Federal Property Seizure Act one's assets can be taken from him even before he is convicted of a crime. All of these excesses have the same chilling effect on the owner. The citizen loses to an all-powerful government that refuses to recognize his constitutional rights.

Brandt Child owned a four hundred acre site near Kanab, Utah. His dream was to create a golf course, campgrounds, and a related recreational water park. During an inspection in 1991 the United States Fish and Wildlife Service found that his land contained a life form protected by the Endangered Species Act. It was called the Amber Kanab Snail, and its presence altered Mr. Child's dream.

The Endangered Species Act can be very punitive. Just as in the shooting of grizzly bears, the law calls for heavy fines for violations. In this case a penalty could be assessed at *$25,000 for each Amber Kanab Snail killed on Mr. Child's land*. While the state unilaterally determined that these snails shall be protected, no thought was given to the competing rights of the property owner. We have grown up under the false assumption that each of us is endowed with the right of private property. When a law prohibits the use of that property, that law, in a practical sense, simply takes the use or enjoyment of it away. The owner must still insure it, pay taxes on it, and fret over it — but he can no longer use it. He owns it in name only. In this case, if a developer just stepped on one snail — or better yet, cleared a road with a hundred snails, he could be fined out of financial existence.

The power of our regulators is vast, and if left unchecked could destroy our freedoms. The most dangerous regulations are those that are cloaked with good intentions, because we relax our guard. Good citizens want to do good things and good causes can quietly subvert our liberties.

There is no question that there is a legitimate interest in protecting wildlife and natural resources. But that interest must be balanced with the rights of property owners. If we as a society want to protect snails, then we must be willing to pay the price by condemning or otherwise purchasing the property under consideration — at a fair market price. It is outrageous to unjustly impose the cost of protecting selected species by selecting innocent property owners who are unlucky enough to own the land where the species reside.

In Columbia, Mississippi, an unnecessary superfund project was completed at a cost between twenty to thirty million dollars. A sawmill and chemical facility, formerly located on slightly less than one hundred acres of property, was the reason for this large expenditure.

Soil testing had revealed small traces of hazardous chemical compounds. If one pictured a ten-ton dump truck filled with dirt, the equivalent concentration of these chemicals would have been twenty ounces of dirt per truckload. Scientists told the EPA that such small chemicals were harmless in such low concentrations, unless people literally ate the dirt. But the Columbia, Mississippi, site barely exceeded the federal minimum standards. Hence, it was placed on the National Superfund site list. Dumping clean dirt or fill on the top would have formed a layer that would have been a simple, effective, and practical solution. Instead, the former owner, Reichold Chemical Company, was forced to dig up more than ten thousand tons of dirt and truck it to Louisiana. The same tainted dirt was somehow less hazardous when dumped in Louisiana than remaining covered in Mississippi. Once on the superfund list, however, simple, logical answers seem to be no longer possible.

In another similar superfund case, over ten million dollars was spent to cover a site that was purported to be hazardous. Most of the community was up-in-arms for years because they lived next door to a *perceived chemical waste dump*.

When I investigated this case, it became apparent that most of the fears and rumors about it were exaggerated. First, the site was a landfill that received ninety percent of its material from household garbage sources. Second, the site was closed years before and only limited leeching had occurred. Third, it was found to contain only one contaminant.

The official who told me of the contaminant did so on the basis that I would not reveal his name or the site. He said, "Bruce, the only contaminant here is (other than the household garbage) is baby oil, the kind you purchase in a drug store, which was picked up from a local packing plant years earlier."

Over ten million dollars was spent to cover the site with dirt because, once on the superfund list, it had to be handled *according to federal guidelines. But no actual threat existed.* Worse yet, the town was never told of the real facts, hence the citizens lived in fear because of the alleged threat.

A founding principle of our own new government in 1789 was that any rights not expressly granted to the government were reserved for the people. This principle was embodied in the spirit of the Ninth Amendment. Notwithstanding this constitutional bulwark against unwanted state intrusions, attacks on personal liberty still remain.

Unfortunately, the subversion of liberty continues to proceed under the banner of wetlands, health, safety, the environment, or some other well-meaning cause. The American people are far removed from the historical circumstances that gave rise to the Constitution. They are unfortunately all too ready to cave in to the demands of these reformers. They believe in the principle that the ends justify the means despite the erosion of long-held precepts of due process and fair play.

Bureaucrats have used these worthy-sounding issues to impose their preferences on others. The nonelected officials are saying "we know better." But this is the conceptual antithesis of the freedom. The proper role of government is to protect public safety, not to *invent crimes without victims*. We are permitting our government to legislate morality and culture. Much contemporary regulation is simply Orwellian "misspeak," which, if unchecked, could lead to a tyranny of the majority. Our founders took great pains to avoid this tragic possibility; evidently their efforts were not good enough.

If we were to be completely honest with ourselves, we would have to admit that the curtailment of individual freedoms has been sponsored by our own elected officials. What was originally conceived in the eighteenth century as one man getting on his horse, riding to Washington to vote, and returning to his constituents has changed radically in the twentieth century. This idea of representatives close to the people has been replaced by elected representatives treated as near royalty.

Since the 1960s, to be elected to congress has been to be elevated in class. Congressmen receive liberal pensions, health care, substantial benefits, a good salary, and emoluments that are, in many cases, above private industry standards. While our elected officials tell us that government can't be run like a business, most elected official take their own enrichment from the public trough, as if they worked for a large, very rich company. At the same time any congressman working for a private business would be held responsible for his actions. Not so in government. Few are judged by their actions, and apologies are not proffered for misdeeds.

While the rest of us drown in red tape, rules, regulations, paperwork and inspections, congress does not. They have used their near royalty status to exempt themselves from *many of the laws that they pass*. No private person or business enjoys such an exemption, and Congress cannot provide a sound reason for the existence of such self-aggrandizement.

Here is a partial list of laws (passed by Congress) that *we citizens must obey*, but from which Congress is totally exempt:

>   Americans with Disabilities Act
>   Age Discrimination Act
>   Civil Rights Act of 1964
>   Ethics in Government Act
>   Family and Medical Leave Act
>   Freedom of Information Act
>   Higher Education Act, Title IX
>   Independent Counsel Act
>   National Labor Relations Act
>   National Labor Standards Act
>   Privacy Act
>   Occupational Safety and Health Act
>   Rehabilitation Act
>   Social Security Act

The logic behind these congressional exemptions is that elected representatives should not be impeded in their performance by another government branch (the Executive). But the realities of today's Congress is much different than that rationale. Congress is a big business with about twelve thousand employees and a two billion dollar budget. In practical terms Congress has twisted the separation of powers doctrine to set up a privileged, unregulated class. Today, they are the only unregulated Americans, and they never miss an opportunity to keep it that way.

Congress has grown into a major entity. Until the 1930s its size remained quite close to its 1789 intention. But how the congressional tree has blossomed since then.

Federal staffing has increased dramatically over the last twenty years. In the 1930s a United States Representative was entitled to the services of two congressional aides. Twenty years later the number had grown, but it was still only five per representative. The number of aides had stayed fairly constant from 1789 to 1935, and slowly rose into the 1950s.

The depression years coupled with World War II awakened new bureaucracies, some of which died at the end of World War II. But the growth of government beginning with the Lyndon Johnson Administration caused a significant expansion in all areas. Congress was no exception.

A congressman today is entitled to four part-time and eighteen full-time aides. Senators have more assistants than most presidents of the largest American corporations. Their number is now forty! This does not reflect the staffing of their respective committees *or the general employment of Congress as an organization.* Each committee has its own aides and Congress has general staffers, like post office, and food service workers. While the latter is difficult to calculate, an average staff-to-Congressmen ratio is over two hundred to one. The House and Senate have a payroll of more than 12,000 employees for only 535 members.[20]

The problem with this enormous organization is not that the staff is required to assist with the growing paperwork. This in itself would be unfortunate. The problem is that the sheer size of the staff serves to distance elected officials from the voting public. As the elected government officials move further into the coziness of higher executive status, they remove themselves from their constituents. With this in mind, the types of persons who seek the job have changed from thinkers and shakers to those interested in deal making, bartering, blustering, and making a career out of *serving themselves, not the public*.

A review of the Congressional budget shows over one thousand offices located in home congressional constituencies, yet there are only 535 districts. These represent a cost approaching thirty-five million dollars per year.

Your interests cannot be the concern of 535 elected officials buffered by 12,000 employees. A bureaucracy of that size tends to take on a life of its own. The representation of an elected constituency cannot be effectively performed by regiments of individuals seeking their own agenda and blocking ours.

Many regulations, both federal and state, are well-intended, well-meaning, and even sensible. But, unfortunately, excess can undermine the precept. For example, during the Bush Administration the "War on Drugs" was accompanied by the kinds of searches and property seizures that were feared in 1789.

The erosion of our rights occurs not only through overregulation, but through the "power to delay." "The power to tax can be the power to destroy," observed Oliver Wendell Holmes. The power to delay can likewise destroy.

In New Jersey the developer of a 9.4 acre site off of State Route 202 had filed its plans in 1987. The plans included requests for a site plan approval, a wetlands application, stream encroachment permit, sanitation hook-ups, etc. The developer, Kalkin & Company, had continually met with procedural delays for a five-year period. The developer had to review (not file) a total of 137 potential individual permits or agency filings as follows:

    49 - Municipal/Permits/Proceedings
     5 - Private   "   "
     7 - County   "   "
     7 - Regional   "   "
    64 - Agency   "   "
     <u>5 - Federal</u>   "   "
   137 Total

While the project did not require 137 actual filings, all permit requirements had to be checked for relevance. When the builder, his attorney, and an engineer determine which thirty to forty filings they must make, they must keep them in a juggler's balance to effectively complete the project. It was this very balancing act that became Kalkin's problem.

As the hearing for one permit moved ahead, another permit would become due for review or revision. Since there was a constant interlocking relationship between city, county, state, and federal agencies, Kalkin found itself in a proverbial Catch-22 position. Over the course of the five year process the standards changed; so while the developer was waiting for various approvals, the criteria for such consents underwent modifications:

> The township is withholding a soil grading permit needed for Kalkin to fill in about a third of an acre of wetlands on the 9.4 acre site between Routes 202 and 287, just south of Glen Alpin Road. The township contends Kalkin must first obtain final site plan approval, but the company says it cannot hope to do that until February because of procedural requirements that will delay public hearings on the project for two more months.

Meanwhile, a federal wetlands permit that allows the small area to be filled in is due to expire Jan. 12 and Kalkin cannot, by law, get an extension on that approval. The requirements to get the same permit today are much tougher.[21]

Should the wetlands permit expire before local approvals were granted, Kalkin would be required to start the process again. Of course, each bureau had its own reason for delay. The New Jersey Department of Environmental Protection and Energy said its delay was related to sewage treatment approvals, which were awaiting Harding Township wastewater management plans. On the other hand, the township engineer said that he was waiting for a grading plan. The planning board stated that they were waiting for information from Kalkin and the township engineer.

How can a petitioner balance one agency against another? How does one make continual adjustments to a permit application, adjustments that can be overruled by a higher authority such as the EPA? Even if ten of eleven permits are okay, a voided eleventh permit can force the applicant to start over.

People can be demoralized and ruined financially in such a process. We have developed a system that cares only about abstractions, not about people. One is reminded about totalitarian regimes where, in the interest of a perceived public good, individual rights are abrogated.

The problems exemplified in the Kalkin case are certainly not limited to New Jersey; rather they are symptoms of a nationwide problem. Some states are better and some are worse, but all have contributed in this paperwork explosion. The Kalkin case clearly shows that the power to delay, addle, and confuse is nothing more than deprivation of one's property rights, and in a larger sense, a disincentive, if not an outright impediment, to individual initiative, progress, and economic development. Sadly, there are other impediments to initiative and achievement.

Two laws, the Endangered Species Act, and the Wetlands Protection Act, engendered a major shift toward government takeover and management of private property. But more recent expansions of these environmental initiatives may be even more threatening to property rights. Under the "Ecosystem Management" designation a "National Biological Survey Act" (NBSA) has been proposed. In 1993 a proposed new regulatory vehicle with the bogus name of "Ecosystem Management" was promoted. Since everything and everyone is part of an "ecosystem," this is another invitation for mischief. An ecosystem is defined in *Webster's Collegiate Dictionary* as "the complex of a community and its environment functioning as an ecological unit in nature." All of us could be subjected to intrusions of our personal liberty if this idea finds its way into our statute books. Kent Jeffreys gives us a chilling description.

> The Act would override state trespass laws. Landowners would be powerless to prevent federal agents, or their paid "volunteers," from entering their property. The data gathered from such invasive surveys could be used against landowners under future "ecosystem management" regulations. Worse still, the administration specifically requests that the Freedom of Information Act be waived in the Act. Landowners would not be permitted access to the data gathered by the NBS, nor would they be entitled to an explanation of the government's plans for their property. Without such information, landowners would be unable to defend themselves against their government.[22]

If the NBSA were to become law, it could be a significant step toward thought control in America. Individuality matters little to

Our Regulatory Nightmare 41

people who do not concern themselves with "trespass," or the private property rights of others. Representative Bill Emerson (R. Missouri) debated the issue in October 1993.

> According to this insidious measure...we are going to do a census on bugs and ants.
>
> The thrust of this legislation sounds more like a science fiction novel, and I am indeed deeply troubled that today this body is moving to make this far-fetched notion a reality.
>
> This National Biological Survey is nothing more than an attack on the principles of the fifth amendment of the U.S. Constitution, and it is everything that a radical preservationist could ask for. It could easily prove to be a private property owner's worst nightmare. Ultimately a National Biological Survey will lead to the establishment of a militant eco-Gestapo force....
>
> Soon the day could come when a Government bureaucrat steps on a farmer's land and shuts down his farming operation; or, worse, seizes private property in the name of environmental protection.
>
> A National Biological Survey potentially will cost taxpayers millions, enhance yet another unrestrained Federal bureaucracy, and give radical environmentalist elitists greater control over private property and what you can, or cannot, do with it.[23]

Environmental regulatory complexities could be elevated to a new level of mischief. "Ecosystem" appears to be a catchword for collectivism. Being a part of an ecosystem to a bureaucrat does not foster independent action by individuals.

The citizens of Wolcott, Connecticut, learned about regulatory problems the hard way. In the early 1970s an investment group sought to establish a thoroughbred racing operation in that community. This project promised jobs in construction, hotels, restaurants, and related activities, all of which would have greatly benefited Wolcott. At the time, it was a welcome thought for a faded manufacturing area.

Over the seven-year period that the developers drew up plans, the environmental community was brought into the process in the hope of obtaining support and approval. During the half decade of planning, the investment group spent over five million dollars, only to lose in the end to a myriad of rules and regulations.

In 1994 the three-hundred-acre tract still looks the way it did in the 1970s. Not being able to meet the requirements of environmental regulations, the project failed. Today the site is still grassland, trees, and a few dirt roads. While the project was defeated by environmental regulations, it wasn't the threat to the environment that killed the project. To save the project, the developers agreed to do all sorts of things that would enhance the environment. Few residents opposed the project on environmental grounds. Few complained of potential environmental damage if the project went forward. But, in the end, it was the permits, paperwork, and forms that couldn't be satisfied.

The people lost. Jobs were not created; a town was not revitalized; restaurants and motels were not erected. In the sense that people share the environment, everyone lost. The failed project cost more than five million dollars, proving that bureaucrats can halt anything, including the revival of an old industrial town, even if the objections are not scientifically rooted.

While property rights have been eroded with the knowledge or tacit consent of the American people, few citizens are aware that this erosion has also touched the sacrosanct area of free speech. The First Amendment has been assailed in various legal interpretations. The First Amendment states:

Our Regulatory Nightmare

"Congress shall make no law respecting an establishment of religion, or prohibiting the free exercise thereof; or abridging the freedom of speech, or of the press, or the right of the people peaceably to assemble, and to petition the Government for a redress of grievances."

The First Amendment begins with the words "Congress shall make no law". . . Does that mean that the First Amendment is only a restriction on Congress? Not any more. Before the Civil War the Bill of Rights did not apply to the states. But under the Fourteenth Amendment, adopted in 1868, the Bill of Rights does apply to the states.

The amendment says Congress "Shall make no law. . ." Does that mean there can be no restrictions of religion, speech, press, or other forms of expression? No. A majority of the Supreme Court has always allowed some restrictions on speech, press, and assembly. In addition, the meaning of such terms as "establishment of religion" forces the Court to constantly reinterpret this Amendment. "No law," apparently, does not really mean no law.

Does that mean that the words of the amendment are unimportant? No. The Supreme Court has said that the First Amendment embodies the preferred freedoms necessary for the functioning of a free society and, therefore, must be carefully protected.[24]

We all understand that freedom of speech does not permit anyone to yell "fire" in a crowded theater and thereby create a panic. We also understand that freedom of speech does not permit anyone to put his finger in someone's back and say, "I have a gun and I'm going to kill you." Those two examples of unprotected speech are quite obvious.

On the other hand, can a person be kept from expressing his or her opinion? The answer, sadly, is yes. On October 1, 1992, a federal rule was enacted that would deny federal financial assistance to any health care provider who attempted to counsel women to have an abortion. The real issue, however, is not the desirability of abortion; that decision can be left to the reader. The relevant issue is the right to speak, counsel, or aid a person with positive or negative advice, i.e., "Freedom of Speech."

Since many of these clinics were funded through federal grants, the use of purse strings to suppress information on abortion was obviously extremely effective. Money could be withheld if the guidelines were not followed. Under those federal guidelines clinics providing family guidance services were stopped from talking with clients about abortion or even making a referral on the issue. The "gag rule," as it came to be known, permitted only medical doctors, operating in the agency, to speak with female clients. As the majority of counselling usually occurs through nurse practitioners, this proved to be an important distinction. Sadly, most of the affected individuals were poor or needy people, and they could not readily obtain other advice, referral, or help.

If one views this issue objectively, it is apparent that this gag rule limits freedom of speech and creates a two-tiered health care system at the same time. There is the public tier for poor people who need to know about the option of abortion but cannot be counselled legally. Then there was the private tier for patients who could pay for and receive private consultations including advice on abortion. Putting a clinic in the position of losing its funding if its employees speak freely should be called what it is, plain and simple extortion.

> It would be nice to say to the federal government, "I'm not interested in your money," but there is no way I would jeopardize any funds available for the women who so desperately need it," said Ellen Samuel, executive director of Planned Parenthood.

Noting the office receives $300,000 in Title X funds, Samuel said, "We will reallocate and separate out services, even though that flies in the face of every forward-looking health care plan. . . . The staff "is appalled that they live in the greatest democracy in the world and in this democracy, one small segment of the population is being told they don't have free speech."

What's ironic is that Title X originally mandated offering a full range of family planning options (the rule defeated that mandate) to poor women.[25]

The First Amendment was written to protect bad speech, good speech, and outrageous, offensive, or immoral speech. When the federal government takes a side as to the proper speech permitted and uses money as the coercive force, the approach violates everyone's rights. This argument is unrelated to whether one is for or against abortion. If we do not protect the rights of both sides to express their position, then we all lose. In a democracy the ends cannot justify the means.

On Friday, January 7, 1994, a United States federal judge found attorney, Bruce Cutler, guilty of contempt of court. The conviction, if upheld, could cost Mr. Cutler $5,000 in fines and a possible six month jail term.

Was Mr. Cutler found guilty of being a mob lawyer, as he did represent John Gotti, Sr. in a 1993 trial? The answer is no. Mr. Cutler was found guilty of publicly speaking out prior to the trial. His offense was that he talked to reporters before the Gotti trial began. Cutler's statements were directed at his view of the government's campaign against his client, John Gotti, Sr.

While the conviction was appealed, if upheld, the intrusion into freedom of speech could be extensive. Since the statements were made prior to the trial, hence, did not interfere with the trial itself, the conviction could serve to muzzle trial attorneys and lessen aggressive representation of accused citizens, mobsters or not. The executive director of the New York Civil Liberty Union observed: "This will have a chilling effect on zealous advocacy by criminal defense lawyers.[26]

Should this conviction stand, another weight of imbalance will be added to the current attack on individual liberties. Since the government possesses unlimited funds and endless use of manpower in all federal court cases, it has a larger arsenal than most defendants. The defendant must protect himself with far less resources. If defense attorneys are now to be kept on a short leash by the courts, then the imbalance becomes even greater than heretofore.

It is not only free speech that is imperiled, but also the protection of a citizen's rights by an aggressive defense attorney.

As our government has increased its power to control our lives, the individual has become of secondary importance. Government rules have been elevated far above the importance of the rights of individuals. Here is an example from California.

The Emergency Medical System (EMS) is a nationwide program covering ambulance personnel and paramedics. Each state adds its own requirements to the minimum federal standards. Some of these additions make good sense. In Maine, training of personnel is enhanced to include more water-rescue techniques. Since ski accidents are common in Colorado, movement of people with fractures is highlighted in practical exercises as well as in classes. The bureaucrats of California, however, have evidently decided that the care of their population is less important than the generation of fees, regulations, duplicative testing, and red tape. In 1990 that state promulgated a set of new regulations for paramedics under Title 22 of its Health and Safety Law. The law created a paramedic certification requirement as well as a statewide test. The fee was set at $42.50 per year, which permitted a licensed paramedic to practice his or her life saving technique in California.

But there are fifty-eight counties in California. Each county chose to determine its own additional duplicative authorities and fee structures. The criteria differed somewhat county by county and so did the fees. The permitting cost varied throughout the state from $50 to $400 to become licensed.

While doctors, nurses, and EMTS (Emergency Medical Technicians) can work in California statewide after passing one certification, paramedics cannot. If they move their employment just one county away, they must take a new test, pay a new fee, and fill out more papers. The counties of California have acted in the mistaken notion that human experience, education, and competence will be vitiated when one crosses the county line. Other than creating a revenue stream and an attendant employment opportunity for a county bureaucrat, who or what does this duplication absurdity benefit? Does it help the patient or the average citizen? Does it create jobs? Does it enhance the health care system? Does it reduce paperwork? No, the system exists for itself, to benefit itself.

Chapter 2

The Bill of Rights and Freedom

"Our elected representatives are supposed to have the same concerns at stake which those have who appointed them, and who will act in the same manner as the whole body would act were they present

Thomas Paine
Common Sense, 1774

The American "Bill of Rights" is rooted in the Magna Charta (1215 AD), the English Bill of Rights (1689), and various other writings and experiences. The Bill of Rights are the first Ten Amendments to the United States Constitution.

While the Bill of Rights obviously has its roots in the realities of its time, it was also generated by the fear of big government that was held by many of our forefathers. The American colonists did not wish to trade one master for another, once they had gained their freedom from England. While many Federalist delegates to the constitutional convention felt that the Bill of Rights was extra baggage and unnecessary, the anti-federalist position (those fearful of big government) luckily won the day.

Unfortunately, in the two hundred years since the adoption of the Bill of Rights, many of its protections have come under subtle but continual attack. For the first one hundred and fifty years, small government was the rule and the Bill of Rights was not seriously jeopardized. But the situation changed in the last half century.

The Bill of Rights and Freedom 49

James Madison, who was fearful of an overzealous government, made own feelings quite clear at the constitutional convention when he said:

> In time of actual war, great discretionary powers are constantly given to the executive magistrate. Constant apprehension of war, has the same tendency to render the head too large for the body. A standing military force, with an overgrown executive will not long be safe companions to liberty. The means of defense against foreign danger, have been always the instruments of tyranny at home.[1]

Madison was quite precognitive, since his words foresaw the future's precise danger.

The American constitutional experience was unique in history. It was a time when great intellectual capacities came together and debated. Indeed, it was a rare moment in history. The battle was so intense that a civil war could have erupted, but it did not. Compromise, with upheld principles seized the day.

Communication was limited. Polls were nonexistent. Experience was the teacher. The delegates at the constitutional convention had to think for themselves. Fortunately, for future generations, they possessed the necessary intellectual gear to envelop the issues and attempt to protect liberty while agreeing to a federal system.

In the two thousand pages of federalist and anti-federalist arguments there were many writings that turned out to be accurate predilections of human behavior. One columnist who wrote under the name of "Brutus" published an article in the *New York Journal*, in 1787, that "a power, if given and exercised, will generally produce evil to the community and seldom good." The words of "Brutus" rings true two centuries later.

In retrospect, our freedoms have imploded from within, not from without. Our country has not been taken from us by a foreign enemy. In many cases we have been challenged by our own elected representatives, who have not upheld the gift of our forefathers.

For a century and a half, individual protections withstood assault. Shortly after World War II the liberty battlefield took a marked shift. A massive change in the size and scope of government, paperwork, rules, laws, and committee staffs began. Since it happened gradually, many people did not realize the scope of these changes. The conversion had its roots in the New Deal during the 1930s, and World War II kept the condition alive.

The process slowed in the 1945–1950 period as World War II agencies were dismantled. In the early 1950s the entire staff of the committees of the United States House of Representatives totalled under two hundred persons.

The explosion gained new momentum during the decade of 1960–1970 when the number of congressional employees increased — yet, it still totalled just under 750 persons for the committee staffs of the Senate and House. By the early 1990s both houses, combined, have nearly three hundred committees in total, and the staff for these committees now totals nearly four thousand individuals, not counting the committee chairmen and vice chairmen.

While this book is not a treatise on government waste, it is incumbent to alert you to the salaries of some of these same staffers. In 1992, the top salary of a Congressional Committee staffer was approximately $110,000 per year. This does not take into effect a host of superb benefits, such as a free pass on the Washington Metro rapid transit system.

As stated in Chapter 1, Congress in 1993 had 11,800 people on the payroll. The cost of this army exceeded 1.5 billion dollars a year, when calculated with all employment costs.

Today's mammoth Congressional payroll was certainly not to be found in the minds of our founding fathers. They fretted about

The Bill of Rights and Freedom 51

tyranny while Madison accurately forecast dangers from within. No one pictured a federal government of the size it is today.

Because of the decision to create a federal government in the United States Constitution, several important members of the convention threatened to withhold their support unless a Bill of Rights was added and granted to the people. Some of these gentlemen were: Elbridge Gerry, of Massachusetts, Edmund Randolph and George Mason, who were both from Virginia.

So many citizens of the fledgling republic feared the central government that even James Madison, a federalist, agreed to support a Bill of Rights. His Virginia constituents prevailed upon him to support these amendments to the Constitution. He finally agreed, and stated in July 1788 that if he were elected to Congress, he would work for a Bill of Rights to protect the people. The people had prevailed upon Madison, and as a true statesman, he modified his views.

In 1789 the Bill of Rights was sent to the states for ratification. Within two years, on December 15, 1791, the Bill of Rights was ratified.

An interesting sidelight to history is that, while the states ratified most of the amendments, they did not agree to the original first and second amendments:

   1st   One representative for every 50,000 people. (This would have been a colossal error. If it had been accepted we would now have 5,000 members of Congress.)
   2nd   No salary raise for members of Congress could be effected until after the next election for Congress.

In a strange twist the 1st Amendment to the Bill of Rights correctly headed for oblivion, but the 2nd did not. Rather, its two century progress clearly demonstrates to any doubter that the idea of a Bill of Rights is as *valid a concept today as it was when proposed* in 1788. Follow the incredible progress of the 2nd Amendment, which began in 1791.

On May 7, 1992, 201 years after the ratification of the Bill of Rights, the original second amendment returned to see daylight as our Constitution's 27th Amendment. What James Madison's efforts started, the 1992 House and Senate ratified, after Michigan became the 38th State Legislature to vote an acceptance. While Madison's brain child was every bit as valid today as it was two hundred years previous, it nevertheless took two centuries to adopt.

While the Second Amendment (now our 27th) to the Constitution showed the remarkable staying power of the document, we have as a nation permitted erosion of many protected liberties, which we will explore and discuss. In a later portion of the book (Chapter 10) our rights will be evaluated in a bar-chart format to contrast our founder's vision to present-day circumstances. The counterpoints may surprise you.

In order to place all of us on a common ground, the Bill of Rights is reprinted here.

The Bill of Rights

1. Congress shall make no law respecting an establishment of religion or prohibiting the free exercise thereof: or abridging the freedom of speech, or of the press, or the right of the people peaceably to assemble, and to petition the Government for a redress of grievances.

2. A well regulated militia, being necessary to the security of a free State, the right of the people to keep and bear arms, shall not be infringed.

3. No soldier shall, in time of peace, be quartered in any house, without the consent of the owner nor in time of war, but in a manner to be prescribed by laws.

The Bill of Rights and Freedom 53

4. The right of the people to be secure in their persons, houses, papers, and effects against unreasonable searches and seizures, shall not be violated, and no warrants shall issue but upon probable cause, supported by oath or affirmation, and particularly describing the place to be searched and the persons or things to be seized.

5. No person shall be held to answer for a capital, or otherwise infamous crime, unless on a presentment or indictment of a Grand Jury, except in cases arising in the land or naval forces, or in the Militia, when in actual service in time of War or public danger; nor shall any person be subject for the same offence to be twice put in jeopardy of life or limb; nor shall be compelled in any criminal case to be a witness against himself, or be deprived of life, liberty, or property, without due process of law; nor shall private property be taken for public use, without just compensation.

6. In all criminal prosecutions, the accused shall enjoy the right to a speedy and public trial, by an impartial jury of the State and district wherein the crime shall have been committed, which district shall have been previously ascertained by law, and to be informed of the nature and cause of the accusation; to be confronted with the witnesses against him; to have compulsory process for obtaining witnesses in his favor, and to have the Assistance of Counsel for his defence.

7. In Suits at common law, where the value in controversy shall exceed twenty dollars, the right of trial by jury shall be preserved, and no fact tried by a jury, shall be otherwise re-examined in any Court of the United States, than according to the rules of the common law.

8. Excessive bail shall not be required, nor excessive fines imposed, nor cruel and unusual punishments inflicted.

9. The enumeration in the Constitution, of certain rights, shall not be construed to deny or disparage others retained by the people.

10. The powers not delegated to the United States by the Constitution, nor prohibited by it to the States, are reserved to the States respectively, or to the people.

The Bill of Rights are enumerated in this chapter for one central reason. It is important for every American to realize what he is supposed to have, what he did have, and what he has given up through the erosion of these principles. The importance of these protections were so paramount to the ratifying of the United States Constitution that the insistence on them nearly caused its approval to fail at the final vote.

In 1787 Delaware ratified the Constitution. It was the first state to do so. This was quickly followed by Pennsylvania, Georgia, and Connecticut. Then the process became more difficult. In Massachusetts, for example, a battle between the Western farmers and the Eastern merchants of Boston became quite emotional causing the passage in Massachusetts to be very close, 187 yea to 168 nay.

Without the promise of a Bill of Rights, not yet attached to the Constitution, ratification might never have occurred. To the founders of our new country individual rights were that important. Many were willing to sacrifice the start of a new nation if personal guarantees were not assured.

Individual rights continued to be so important to the founders of our country that in Virginia, passage of the Constitution itself might have failed. The only way passage eventually occurred in Virginia was by the promise of the Federalists such as John Marshall and James Madison to support a Bill of Rights as an appendage to the Constitution. Virginian Edmund Randolph, who had opposed ratification, changed sides and supported it with the new amendments.

New York could, at first, only produce nineteen of its sixty-five delegates in favor. Passage was later approved because the Federalists, led by Alexander Hamilton, found the amendments acceptable to them.

Feelings for individual rights ran so high that North Carolina met on August 2, 1788, but refused to vote on the Constitution until the Bill of Rights was added.

It is important to understand that our rights were born with much pain, much rancor, owing to the visions of the recent experiences by our founding fathers.

With increased size, power, and stature, the federal government began to assume a more expansive role in regulating the day-to-day affairs of the average citizen. With this increased role came both increased authority and decreased contact at local levels. Slowly, the powers once exerted with common sense and restraint by bureaucrats, who saw themselves as part of the mainstream, were later exerted by political ideologues. These tenets were later exerted by political partisans, insensitive to the Bill of Rights and consumed with their vision of a reordered, perfect society.

As we have already passed two centuries as a nation, we must reflect on the covenant with our forebears. This reflection must include the realization that we have permitted the diminution of our rights with little protest and hardly a whimper.

Chapter 3

How Regulation Affects Our Lives

"Men, when they first enter into magistracy, have often their former condition before their eyes: They remember what they themselves suffered with their fellow subjects from the abuse of power, and how much they blamed it; so their first purposes are to be humble, modest and just; and probably, for some time, they continue so. But the possession of power soon alters and vitiates their hearts, which are at the same time sure to have leavened and puffed up to an unnatural size, by the deceitful incense of false friends and by the prostrate submission of parasites. First they grow indifferent to all their good designs, then drop them. Next, they lose their moderation. Afterwards, they renounce all measures with their old acquaintance and old principles, and seeing themselves in magnifying glasses, grow in conceit, a different species from their fellow subjects. And so, by too sudden degrees become insolent, rapacious and tyrannical, ready to catch all means, often the vilest and most oppressive, to raise their fortunes as high as imaginary greatness."

John Trenchard and Thomas Gordon
"Catos Letters" 1774

While regulations controlling dust, blowing leaves, or grass clippings are infuriating, they are not themselves the enemies of individual freedom; they are merely the manifestations of a more fundamental ill — the mindset and attitudes of both our legislators and regulators.

How Regulation Affects Our Lives 57

Since the 1960s, our legislators have enacted more and more laws, while our "regulators" have found more and more ways of regulating. To save our liberty a change in this very thought process is required. The problem has become so significant that some of our more enlightened elected bodies have placed limits on themselves. The Colorado Legislature, for example, realized that more bills were being introduced than could be rationally acted upon, so they limited each lawmaker to a yearly quota. This was accomplished in a simple and rational manner. The leadership took the number of bills that could be dealt with through committees, divided it by the total of legislators, and came up with a number. That final quantity, which was approximately eight hundred, became the maximum number of introducible bills in any one year.

Contrast Colorado with New Jersey where legislative excess is rampant and irrational. In New Jersey between January 1, 1990, and January 1, 1992, there were over ten thousand resolutions and bills introduced into the legislature. That number represented nearly eighty-five items per legislator. Because no legislator could be expected to know, let alone understand, the content of all these bills, it is apparent that laws were either approved or disapproved in almost total ignorance much of the time.

According to the New Jersey Office of Legislative Services, the number of resolutions and bills introduced were as follows: 1980-81, 6,034; 1982-83, 7,224; 1984-85, 8,721; 1986-87, 9,303; 1988-89, 9,918; and 1990-91, 10,612. Dr. George Sternlieb, of Rutgers University, stated that the problem shook the viability of the legislative process itself. "There are too many committees, the homework assignments are just too heavy for legislators, and there are very few people who can really master the legislation."[1]

Is the answer to force more through the eye of a needle? No, the answer is to concentrate on major laws, with less effort spent on issues of limited urgency or applicability. The regulatory thought process that "more is better" is self-defeating. Every new rule or law takes something away from its targeted community. While elected legislators and unelected regulators say they pay attention to our individual liberties, it is a fallacy to believe that they actually spend much time worrying about the effects of their actions on the freedom or economic well-being of their constituents.

There are a few stories of a runaway bureaucracy that tell more about what we have lost than the saga of Bill Ellen. In 1987, Mr. Ellen embarked on an environmental mission to transform 103 acres of open land into a sanctuary for waterfowl. The estate belonged to P. T. Jones, II, and was located in Maryland. Mr. Ellen took on the job for Mr. Jones with great anticipation.

The plan called for the building of ponds, grassy areas, and sheds. The overall idea was to provide migratory waterfowl with a comfortable stopover on their north-south route, which naturally traversed Mr. Jone's property.

By 1988 Mr. Ellen had obtained over thirty permits from various agencies regulating the project, including the United States Army Corps of Engineers. During the construction phase of the project, new wetlands regulations were issued by the Federal EPA. These regulations increased federal controls to encompass everything from a wet spot between railroad tracks to a river bank. In other words, the definition of wetlands was expanded to cover almost any property and, accordingly, regulations were being promulgated wildly.

In early 1989, the United States Army Corps of Engineers told Mr. Ellen to halt work on the project since the new, more stringent, regulations were different from the ones on which his permits were based. Using this approach, every construction job in America could be halted. If a person had to function within changing rules, he would never complete the task.

Mr. Ellen, who had previously worked for the Virginia Resources Commission, was upset by the order but nevertheless agreed to stop work on the water-sensitive (wetlands) areas. There was a small area, however, which had been indicated on the map as not under wetlands regulations, so he continued the project on that corner of the Jones Sanctuary. This area consisted of the property manager's shed and storage unit. The continuation of work at that location only consisted of the delivery, receipt, and dumping of two truckloads of top soil over a few days. Otherwise, the project had been shut down to revise the permits.

The Army Corps of Engineers saw these two truckloads of dirt as a clear violation of their order. They recommended prosecution of Mr. Ellen on criminal charges relating to violations of the revised federal wetlands regulations.

Mr. Ellen did not feel that he violated his permits or any other rules. He also did not see the dumping of two truckloads of soil at the same level of importance that the Corps did. His views appeared supportable since the regulations that he was being charged under *were promulgated two years after he commenced his project with all necessary permits.*

The Constitution, under Section 9 (the Limitation of Powers Passage), states: "No bill of attainder or *ex post facto* law shall be passed." Americans have generally assumed that acts performed previous to a law or rule, would be "grandfathered" since they were accomplished before the enactment of the new rule or law. I am sure that Mr. Ellen felt this way also. But traditional American justice was not to be reserved for a person building water fowl migration ponds.

The result of these violations proved to be quite severe. Mr. Ellen eventually received six months in federal prison for the aforementioned "wetlands violations." Mr. P. T. Jones, the property owner, who had graciously given over one hundred acres to the cause of migrating birds, was fined $1,000,000. In addition, as part of his settlement, he agreed to donate another $1,000,000 to an environmental cause. The prosecution of the case was pursued by the federal government even though Mr. Ellen and Mr. Jones had succeeded in adding nearly fifty acres to our nation's wetlands arsenal.

But this case is more than simply a picture of bureaucratic excess. This excess has real human consequences.

> It cost *We The People* tax dollars to house, feed, clothe and, of course, guard for six months this supposed threat to society — a man who harmed neither man nor beast. It cost his community the loss of one of their workers. And it deprived Bill and his young boys of precious moments of their tender years.[2]

Are we so humbled and so at the mercy of our unelected bureaucrats that their rules are enforceable even if they violate the spirit of the Constitution? Is it within the spirit of America that someone go to jail for a technical violation, which intended (and caused) no harm? Has environmental hysteria become so pervasive that what was born of a legitimate desire to curb the excesses of development in an industrial society has become nothing more than a witch-hunt? Is it the object of the government to achieve a balanced regulation of human affairs or to impose paperwork, rules, and regulations on us for *their own sake*? After reviewing the Ellen case I question both the objective and the desired result of regulations of this nature.

Since the 1960s, our collective psyches have been altered. Our sensibilities have become jaded. Mr. Ellen and Mr. Jones tried to perform a valuable public service and were humiliated for their efforts. It wasn't the environment that was impinged, it was sensibility. Traditional American fair play didn't even act as a counterbalance to this tragedy.

How Regulation Affects Our Lives

During the last several decades, we have permitted regulation of our businesses, lives, and personal behavior to become institutionalized. In a way, Americans seem to suffer from a kind of Stockholm Syndrome. In psychological terms it means surrendering part of your will to your kidnapper. Instead of saying to our government — "NO — you cannot regulate the totality of our entire personal lives," we have accepted passively. Even when regulations are so severe as to provoke opposition as an intrusion on personal liberty, winning means that only the most egregious regulations may be modified or eliminated. The bulk, however, remain and are accepted by a humbled populace. As long as we keep our jobs and a modicum of comfort, we seem to be indifferent to the erosion of freedom.

Nationally, the amount and cost of regulations are staggering and impact negatively on our business community as well as our personal liberties. In 1970, the estimated annual cost of government regulation of business was $3.4 billion dollars. In 1991, in constant dollars, the cost was estimated at $9-$10 billion dollars. In the 1990s Congress passed new regulatory laws (the Clean Air act, etc.), which are estimated to place the regulatory costs in excess of $100 billion per annum until the end of the twentieth century.

The dramatic growth in dollars is paralleled by the size of the books needed to house these regulations. The current size of "The Federal Register," which lists all new federal rules, now exceeds seventy thousand pages.

In 1992, a much criticized Vice President Dan Quayle correctly summed up the problem.

> First: A free market and a competitive economy are the best allies of the American people. Second: The less regulation — the less government intrusion into [peoples'] lives, the better off they are.[3]

If the Federal Register can contain seventy thousand pages of new regulations, what's next? Bureaucrats make little distinction between business and personal behavior, and they are hard at work fashioning new ideas to control every mode of our behavior.

An example of regulatory excessiveness can be drawn from a 1992 booklet the "Summary of Fishing Regulations and Laws" for the Commonwealth of Pennsylvania. First, it is notable that the summary of these regulations totals sixty pages. A note in the fishermen's manual on page 2 alerts the reader that "the booklet represents a summary of these laws. . . . The official text of the fishing regulations summarized in the booklet appears in the "Pennsylvania Bulletin."[4] In other words the full text is much longer.

Why does one need a sixty page summary of rules that tells the reader how to fish? On page 4, there is the Commonwealth of Pennsylvania's definition of fishing itself; "The act of angling, or to catch, take, kill or remove from any waters or other areas within a bordering on this Commonwealth any fish by means or method for any purpose, whatsoever."[5]

On page 7, another "much-needed" definition is indicated for the "complicated" word "ice." On the same page are also found rules that prohibit "swimming" in the rivers covered by the Commission's jurisdiction.[6] The booklet continues with a massive collection of trivia; except that it also states that for violating a trivial rule, one can be fined and even arrested.

While sixty pages of fishing regulations (in Summary form) demonstrate how firm a hold bureaucrats can exert on simple behaviors, has anyone ever asked why? Why has there been a proliferation of rules, regulations, and forms that regulate almost everything we do? As the institutionalization of rules run unchecked, the rule makers continue to reduce our freedom of action. Where are the ideas to enhance personal liberty?

In June of 1992, Mayor Raymond Flynn of Boston suggested that water pistols with large chambers be banned in his city and removed from store shelves. A week later a New York City man playfully squirted water at the wrong guys. One of the group drew a handgun, fired a few shots, one of which hit its mark. The playful water squirter was killed.

Why is an inanimate object, i.e., the water pistol, held responsible? Wasn't it the act of a person that caused the problem? Can every human interrelationship be solved by a new law?

Obviously, if a person fills a water gun with lye or chlorine and shoots someone with it, that person is probably guilty of assault. If someone fills a milk or soda bottle with gasoline, inserts a cloth and lights it, the bottle then becomes an explosive. Is the answer to outlaw lye, chlorine, soda, glass bottles, and gasoline?

The rule makers are often gifted rhetoricians whose promises and platitudes are often taken at face value. Even after the political promises are unkept, citizens do not insist on future performance or apologies. In business, the repeated failure to deliver leads to firing. But in government there is little if any accountability or responsibility.

In 1992, following the Los Angeles riots, politicians rushed in with promises to rebuild and help the city recover from its misery. After they left, the process of rebuilding was left to paperwork-oriented, insensitive bureaucrats. Many treated the Los Angeles citizens with suspicion rather than compassion. Then they laid out guidelines for compliance, guidelines that included mountains of paper, an appeal system, and a bureaucratic maze.

It soon became obvious that more applicants for aid would be deemed ineligible than those accepted for aid. Then as the process continued, more difficulties plagued the aid applicants.

> Burned out of homes and businesses, violently stripped of possessions gained through years of sacrifice, thousands of victims of the Los Angeles riot are finding that help may not be on the way after all.

> Nearly four months after the city erupted in anger, there is a dawning realization that comforting promises of relief made in the riot's emotional aftermath came with an asterisk — the fine print laying out criteria for federal assistance that many will never meet.
>
> Denial rates for nearly all of the federal grant and loan programs are running at fifty percent or more, leaving many victims and their advocates with the sense that the aid process is not working. They say the Federal Emergency Management agency (FEMA), more accustomed to dealing with natural disasters, has not adapted its programs to meet the special needs of riot victims.[7]

While victims awaited assistance, they learned the difference between sound bites and the reality of help. This is no longer the country where townspeople gather to rebuild a house burned in a fire. No longer do people see Sunday as the day to attend a "barn raising." Instead we look to Washington for a sacred message. But Washington often disappoints the victims. Neighbors might still help neighbors, but government is not our neighbor.

The rule makers are also propagandists, manipulating words beautifully to put the best face on bad news and programs. Under the credo of "perception is reality," words are substituted for accomplishments.

It was this use of spin that helped Congress get sufficient support to pass the "Americans With Disabilities Act" in 1992. It is beyond cavil that disabled people deserve a chance in our society, and that all of us should attempt to assist those who are less fortunate.

However, when attempting to redress inequality of opportunity, there still must be an effort to achieve the results without jeopardizing the legitimate rights of others.

First the law went astray by expanding the definition of "disabled" so broadly that the Act could cover over forty million Americans. Immediately, there were forty million potential law suits. "The Act includes all who suffer from emotional or mental illness, drug addiction, alcoholism and AIDS. . .they now have the right to sue for compensatory and punitive damages."[8]

The United States Justice Department publicly averred that by mid-1993 over three hundred lawsuits had been filed and expected many more. Like many laws this one has created a minefield for punitive action. As often happens, a strict enforcement often works against the spirit of the concept behind the law. Because of the high legal risks in hiring disabled people, some employers will find ways not to fill the positions.

Did Congress assess the potential fallout, or just cave in to pressure from one side of the issue? In Monroe County, Pennsylvania, this legislation put the library board in a quandary. They had problems complying with the AWDA requirement that all buildings open to the public shall provide access to the handicapped.

The Monroe County library in Stroudsburg, Pennsylvania, is located in an old house at 913 Main Street. The county did not have the money in the recession year of 1992 to fund a move to roomier quarters. The library, unfortunately, has narrow hallways, shelves that are too high, and steps that are difficult to traverse. The library's acting director, who is fighting to keep it open for all citizens, said: "The AWDA is just another nail in our coffin. . .a handicapped activist could force the library to close."[9]

The library board understands that they cannot bring the building into compliance with the AWDA and wanted to erect a new building. But the money wasn't available in 1992 or 1993 and may not be there in later years.

What is the solution? In our efforts to help the disabled, should we close the library so no one can use it? Or, perhaps, instead of turning the whip of the AWDA on the remaining citizens, we could be less punitive with each other. Perhaps a librarian could obtain the books for someone who could not get to the book stacks? This would allow one citizen to help another — without giving one the right to sue out of misdirected anger, for the wrong (though politically correct) reason. Why must common sense be legislated out of existence?

The granting of rights is a zero sum game. When a government gives rights to someone it is safe to assume that another person's rights are being impinged or removed.

The AWDA, on the face of it, corrected injustices for many Americans. But a fair question is how many? Are we all victims? How far should these corrections go? How does the AWDA affect the rights of others?

While most people favor wheelchair ramps for disabled persons, the American tendency to expand a good thing is already evident in the court cases being filed under AWDA. Here are two examples of excess:

A young law school graduate completed the bar exam in Connecticut but was denied admission to the state bar. The graduate had suffered from bouts of depression. The State Bar Admissions Committee felt this made him unfit to practice law in Connecticut. The prospective lawyer has sued the Bar Association seeking admittance under the AWDA umbrella.

In Ohio a Cleveland Browns football fan has launched a suit against the NFL and the major television networks because they black out home games when they are not sold out. The fan, who is deaf, says that this fails to recognize that deaf people cannot listen to the radio, hence are shut out of the games. His attorneys seek $350 million in compensatory damages in their lawsuit.

By December 31, 1993, there were nearly 16,000 discrimination cases filed with the Justice Department and the Equal Employment

Opportunity Commission. What started as a law to assist disabled Americans and to achieve equality may wind up hurting all of us, including those it originally sought to assist.

It has become the modern nature of regulation that rules seem to expand out of common sensibility, as a western town found out.

The people of Colton, California, learned a real-life story about its town and its sense of caring. This San Bernardino County community was considering the construction of a new hospital in 1993. The hospital building project was to have provided jobs and an economic uplift to the community.

In addition to the construction of a six-story hospital building, the town had also planned a three-hundred acre enterprise zone in order to attract industry to an area suffering from the shutdown of Norton Air Force Base, located nearby. The shutdown has touched the lives of more than three hundred Colton families.

But the town's hospital and the proposed enterprise zone could be threatened permanently by the "Endangered Species Act," which provides for penalties of up to a year in jail and $200,000 in fines for its transgressors.

In the fall of 1993 the Delhi Sands fly was added to the list of species protected by the Endangered Species Act. It was the first fly to achieve this distinction. While there is some humor in this, its allegorical implications could be gigantic. Flies take to the air and migrate. They can nest or reside anywhere. Unfortunately for Colton, several acres of the Delhi's habitat are inside their delineated "enterprise zone." Both the hospital and the attraction of new industry are threatened by the Delhi Sands fly, an insect no more than 7/8ths of an inch in size, which would normally be swatted if it landed on you. But the fly is more important than the people sharing its space. If the endangered fly blocks the construction of the Colton Hospital, who loses? Who wins? Is such a decision rational? The movers and shakers propose solutions to problems that sound good when enacted but create practical havoc for the remainder of society.

A library in an old building is not such a bad thing. A hospital and the revitalization of a town are positive steps for a community. Rather than accommodate these legitimate public interests with those of disabled individuals and endangered species, the lawmakers and regulators regularly choose draconian, one-sided solutions while ignoring the interests of the larger society.

A good example is that of the Keene Corporation located in New York City. Keene owned a subsidiary that manufactured insulation that utilized asbestos in its manufacture. About ten percent of the product's final composition was asbestos. The subsidiary was small and sold approximately $15 million of asbestos-containing materials during its existence.

Due to asbestos-related lawsuits, the Keene Corporation was forced to pay out nearly $400 million in related claims. But that figure doesn't tell the whole story. Of the $400 million, $265 million went to pay legal fees. The award had to be paid even though very few of the plaintiffs became ill from Keene's product line.

Under our current system of justice, large contingency fees in class action suits seeking hefty punitive damages have made companies like Keene Corporation sitting targets. At the time of the Keene case, sixteen of the other companies named as co-defendants were bankrupted during the legal process.

This kind of litigation is not justice but extortion. If we don't change our ways, we will retard the growth of technology because of the fear of being sued.

Another parallel exists and should be considered, the economic effects of the 1991 Minimum Wage Increase. It was an attempt to help the underprivileged and mirrors the AWDA in its attempt to assist the disabled. But it has also produced some problems.

From 1981 through the late 1980s the minimum wage was set at a federal floor of $3.35. During that time the percentage of teenagers who had employment increased from 41% in 1981, to almost 50% in 1988.

However, after the federal increase went into effect, employment of teenagers began to drop significantly, reaching 43 percent by late 1990. After the minimum wage rate increased to $4.25 in 1991, teenage employment percentages dropped again. It is safe to assume that if one were to raise the minimum wage each year from 1992 until 2002, there would be more teenagers shut out of jobs.

Of course, the reason for raising the minimum wage is to keep the working poor, not teenage workers at fast-food restaurants. But our working poor have not been helped much either. A balance must be achieved between the rights of our handicapped and the rights of the able-bodied; between the protection of our environment and the recognition that people are part of our environment also; and lastly between teenage workers who wish to supplement their family income, and those adult working poor who deserve a living wage to support themselves and their families.

You cannot give rights to some by taking someone else's rights away. These goals can only be achieved when rationally planned and cooperatively executed.

Chapter 4

Freedom's Worst Enemy — Environmental Hysteria

"All substances are poisons, there is none which is NOT a poison. The right dose differentiates a poison and a remedy."

Philip A. Paracelsus (1493-1541)
Swiss Physician

The effect of runaway environmentalism has frightened many freedom-loving Americans. Many recent environmental laws and regulations have seriously eroded the long-held sanctity of private property, of due process, of laws against self-incrimination, of the right of habeas corpus, and of the prohibition against *ex post facto* legislation.

A citizen's ability to speak out against or resist this extremism is difficult. How does an average property owner, often with limited financial resources, fight a powerful state agency, the EPA, or the Army Corps of Engineers? How does he confront the charges that he is indifferent to or even opposed to the public good by challenging or resisting oppressive and unfair laws and regulations.

Many citizens are unaware of the extent of the diminution of rights that recent environmental regulations have imposed on farmers, manufacturers, developers, property owners, businessmen, and even homeowners. No area of economic activity is immune from these attacks on our traditional values.

One region that has become a target of considerable environmental activity is South Central Florida. This area, which is primarily agricultural, grows and harvests sugar cane, fruits, and vegetables. Naturally, the growers use water. But farmers, or other users of water, are under unrelenting regulatory attack nearly everywhere in the United States.

In 1988 a United States Attorney, Dexter Lehtinen, sued the State of Florida because too much fertilizer residue was leaving Florida farms through various waterways such as rivers, streams, and channels. Vegetable and sugar cane growers fought back, incurring large legal bills in the process. Because they are highly technical in nature, environmental lawsuits are very costly to pursue, as the farmers quickly learned. The results of this federal attack were delays, frustration, and heavy costs to farmers and taxpayers without any real solution.

When environmental zealots joined in on the Florida case, it grew even more embroiled, resulting in increasing insensitivity and indifference to the rights and values of others.

What the federal government really wanted was to convert the 35,000 acres of South Central Florida crop producing land back into the marshes of antiquity. This plan could have cost tax payers nearly $400 million dollars. If the actions of the government and the environmentalists were permitted, it would have meant the taking of farmers' land, destruction of their businesses, homesteads, and their ability to farm land that many of the smaller farmers had been doing in Central Florida for generations.

The South Central Florida case grew to such a level of absurdity that the EPA said it would arrest any independent scientists who attempted to gain access to the rivers to measure the water quality under consideration. When the Wetlands Center at Duke University attempted to gain access for testing, it was told by the EPA that their scientists would be arrested for trespassing if they persisted in these efforts.

Finally, the lawsuit was settled. It was agreed that both federal and state agencies would implement more stringent regulations in the future, but that a period of time would be granted to achieve these goals. In other words a cooling off period was placed in effect. Neither side won.

The most incredible part of this Florida case was that the farmers had not been proven to be polluters, or to be harming the environment. The farmers contended that "the amount of phosphorus per billion in the runoff was less than the phosphorus content of the leading bottled waters."[1] This bout of overregulation, based on fear, not science, could have cost thousands of jobs. The environmentalists who embroiled themselves in the case had not done their homework or their science well, and spread false issues about the case.

While farmers in Florida were being pilloried for supposedly polluting waterways, an arbitrary rationing of water occurred in California in a dry region of the state.

From 1987 to 1993 a drought in California crippled the state's 18 billion dollar agricultural industry. Fortunately, the winter of 1993 was quite wet and the drought was declared over. But then a new tug of war began to unfold.

Under extreme pressure from environmental groups, the EPA began a fight to save the fish in the Sacramento River. The Sacramento runs through the richest farming areas in the state known as the San Joaquin Valley. Even though the drought had ended, the area's farming community was notified that it would only receive forty percent of the pre-drought water allotment for irrigation purposes.

A farmer without water is like a rowboat without oars. Because of this expected reduction in water, the jobs of three thousand area farm workers were imperiled. Of course, produce distributors, farm stores, tractor dealers, banks, and landlords also became edgy. Economic impact is always concentric; less water, less planting, less work, and less jobs translate into a threatened area economy.

The prospects of fighting back were not encouraging. It seems that more power can be brought to bear for the delta smelt and the Chinook salmon than for the poor farmer or the embattled consumer. The Endangered Species Act of 1973, while protecting wildlife and fish, totally fails to take into account or to protect the dominant species on the planet — the Homo sapiens. Those two fish turned out to be the reasons for the reduction in water allocations to the San Joaquin Valley farmers.

Like most problems, a fair solution is usually a question of balance. But we have careened off the scales *illogically in favor of wildlife* — without a balance for people. We have treated the Constitution as if it does not exist, since environmental priorities often have superseded property rights and human rights.

Perhaps the impact statements, which are necessary for development, should contain additional factors. They should not only inquire as to the effects on wildlife and endangered species, but also the effects on jobs, the economy, the people involved, as well as constitutional protections. Certainly, humans should be permitted to share the same rights as animals.

While farmers can be hurt economically and perhaps lose their businesses, others have been threatened with the loss of their homes. A homeowner residing in Morris County, New Jersey, found out how excessive and unfair environmental regulation can be. Robert Carpenter bought his house in 1986, believing that the toilet and drain problems were correctable. He contracted with a tank suctioning company that pumped his septic unit but to no avail. To his dismay he found that pumping the tank was not the solution.

Being a responsible citizen he approached the health officer of Montville and openly discussed the problem. The Health Department stated that he would have to redesign the system. Following these instructions he submitted two engineering drawings in 1987.

Both drawings were rejected because of a possible encroachment onto a deeded right of way.

The homeowner hired a second engineer who designed a more elaborate system. The new drawing created a mound, located above the water line, thus avoiding seepage. This new design was sent to the NJDEPE (New Jersey Department of Environmental Protection and Energy) in 1988. The DEPE returned the submission, stating that it should be left in the hands of the township Health Department.

Mr. Carpenter resubmitted the plans to the local authorities. Shortly thereafter, Mr. Carpenter received approval from the township, gave the contract to an excavation company, and finished the project in 1989 at a cost of almost $100,000.

Several weeks after the project was finished, the homeowner received a letter from the DEPE alleging that the project "involved building in a flood plain, a flood way, and a federally designated wetlands, in addition to encroaching on a stream without a permit, and (illegally) adding soil to the Passaic River Basin."[2]

Now, the only solution to the homeowner's problem appeared to be the removal of the system. A second more expensive choice was the filing of a stream encroachment permit. Unfortunately, environmental consultants informed him that he probably wouldn't qualify for a permit since there were so many alleged violations.

Mr. Carpenter was quoted costs in excess of $100,000 as the price of removing the newly installed system. To make matters worse he also faced possible fines of $2,500 per day if he took no action. In another set of communications the township said the system couldn't be in the front of the house, and the DEPE said it couldn't be in the back.

The homeowner, who couldn't personally afford to solve the problem, has stated that he probably won't be able to keep his house. The stress of the situation took its toll on Mr. Carpenter who stated that he, "[didn't] care if he [lost] the house... he just [wanted] to settle this and get out of Montville."³

The Carpenter case is one of many such situations occurring in America at this time. The tyranny of hysterical environmental regulation has affected Americans in every walk of life. In lieu of an evenhanded approach, these regulations have been promulgated without respect for individual rights or the Constitution.

Lest someone believe that once caught in this situation he can fight back, think again. One particular case went on for nearly six years. The company official responsible for its "progress" tried to keep his sanity by making a game of it. As each bound book and new file was presented, he stacked them vertically against a wall. He placed a measuring tape behind the pile of records to evaluate the work in feet and inches. I visited the gentleman's office when the case was in its fifth year, still unsettled. At that time the height of the paperwork was eight feet, six inches. I call it the "Count of Monte Cristo" case.

A widow found out about the unfairness of *ex post facto* liability. This kind of liability, which is generally referred to as "joint and several without regard to fault applied retroactively," has crept into federal and some state regulations. Its usage stems from the Comprehensive Environmental Response, Compensation and Liability Act (Superfund) legislation and it has stirred a witch's brew. Ask yourself how one can be responsible "without regard to fault," for anything in America. The word "environment," however, appears to obviate any requirement that constitutional protections be considered.

In the summer of 1993 a Connecticut court case held that the widow could be held liable "without regard to fault." A lower court in that state had ruled that the widow, who had inherited polluted land from her husband's estate, was not liable for cleanup costs. The Connecticut Supreme Court ruled otherwise.

The widow, who had never had an active interest in the property or the business, was held personally liable, without regard to fault, even though she didn't pollute the property or have knowledge of the pollution. In this particular case, "Starr v. Commissioner, Department of Environmental Protection and the Scantic Neighborhood Association, (legal reference 226-CONN-358-1993), it was ruled that her assets could be taken from her even though she did not cause or know about the pollution.

A small company located in Philadelphia also learned firsthand about unfair liability. The business was known as the Gilbert Spruance Company. Their product was paints and coatings used in the manufacture of furniture and cabinets. Their products had been in use for many decades.

The company contracted for its waste haulage with licensed contractors who also served large corporations such as DuPont, Hercules, and Texaco. During the 1960s and 1970s, Gilbert Spruance *had legally consigned their waste products* to that contractor. The garbage disposal carter had, without his customer's knowledge, dumped some of it outside of the state of Pennsylvania.

Though Gilbert Spruance legally consigned its waste, and though no records ever showed that it illegally dumped those wastes, it was brought into the web of litigation. Under the infamous doctrine of "jointly and severally liable without regard to fault" (applied retroactively), the EPA claimed that Gilbert Spruance's waste found its way into ten or eleven sites. As a result, Gilbert Spruance was named as a responsible party in various Superfund actions.

Once such an accusation is made, and once a person or company is named a responsible party (even if innocent), the only way out is via the courts. Gilbert Spruance faced *a per site settlement cost* of between $175,000 minimum to $1,000,000 maximum. Hence, the company felt that it had no alternative and chose to fight. From 1985 to 1990 Gilbert Spruance spent over $250,000 in legal fees defending itself. The allegations and related defense costs threatened to force Gilbert Spruance into bankruptcy. It had only two choices, bankruptcy or sell out cheap. It chose to sell out.

The lesson learned was that, unless you have very deep pockets, you can't fight errant regulations even when you have done no wrong. The ability of the EPA to assess retroactive liability — even when the actions taken were legal at the time — is appalling.

Just how extreme can the concept of Superfund liability become? Well, under the "joint and several liability" concept a legal dumper of one fifty-five gallon drum of waste in 1960, can become (retroactively) the responsible party (P.R.P.) for that drum and one hundred others. Since Superfund causes a scapegoat reflex, lawsuits become the normal — not abnormal result.

A Superfund site located in Glenwood, New York, caused the notification of approximately 260 P.R.P.s, consisting of mostly companies and some individuals. The E.P.A. charged this group (retroactively) with illegal waste dumping.

Next, the defendants hired over one hundred law firms who, in turn, sued other P.R.P.s. Four of the law firms then sued over four hundred insurance carriers, brokers, and co-insurers. The insurance companies were forced to hire over fifty law firms to represent them.

Such a result is not surprising when it applies liability in an un-American way. If the liability applied here were criminal, it would by prohibited by the *ex post facto* doctrine of the United States Constitution. Since it generally bears civil penalties (i.e., fines, not imprisonment), the *ex post facto* provision does not apply, according to a federal judge queried by this writer.

These two Superfund liability issues are:

(1) Making a citizen or company pay for contamination caused by conduct that was legal at the time it was done, e.g. hauling to approved landfills, discharging to permitted lagoons, etc., and
(2) Joint and several liability which makes a person who contributes one percent of the problem pay for one hundred percent of the cleanup.

Superfund, which snagged Gilbert Spruance in its web, has proven to be a disaster cloaked in the name of environmental cleanup. Gilbert Spruance's Trade Association has attempted to assist its members who have been caught in this web. It has published numerous pamphlets on the subject, a small extract follows.

WHAT'S WRONG WITH SUPERFUND

The National Paint and Coatings Association (NPCA) has always contended that Superfund's failure is caused by the program's emphasis on confrontation instead of cooperation. At an average of $30 million in cleanup costs per site, the stakes are very high and the liability system is designed to exact the maximum contribution from each potentially responsible party (PRP), regardless of the consequences. Often a PRP's only recourse is to spread its potentially ruinous liability costs among other PRPs at the site. This process invariably pits PRPs against each other as well as against the United States Environmental Protection Agency (EPA), touching off a cycle of litigation that consumes enormous resources, virtually cripples cleanup and further strains our already overburdened legal system.

Superfund's Liability System

At the heart of the problem is Superfund's strict, retroactive, and joint and several liability system. It was designed to

Freedom's Worst Enemy—Environmental Hysteria 79

address a much simpler, much smaller problem than Superfund is today. Many people view as "un-American" its misapplication to a situation embroiling more than 20,000 PRPs who typically engaged in perfectly legal and legitimate behavior. Indeed, we have no other legal statute that is as severe or that routinely denies law-abiding citizens and institutions the basic constitutional right of being innocent until proven guilty. New standards of conformance in virtually all other laws, including environmental controls, are designed to be prospective and to differentiate between wrongdoers and the conscientious.

The extraordinary punitive nature of Superfund liability comes from the combined severity of its individual provisions. These include:

- **Strict liability** means that a party may not have to have done anything wrong in order to be held liable. PRPs simply need to be associated with a Superfund site. Despite the popular myth that Superfund targets midnight dumpers, most PRPs are law-abiding businesses and institutions which did nothing illegal or even irresponsible. Ironically, many PRPs — and many NPCA members — find themselves facing huge liability costs because they sent their waste to government-licensed recycling facilities.

- **Retroactive liability** means a party can be held liable for any environmental contamination with which it is associated, regardless of when disposal occurred. Many PRPs are being held liable today for waste disposal that occurred decades ago. At the time their wastes were disposed of, most PRPs were simply complying with the law. Few people, including state and federal governments, understood how to treat hazardous waste.

- **Joint and several liability** means any single party or group of parties can be forced to pay the whole cost of cleaning up a site, regardless of their specific contribution to the site. Typically, this means that EPA designates a handful of PRPs — even at sites involving hundreds of waste generators — to bear the entire burden of cleanup. In return, the law specifically allows those PRPs to recoup the unfair portion of their costs by suing other responsible parties at the site for contribution.[4]

Obtaining justice is difficult to say the least. While some well-heeled companies have the ability to mount a spirited legal defense, small companies and farmers do not.

The congressman who first proposed Superfund was James Florio, who later was governor of New Jersey until 1994. Florio, in a newspaper article, decried the outcome of Superfund. He agreed with critics that "his" law had become misused and foundered in endless delays. He further stated that legal gridlock had set in and created a disaster for toxic cleanup.

In his own words, "Superfund, as implemented, provides us with a classic case study of how the laudable purposes of a program can be thwarted by an agency."[5]

When Sarah and George Perkins purchased a parcel of timberland in Tennessee, they expected no difficulties. Their aims were simple and clear. Mr. Perkins began to clear his land so as to bring it into agricultural production. Approximately two years later he was visited by a representative of the United States Army Corps of Engineers. The representative informed him that he could not build ditches on his land because such a modification to the drainage was forbidden under the Federal Clean Water Act.

After discussions, George Perkins (now deceased) was permitted to farm approximately sixty of his seven hundred acres. Perkin's choice was to agree to the demands or subject himself to hefty

Freedom's Worst Enemy—Environmental Hysteria

fines (and legal expenses) for farming his own land. His widow, Sarah, put it this way:

> My money is tied up in 642 acres of land that I can't farm and no one else wants to buy. I pay taxes on it. It is a great place for the birds, bees and wildflowers, and I understand why it should be preserved. But if the land benefits everyone, why should I have to pay the whole cost? To me this is confiscation by legislation.[6]

The regulations covering farmers are so Byzantine that agricultural consultants are urging their clients to check with the relevant state bureau or the United States Army Corps of Engineers *before performing farming activities on their own land*, activities that include tilling, clearing, filling, surface drainage, building of ditches, creeks, etc.

Farmer Wayne Sholtey, of Indiana, was told that he would not be able to use one and one-half acres of his property for agriculture or anything else. The two one-half acre pieces had been determined to meet the definition of wetlands, while another one-half acre was in the middle of a field but could not be farmed.

Many farmers believe that these kinds of determinations violate their ownership rights and are, at the very least, an unjust taking of property without compensation.

Most citizens believe that Wetlands regulations refer to marshes, bogs, aquifers, rivers, deltas, etc. However, under the Federal Government's sweeping definition, nearly forty percent of the state of California could be federally designated as wetlands. Since 1972, when the word "wetlands" was first defined, the definition has been expanded exponentially from its original meaning to cover property, which by any rational standard, should not be so designated. "Under the new designations "wetlands" now include a North Dakota corn field where pools of water collect for a week each year during normal spring; a muddy patch between railroad tracks; and irrigation ditches dug by farmers."[7]

This expanded definition, as enforced by bureaucrats, has already impinged on the rights of thousands of land owners. No agency should have the unbridled power to interpret the law without regard to the intent of the legislators and without fear of legislative oversight.

While the effect on one's rights can be chilling, the devastating economic impact of overregulation must also be explored. If your property is designated as being on or abutting a wetland area, you could suffer many economic problems. You can't touch it without numerous permits; you can be prohibited from building on it in whole or in part; you cannot alter it; you can be fined heavily for working on your own land; and you can be jailed for erecting dams, drains, or ditches on your own property even if you have an approved site plan. As a result of these impediments and potential liabilities, the market value of wetlands-designated property is a fraction of what it would otherwise be. Yet the owner remains responsible for all taxes.

More than thirty years ago the Exxon Corporation built a manmade ditch to transfer cooling water from their Bayway, New Jersey, facility to the Arthur Kill Bay located on the western side of Staten Island, New York. The manmade creek is one and three-quarters of a mile long. Its function is to draw clean ocean water from the bay in order to cool the Bayway Refinery's processing unit. No other substances or waste materials are added from the processing unit. Due to the heat exchange process the water does warm up by ten degrees to twenty degrees fahrenheit over its intake temperature. The water is then discharged into the manmade creek flowing back into Arthur Kill Bay. The manmade creek is, in

Freedom's Worst Enemy—Environmental Hysteria

essence, a concrete sluiceway used for one purpose. It serves as an outlet for the cooling water.

Even though the manmade creek was never intended to provide a habitat for marine life, NJDEPE officials have noted that "most species of fish in the New York New Jersey area cannot survive in water at such high temperatures."[8] Since the creek was manmade and never was intended to provide a habitat for fish or wildlife, you would think that this to be irrelevant. Not so. NJDEPE officials threatened to enforce regulations that fish must be capable of living in all streams. If required to comply, Exxon could be required to construct a cooling tower costing between $100-$200 million dollars.

New Jersey Commissioner of Commerce, Barbara McConnell, appealed to her sister agency, the NJDEPE, to recognize the economic and practical side of the dilemma.

> [New Jersey] forms the core of the East Coast refining region and that Bayway is the largest refinery in the 17 East Coast States. The facility accounts for 31 percent of the state's refining capacity. A shutdown of the Bayway refinery would result in a $2.5 billion dollar loss to the petroleum industry and would lead to a direct job loss of 1,369 persons and an indirect loss of 5,422. The closing of this production facility is an event that the state's economy can ill afford.[9]

Some might dismiss the Exxon Bayway affair as an aberration. But it is still another instance of bureaucratic overkill.

The Fifth Amendment to the Constitution guarantees citizens just compensation if the government acquires private property or renders it unusable for its intended purposes. Our environmental regulators must be made aware that citizens have rights, but property, itself, does not have rights. Environmental regulators must learn these constitutional distinctions.

In 1991 a city agency in Columbus, Ohio, discovered small amounts of oil and chemicals on a site selected for the parking of municipal vehicles. The city intended to pave over a vacant lot to make it useful again. The amount of contamination on the entire site was estimated by engineers to weigh less than ten pounds. The area of contamination was only a few hundred feet square.

The city's engineers believed that the problem could be easily solved by simply paving over the site with macadam. The paving of the lot would have encapsulated the contamination within the site. When the town officials selected it to be a parking area, they were aware of slight contamination, but believed it could be handled on a practical basis. The federal environmental regulators thought otherwise. The applicable regulations required that the City of Columbus excavate more than a million pounds of the soil, ship it to incinerators, and then monitor the site for the next twenty-five years.

The idea of a revitalized low-cost parking lot had turned into a potential $2,000,000 environmental cleanup boondoggle. The engineers could see no meaningful difference to public health if they simply paved the lot over and controlled the migration of the purported contamination. After all, macadam is hydrocarbon-based and is, in essence, a contaminant also. Why clean up beneath a layer of contaminant if the problem can't migrate? Done sensibly, the project would not negatively impact public health, and the cost to the taxpayers would be nominal.

Once the municipal officials examined the situation, they quickly saw that the parking lot was only the tip of the iceberg. A study then conducted by the same city showed that the parking lot was not its only problem since the city's

> 1991 City Budget delineated $62 million or 11 percent for environmental protection. . . . By the end of the decade (if

every federal regulation were met), Columbus, Ohio's, environmental budget would more than triple to $218 million or 27 percent of the then projected budget.[10]

The environment itself is not the issue. In the decade of the 1990s there are very few people who openly favor a dirty environment. The question is how practical, how impractical, how fair or unfair the solutions have become. Environmental problems can be resolved without creating rules that engender unreasonable costs and achieve little actual cleanup.

A good example of environmental excess is the nearly universal hysteria created by the mention of the word "dioxin." Some scientific facts must be observed, however, or the truth can be totally buried from our view. Recently a chemist shared some facts about dioxin with me, facts that are not generally known to the public.

1. Dioxin decomposes rather simply; it is not difficult to destroy.
2. Simple exposure to sunlight makes dioxin nontoxic to humans.
3. Dioxin is already a part of our soil. Its level per gram of soil is one-half billionth to one billionth of a gram.
4. Dioxin is produced by fire. Since lightning and forest fires preceded man, dioxin has been here before Homo sapiens inhabited the earth. Chemical companies did not create the problem.

If facts about dioxin were made part of the general public debate, people could better evaluate any proposed solutions and thus reduce the unnecessary fears often promulgated by environmental alarmists. But rather than be governed by national inquiry, we have allowed ourselves to be stampeded into hysterical agendas and regulations based solely upon surmise.

The state of Indiana has rules that require the placement of bales of hay around soil if it is to be dug up from the ground. The cost of a violation is a $10,000 fine. A companion Indiana law humorously referred to as the "fugitive dust act," has serious ramifications. Under this law a person can be prevented from developing his or her property if it is believed that doing so *would permit dust to be transferred from the unpaved piece of property to a neighboring developed piece*. The rule has been enforced, and property owners have been deprived of the use of their property because of the possible formation of dust during the site usage. Silly? Not to the property owner who cannot use his own land.

The United States Government has created a network of banking regulations that make lenders responsible for potential cleanup costs caused by borrowers. Hence, a bank must concern itself with potential environmental liabilities when making a loan. Many banks across the United States will not loan money to whole classes of business because of this potential liability.

Can you think of a legitimate reason that a lender should be responsible for a borrower's mistakes? The reason is not fairness or justice, but money. The environmentalists have called it the "deep pockets approach," but the real word for it is "extortion." If you have the money, you must pay. To see how "deep pockets" works here is the story of the Jones-Blair Company.

> Officials at the Jones-Blair Company believe that many of their problems and costs associated with the Hardage Criner Superfund site could have been avoided if the Superfund process had a focus on remedy and efficiency rather than litigation. The Jones-Blair Company is a paint manufacturer headquartered in Texas which employs 400 people and has been in operation for over 60 years. The money it has wasted

on Superfund transaction costs has kept it from purchasing new equipment and limited its growth over the last several years.

Like many paint manufacturers, Jones-Blair ships its used solvents to be recycled or stored at licensed facilities. Over a period of one month in 1977, the company hired a licensed waste hauler to transport several truckloads — roughly 26,400 gallons — of used solvents. These wastes were transported to the Hardage Criner Landfill in Oklahoma, the only licensed hazardous waste disposal facility in the state at that time. Some nine years later, Jones-Blair would find out that sending its waste to Hardage was a costly decision.

Over the first several years of its operation, the Hardage facility repeatedly failed to comply with the conditions of its state operating permit, and thus became increasingly contaminated. Evidence from state employees shows that the state knew that the Hardage site had serious problems, but continued to allow it to operate while representing it as an authorized disposal facility. Later, after futile attempts by the state and federal government to restrict the site, the U.S. Environmental Protection Agency (EPA) closed it in 1986.

Following the site's closure, EPA placed Hardage Criner on Superfund's National Priorities List (NPL) and named 32 defendants as potentially responsible parties (PRPs). Most of these parties were waste generators at the site. EPA ordered these PRPs to pay for cleanup of the site and estimated it would cost over $300 million. The remedy's extraordinary costs forced the PRPs to seek contributions from other parties who had disposed of waste at the site. The number of PRPs eventually grew to over 200 companies, including Jones-Blair.

Many PRPs believed that an alternative to EPA's extraordinarily expensive remedy could be developed which would remediate the site as effectively, while minimizing cost. A group of 61 PRPs formed the Hardage Steering Committee

(HSC), which commissioned a study of the site and eventually proposed a cleanup remedy with an estimated cost of approximately $60 million. Although EPA modified its initial remedy over time, it rejected the HSC's original proposal. The HSC then adopted a litigation approach which ensured that the dispute would only be settled in court.

While EPA and the HSC waged their legal battle, the smaller contributing PRPs at Hardage were trying to settle their potential liability. In 1989, Jones-Blair and 178 other PRPs reached an $11 million de minimis settlement with EPA. Jones-Blair qualified as a de minimis PRP because it had contributed a nominal amount of waste to the site (less than 1%). As is often the case in a de minimis settlement, Jones-Blair was forced to pay a premium on the gallons of solvents shipped to the site. The company's de minimis buy out amounted to $206,000, or nearly three times its estimated "fair share" allocation. Jones-Blair officials believed that this premium buy out was worth it, if only to save the company from future transaction costs.

Unfortunately, they quickly learned their problems were just beginning. The HSC had decided that any victory with EPA would allow it to collect a share of its $32 million in transaction costs from the de minimis PRPs at the site, including Jones-Blair. This strategy was aided by a September 1989 district court ruling that Superfund's ban on contribution claims against settlers did not cover claims for "response costs."

In August 1990, an Oklahoma court adopted the HSC's remedy but refused to allow the HSC to recover any litigation costs from U.S. government PRPs at the site. However, the HSC tried again, claiming that the reduced cost of cleanup had benefited everyone, and therefore, all PRPs (except the government PRPs) should help pay its $32 million in transaction costs. The de minimis parties tried fighting the HSC's suit based on the previous court ruling between the HSC and the

United States. Unfortunately, the district court simply refused to rule.

Consequently, to avoid further legal battles, the de minimis PRPs settled with the HSC, except for Jones-Blair and one other PRP. Jones-Blair officials contend that the court's September decision, which stated that their de minimis settlement did not protect them from the HSC's "response cost" claim, completely undermines the de minimis settlement process. They believe it provides a disincentive for PRPs to voluntarily participate, and is further evidence that the Superfund program has become a transaction oriented process focused on confrontation and litigation."[11]

The result of overreaching Superfund regulations has been mostly negative, and few sites have been cleaned up. The language of the rules has simply spurred litigation but has not cleaned up the environment. In a 1993 study the Rand Corporation found that a large percent of [Superfund] outlays went toward legal fees and transaction costs. It studied 108 companies that spent money at eighteen toxic waste sites under the federal superfund law and concluded that, in over a decade, about thirty-two percent was spent on legal fees or other activities not related to cleanup.[12] It also reported that one of every three dollars out of the billions spent to clean up the nation's worst toxic waste dumps is going for lawyers or to shift blame for the pollution.[13]

The reason for this absurdity is that Congress, in writing the Superfund Law or CERCLA (for full Superfund names and definitions see Appendix 1), gave little regard to fairness, constitutional principals, or the practical effects of the imposition of the law. Superfund was passed through emotional agitation, not through reflective thinking.

Companies have been drawn into litigation either for actions that were legally taken years ago, or they have been sued on the basis of "jointly and severally liable — without regard to fault" because of small amounts of waste consigned to defunct carriers. The companies are being sued today for actions at one time legally sanctioned by state, county, municipal, and federal standards.

In February 1994, the United States Senate Superfund Committee held hearings on possible changes in Superfund cleanup regulations. The subcommittee heard numerous witnesses express their opinions on the liability system. One of these experts was an attorney, Lance Miller, who told the subcommittee that:

> The current liability system (of Superfund) has not resulted in a fair system, *but that was also not its primary goal.* It was designed for the purpose of achieving the maximum amount of cleanups.[14]

Several experts offered similar testimony, that the goal was not governmental fairness to citizens, but bureaucratic convenience. Perhaps that opinion might be taken seriously if the unfair liability system had actually resulted in cleanups.

The Superfund record is a near disaster. Since 1980, the EPA has placed just under thirteen hundred sites on its list. These are the sites that are known to require cleanups. As of February 1994, approximately fifty have been dealt with entirely. A large percentage of the $13 billion spent to date has not been used for cleanup but for legal fees and determining who is guilty due to the unfair liability system imposed.

The problem lies in a subtle misunderstanding of our justice system. Under our Constitution, retroactive, joint and several liability is not allowed in criminal cases.

During American legal history liability for wrongful acts has generally been linked to ideas of negligence, culpability, or degree of fault. Strict liability, however, means you are liable without regard to fault. Retroactive liability means that you are liable for actions previously taken, even though legal at the time.

The American legal system has usually recognized that financial responsibility must be based on the degree of harm caused. Joint and several liability means a person may be held liable without regard to the extent to which he or she contributed to an injury.

Historically, the notions of justice and fair play upon which our legal system is based have restricted governmental efforts to, retroactively, hold a person liable for changes in the law made after the fact. Every school child knows, or should know, that this concept is embodied in the United States Constitution as a prohibition on *ex post facto* laws. It is also embodied in concepts of due process. It is certainly true that the constitutional prohibition on *ex post facto* laws applies in the criminal law context. The due process guarantees of the state and federal constitutions impose limitations on retroactive lawmaking in the civil context as well, but not to the same degree.

Numerous legal decisions have held that strict liability in civil cases could be imposed for those engaged in abnormally dangerous activities. The problem arose in the widening of this concept by bureaucratic regulation and convenience. Abnormally dangerous or ultra hazardous activities were broadened to include terms like "hazardous substances." In some states this term can be applied to oil, vinegar, matches, and other benign substances.

It is easy to see what occurred. The courts opened the door slightly, and the bureaucrats opened it totally. As a result of definitions, regulations, and the twisting of intent, the application of unfair liability became an opened floodgate.

Similar to the fair liability myth, the "polluter pays" concept has proved to be a fraud. In truth, most sites have dozens, if not hundreds, of potentially responsible parties. Waste disposal practices that occurred over prior years, sometimes decades, are now examined in hindsight. Records are scarce or nonexistent and in many cases, no laws were broken in the past. However, current liability applies even if the disposal actions were legal or mandated by the government. PRPs are not "midnight dumpers" or negligent dump operators, as environmentalists stated that they would be. Rather, they are businesses, local governments, hospitals, schools, nonprofit organizations and others who disposed of their waste through the normal course of America's industrial and technological growth.

The results of this governmental unfairness can be chronicled to date:

1. Through February 1994, about 25,000 individuals and businesses have been listed as PRPs by the EPA. Additionally, many thousands have been drawn into third party suits.
2. Billions of dollars have been diverted from cleanup to legal wrangling.
3. Retroactive liability has boomeranged. The EPA itself is a victim since they have had to assign over twelve hundred people to the task of determining retroactive liability onto PRPs.
4. Inventors, developers, homeowners, and banks have shied away from Superfund locales due to the potential entrapments of time, money, and liability.
5. PRPs, once designated as such, cannot obtain financing for the business since the liability can affect the lender and/or investor.
6. Insurance companies have entered the fray since older policies were vaguely written. Many companies have difficulty obtaining insurance due to the fear of retroactive liability.

Even the Congressional Budget Office issued a report that illustrated the failure of Superfund in action. In March 1994, the CBO concluded that cleanups were taking twelve to fifteen years on average with the main reasons for delay being complexity, litigation, and wrangling.

In 1994, the Clinton Administration proposed a new tax on insurance companies to create a one-half billion dollar Superfund cleanup fund. The creators of the fund idea felt that its establishment would reduce the lawsuit problems by creating a fund that could be tapped into by thousands of litigants.

But the solution may be worse than the problem. Instead of changing the liability arrangement (joint and several without regard to fault), they chose to create a new government-administered fund that could be adding fuel to the fire.

The basic underlying problems remain. As long as citizens remain retroactively liable for pollution they may not have caused, the issue, itself, remains unresolved.

While the Clinton Administration and the EPA saw the establishment of a cleanup fund as a problem-solution approach, the agency also proposed another rule effected in 1994. That rule covers the reimbursement of government expended Superfund costs by companies and individuals caught in its web. According to the EPA itself, that level of reimbursement will be between $269 and $376 of overhead for each hour of work done. This will apply to EPA secretaries as well as engineers. Using this thought process, Superfund reform does not appear highly probable until the reformers figure out ways to reduce the costs and liabilities — not increase them.

Every new regulation should be examined for reasonableness, a concept seemingly lacking in this country. Thus far we have examined regulatory costs, the erosion of liberty, and just plain inconvenience to the victims. But there is yet another concern. Environmentalists have been pushing for tighter cancer-risk assessments. On the surface this would seem eminently reasonable. But what lies beneath the surface?

Another means of analysis is the risk balanced with the cost of eliminating or minimizing the risk. Using statistical models, economic activity can be measured in deaths per risk taken. For example, everyone knows that there are fatality risks associated in the mining of coal or the building of tunnels or bridges. Rules should be made as reasonable as possible to permit the activity while reducing danger on any job site.

Surprisingly, the changes in techniques brought about by EPA regulations have themselves induced 23,000 deaths in the measured year of 1990. The EPA itself agreed that this total could increase to over 30,000 by the year 2000. To be fair, at this time the EPA has not yet estimated the number of deaths that its regulations prevented on a yearly basis. The point, however, is that for every beneficial action there is a consequence. While some EPA regulations are sound, others are not. In the 1992 "Economic Report of the President," the EPA admitted that its rule regulating wood preservatives was expected to cost a theoretical dollar amount (rate) of "5 trillion dollars per avoided death" (see Appendix 2 for Risk Assessment).

For example, Wood Life, a preservative that was widely used until a few years ago, has been banned permanently from the marketplace. It was banned because chemicals contained in it are harmful to human health. But so is gasoline and turpentine. Care must be used in application of all paints, solvents, and preservatives. However, we must be able to use products that are helpful with precautions and safety instructions.

When a product is banned, it seems reasonable to assume that the formulation is dangerous to human health. Yet few deaths resulted from the actual use of Wood Life. The absurd calculation found in Appendix 2 was the reason for this product's withdrawal from the marketplace. Once banned, even in error, it is a reasonable assumption that the product will never again return.

Throughout the United States we have industrial on site cleanup standards that make good public relations but have little scientific value. Unfortunately, senseless environmental laws often perform in an opposite manner to their intention. Instead of cleaning up pollution mindless rule making costs jobs and harms our economic well-being.

Indeed, despite the economic and social devastation of overregulation, more pollution remains unremedied. Lawyers, environmental consultants, waste removal services, and others benefit from the confusion while many more businesses are driven into bankruptcy. If government worked with industry in a rational way, industry would remain healthy and be in a better position to implement remedies. When you kill the goose, all you have is a dead goose.

While well-intentioned, many environmentalists subscribe to "the sky is falling" science. Some suggest an idea or standard and others blindly follow. But often the science, the need, and the results must be questioned.

We are led to believe that it is practical, feasible, and in the public interest to use a standard for preventing exposure to any pollutant, a standard that is based on a one-in-a-million risk of cancer during a lifetime exposure. This standard has been debated widely in the United States and has found its way into Superfund and some state legislation. While such a standard makes good press and makes us believe that our lawmakers are concerned about our health, the regulations themselves make no sense.

Dr. Bruce Ames, a famed cancer researcher at the University of California, in his study of "Natural pesticides that are Rodent Carcinogens" found that the natural carcinogen level in foods are far higher than the level under which many environmental regulations would have us operate our factories (see Appendix 3). Humans naturally handle carcinogens in their bodily processes. While we must be careful not to overtax these processes, a nominal level of carcinogens appears to be normal. Levels of carcinogens are everywhere. They are found in nature, in food, in the ocean, and in the ground. Man need not attempt to exceed what nature intended. That is where the one-in-a-million effort fails.

Environmentalists expect Joe's and Jerry's Machine Shop to adhere to a one-in-a-million carcinogen level, but it is instructive to learn the carcinogen levels that are found in what we eat. Dr. Ames concludes in part that:

- Apples contain approximately 50 parts to a million in rodent carcinogens;
- Parsley contains approximately 14 parts to a million in rodent carcinogens;
- Mushrooms contain approximately 11 parts to a million in rodent carcinogens;
- Cauliflower contains approximately 12 parts to a million in rodent carcinogens;
- Horseradish contains approximately 4500 parts to a million in rodent carcinogens;
- Pepper contains approximately 100 parts to a million in rodent carcinogens;
- Honey contains approximately 15 parts to a million in rodent carcinogens,
- Coffee contains approximately 1800 parts to a million in rodent carcinogens.

The list is not complete. Did nature intend a one hundred percent clean environment? Is eating more dangerous to your health than going to work? If regulations incorporate the one-in-a-million standard, none of us may be able to retain our jobs! The scientific reality is that carcinogens are a natural everyday presence. Of course the old axiom "nothing to excess" still applies. We must reasonably balance the risk and costs.

Freedom's Worst Enemy—Environmental Hysteria

The perspective of these allegations demonstrate that it is not really the environment that is being discussed. It is the adoption of a different way of life.

The costs of this social engineering under the name of environmentalism are expected to be borne by America's businesses. According to a *Wall Street Journal* story, trustees, either individuals or institutions, may be personally liable for pollution cleanup costs. Trustees are usually given power to act for someone else under varying circumstances such as for the beneficiary of a will. "Judge Samuel Conti, of Phoenix, Arizona, ruled that Valley National Bank could be held liable for the cost of cleaning up a landfill as part of an estate for which the Bank was a Trustee."[16] The judge based his decision on the Superfund law, which does not exempt trustees specifically. He said in the decision that "if Congress had wanted it that way, they would have written it that way."

Taking the case one step further, environmental regulations have become so pervasive that officers, directors, shareholders, and other responsible officials may now *be held personally liable for corporate actions*, even actions of which they were not knowledgeable. Some states have used the words "responsible corporate officials" in their definition of parties liable under various environmental acts. Such language justifies the piercing of the corporate veil. Ordinarily, corporations have been separated from the acts of persons working for or associated with the corporation.

In 1991 the United States District Court, Office of Administrative Law (OAL), ruled that "A parent corporation [can be] found potentially liable for the acts of a former subsidiary under CERCLA."[17]

Most courts have steadfastly upheld the offices of corporations, thus most businessmen and directors, heretofore, have not felt threatened by acts committed by others, believing that their own acts, as long as honest and prudent, would protect them from legal attack. Evidently, that assumption may no longer be true. In the above case the judge wrote: "Interest in protecting the environment. . .is an overriding interest which justifies disregarding the corporate form even though the traditional facts necessary to pierce the corporate veil [are] not present or even alleged."[18] What use are constitutional protections if they do not protect us against "overriding interests of the environment?"

With such a broad interpretation, the environment has provided an excuse to put all of a person's assets at risk by virtue of an action committed by someone else. These actions could be the result of activities, which a businessman is totally unaware.

The negative aspects of this kind of environmental extremism was reported by Gordon Bishop, a noted environmental editor.

> The EPA spends only twenty percent of its $7 billion budget on problems considered by federal scientists to pose the greatest risk to the environment.
>
> The study of EPA's expenditures was conducted by the independent Center for Resource Economics. It shows EPA's mission, which began in 1970, has gone astray.
>
> All told, the expenditure of literally hundreds of billions of public and private dollars is being directed by policies that often misjudge or disregard the seriousness of the risks they are aimed at combatting."[19]

There are two well-known situations in which this gunslinger mentality wasted huge sums of taxpayer money and created waves of emotional response throughout America. One incident made Times Beach, Missouri, famous. The alleged pollution in Times Beach was deemed to be so serious that the entire town was purchased by the EPA for $36 million. Additional costs were incurred in relocating the population. Afterwards, it was learned that the

Freedom's Worst Enemy—Environmental Hysteria 99

levels of dioxin found there may not have been actually harmful to its citizens.

In 1989 apple growers from New York to Washington State were shocked to learn that a product they depended on, Alar, was the subject of a national scare. But after the damage was done to the growers and the manufacturer of Alar, the EPA learned that the problem wasn't as serious as it thought. The gunslingers had fired again, before the scientific evidence was assembled.

A more recent example was the New York City School "asbestos panic attack" of 1993. But after closing the schools for nearly all of September and spending millions of taxpayer dollars, no evidence, scientific or otherwise, ever was shown that a health problem really existed. For more than fifty years, there was no evidence that any teacher or student ever suffered *from asbestos poisoning of any type*. Under the banner of a clean environment, a modern day Pied Piper had emerged. Everyone followed the Piper but did not know why. The asbestos could have stayed wrapped or rewrapped without incident. We believed without questioning and were led to the cleaners for no reason.

Precipitous action is the prevalent mentality in modern day government agencies. Perhaps the agencies feel they can do no wrong; after all, they often lack oversight by elected officials, and the bureaucrats do not personally have to bear the responsibilities for their own actions. This is particularly true when "environment" is the catchword that has become a synonym for "an overriding interest." Why such a word is defined to override fairness, law, our Constitution, and our citizens is unanswerable.

Environmentalists have learned the same lesson that all propagandists have discovered during the long course of human history. If you tell a lie, or half-truth long enough, no matter how preposterous, it will eventually be believed. Most people trust their government and want to believe the public-spirited lexicon of the environmentalists. But bureaucrats have defined some commonly-used words to include an ever-expanding jurisdiction.

I have personally worked on many instances of bureaucratic overzealousness. The story described below comes from my first-hand involvement and shows micromanagement at its worst. It is the case of a thirty-five year old transportation engineer who sought to build his dream house in New Jersey. His name is Mike Strizki. Mike and his wife own their home and live there with their three young children.

His "wetlands" is located in East Amwell Township, which is in southern New Jersey. However, there is no marsh or swamp on Mike's homestead. His wetlands is a wooded, rock-strewn property that is only wet after a heavy rainfall, just like any other land in the area. Except for a stream meandering through it, the land is dry. In order to reach his home from Snydertown Road, Mike wished to reconstruct a long gravel driveway that was formerly used as a logging road.

But the attempt to expand his driveway has cascaded this homeowner into a three-year nightmare. When Mike graveled the driveway, it was alleged by the New Jersey Department of Environmental Protection that he disturbed a three-thousand-square-foot patch of his property defined as "freshwater wetlands." A walk on that property showed the land to be dry.

When Mike was informed of this transgression, he did everything to comply. He considered himself an environmentalist and a patriotic citizen.

In 1989, prior to closing on the homesite, he held discussions with the NJDEPE. The agency then informed Mike that he should file for a permit so that the driveway could be legally constructed.

In May 1990, four months before the scheduled closing date, he initiated the filing for a general permit. Although according to DEPE regulations he was to receive a response within thirty days, three months passed without any notification. One week before the scheduled closing date of September 15, 1990, Mike contacted the DEPE to determine the status of his permit application. He was told that he did not qualify for the permit since the crossing was more than one hundred feet in length. Based on verbal assurances, however, Mike purchased the property in December 1990. Since the permit was neither granted nor denied, he did additional research and concluded that he didn't need a permit at all. Hence, in February 1991 he applied for an exemption from the permit requirement. During his investigation he had discovered that the existing logging road (which was to become his driveway) had been constructed prior to 1987, the effective date of the Wetlands Act. Hence, its existence was grandfathered. Verbal approval for a one-thousand-foot exemption was granted in March 1991. This was given by Mr. John Huryk, a DEPE Senior Environmental Specialist, who advised that he would send a letter to Mike memorializing that approval.

Mike continued construction on the site relying on the verbal approval and his newly-discovered grandfathered exemption. However, on May 16, 1991, he received a letter granting an exemption for only 700 feet of the existing 1,000 foot road, soon to be his driveway.

Although acting on the verbal advice of the NJDEPE specialist, Mike was shortly thereafter cited for violating a 3000-square-foot patch of wetlands. The site was not easily visible on his property, although it was listed on an area map. This citation was served while his permit was pending, even though verbal approval was given by Mr. Huryk to move ahead on the driveway.

As the process heated up, Mike communicated with the DEPE on a nearly daily basis. Once again, he was told that his application would be approved. The DEPE admitted that aerial maps (dated 1980 through 1990) confirmed that the logging road pre-existed. It agreed that the wetlands *were disturbed previously*. On April 16, 1991, Mike agreed to have his attorney write the proposed approval to speed up the agonizing process.

This failed to move the approval forward, although the agency had assured him that the letter was only awaiting a supervisor's signature. On May 16, 1991, Mike was informed that an approval notice was signed and ready to be picked up. His attorney, Ken Clark, rushed over to the DEPE building to review the notice and attempted to finalize the long process.

The letter did, in fact, admit that the driveway was outside of agency jurisdiction. Since the letter stated that the road was outside of the agency's jurisdiction, it, in essence, approved the application. At the same time it raised questions. The DEPE letter mistakenly determined the length of the pre-existing road to be seven hundred feet when it was over one thousand feet by actual ground measurement. Because of this error, Mike was told that the letter would have to be rewritten to approve his application for a jurisdictional exemption. Ken Clark was told that a revised letter would be ready on May 23, 1991. No revised letter was ever received.

On June 21, 1991, Mike received a second "Notice of Violation" from the DEPE stating that he had wrongly placed fill in a stream crossing in advance of an approval. As Mike recalls, "I gave notice to the DEPE of this work, which was scheduled to be done on May 31, 1991. At this point, I did not know about any wetlands in the stream area other than the fringe mentioned in the permit denial dated March 11, 1991. It was never mentioned that a wetland permit was needed for this crossing."

A meeting was scheduled for June 10, 1991, to resolve the issues. At the meeting, Mike recalls that, based on aerial photos, the DEPE agreed that the wetland area in question had been pre-disturbed. But while agreeing to his assertion, they added a brand new caveat. The DEPE stated that because the pre-existing road *had not been used for five years,* it had reverted back to wetlands vegetation and now once again fell under their jurisdiction. "My house was ordered and set for delivery on July 1 based on the verbal exemption approval given by DEPE officials in February 1991." Mike recalls, "those verbal approvals were confirmed by Frank Mazzella; my engineer, Ken Clark; my attorney and myself. While one agency official, Robert Piel, said that verbal approvals are not valid, another, Lynn Blake, who gave a verbal denial the previous September, said they are done all the time. In a conversation with Gene McCulligan in May 1992, he told me that John Huryk gave verbal exemption approvals on almost a daily basis."

At the end of the June 10 meeting Mike was told that if he submitted an individual permit application to the agency within two weeks, the officials would complete the permit approval before the house was delivered on July 1, 1991.

Mike's house was physically delivered on July 27, 1991. He had held off the delivery of the house for as long as possible. On the practical side, he had to be careful not to jeopardize his $10,000 deposit. In order to facilitate unloading, just before the house was delivered, Mike personally replaced a few railroad ties in the temporary bridge. The new pieces were made of timber that was two foot wider to ensure the safe trucking and delivery of the pre-cut house parts.

Shortly thereafter, the DEPE issued another violation to Mike. In August 1991, they charged that he had replaced a few railroad ties, which he did, and permitted the Bell Telephone Company to place a pole in a wetland area. Mike recalled that he did not direct the placement of the telephone pole, the Bell system had picked the spot themselves.

While this was taking place, Mike had received conditional approval for a stream encroachment permit. However, the approval was based on the resolution of the freshwater wetlands issue. Mike, believing that the verbal approval made this valid, sent in his signed construction permit to proceed.

Finally, during October 1991, Mike received a conditional, individual permit from DEPE. Upon reading it he realized that it was different from the discussions. He stated that, "When I agreed to this permit in June, no such conditions were ever mentioned. The permit I received contained eleven conditions that were either wrong and/or unreasonable." Mike sent a letter in answer to the new conditions on May 18, 1992. He received his reply on December 16, 1992, or seven months later.

While John Huryk is no longer with the DEPE, he did provide Mike with a notarized statement (dated 7/14/93) about his own recollections:

> I personally took Mr. Strizki's information to be logged in and, within several days, received the package back for review purposes. It was after being assigned to this case that I discovered that there was an enforcement as well as a permit action on this same property. I went to the enforcement section and spoke to them (name omitted) about the case. She was rather perturbed at the situation and seemed determined to bring Mr. Strizki to justice. . . It was under these conditions that I was forced to make some sort of determination as to whether or not the FWA applied to this relatively small piece of property. I personally purchased county overflight photos of the area in question for the two most recent years available which were, I believe, 1985 and 1987. I spent many hours reviewing these photos as well as the State overflights for the same periods, as well as 1988. . . . Based upon what I could clearly discern in the photographs, I manually measured out the distance from the main street to the point where the accessway "disappeared" from sight. I prepared an "exemption type" letter that explained as well as possible that at least the first 700 feet of

roadway was pre-existing and that it did not fall within the scope of the FWA.[20]

Mr. Huryk's efforts did not stop the DEPE juggernaut. While his recollections are now part of Mike's appeal, the nightmare has continued. Mike now has to defend himself against the potential penalties resulting from the multiple citations by the DEPE, for building a driveway on "dry" wetlands!

As a result of the violation notices, Mike was threatened with a $50,000 fine for his transgressions, including the assertion that Mike was illegally operating a solid waste storage facility. This allegation was made because he attempted to use recycled concrete on the roadway. Mike believed, as an ardent environmentalist, that the use of recycled materials was positive, not negative.

Recently, the DEPE suggested a reduced fine of $24,000, with a "wetlands remediation project" to be sponsored by Mike costing an estimated $100,000 to $150,000. Mike answered, "No deal."

The Kafkalike process has nearly bankrupted him financially, but not spiritually. Where does Mike find himself now in 1994?

> This whole process of application requirements, broken promises and changed positions on the part of the DEPE has been an emotional and financial nightmare for me and my family. . . Since April 1992 when I received the Administrative Order, my efforts and funds have been directed toward defending against the allegations contained therein. . . More than fifteen months have elapsed since the expiration of the settlement offer. . .
>
> I have already given the DEPE thousands of dollars in permit fees since the inception of this ordeal, not to mention the more than $38,000 in engineering expenses and $30,000 in legal fees incurred. In good faith I have applied for all the permits I was told were required. I have not now, nor will I

ever, harm the environment by living on this property with my family.[21]

I took the Mike Strizki case to a large law firm that has a prominent environmental law department. In the past, due to the quality of this firm's work, I had referred more than ten cases to them. Since Mike had run out of money and was attempting to act as his own lawyer, I felt that real representation was necessary. "Pro bono" was the only way it would happen since there were no funds left to pay attorney fees.

Their turndown took me by surprise and was more disturbing when I calculated that I had referred cases to them resulting in more than $100,000 in legal fees. I had never asked for a cup of hot chocolate in return.

Upon thinking about it I recalled words, sentences, and phrases that had been said to me in the past by lawyers.

"Our firm practices before various environmental agencies, both state and federal. In order to get a good hearing for our clients we have to be careful of our position. If we handle too many unpopular cases, we can jeopardize our clients [they meant their practice]."

I took this to mean that good, forceful, legal representation, i.e., strong advocacy, can also be silenced by agency rancor. Although I eventually was able to obtain pro bono counsel for Mike, the average citizen is often left in his rowboat without oars. Very few people can represent themselves in a complicated legal scenario, such as wetlands, and win against a battery of taxpayer-funded agency attorneys.

We have marched so far down the road of environmental extremism that the twists and turns have stopped making sense. The expenditure of regulatory enforcement time and energy on minor infractions, such as the Strizki case, is ridiculous and callously punitive. In a democratic society there should never be a Mike Strizki case!

On May 18, 1994, after a year of newspaper articles, the glare of television, and intercession by lawmakers, the DEPE settled the Strizki case. It cost the homeowner nearly $100,000 including the elimination of his children's college accounts. According to New Jersey Network News, it cost the state over $1,000,000 to pursue its inane bureaucratic path.

The problem with environmentalism is that it is achieving the status of a religion — it can no longer be questioned. But question it we must. Man can live in harmony with the environment. We do not have to despoil the earth, but we must be able to use it in our pursuits. What is required is good science, good sense, and good balance.

Chapter 5

Freedom and the Economy

"If you will not fight for right when you can easily win without bloodshed; if you will not fight when your victory will be sure and not too costly; you may come to the moment when you will have to fight with all the odds against you and only a precarious chance of survival. . . . There may be even a worse case. You may have to fight when there is no hope of victory, because it is better to perish than live as slaves. What will you do?"

Winston Churchill, 1936

Since 1978 the United States has continued to depend on increasing quantities of foreign oil. Oil imports have risen, while, at the same time, United States domestic oil production has fallen to a thirty year low. Prospects for revival are not encouraging.

Oil production in the United States was running between eight and nine million barrels per day between 1980-1985. In the ensuing five years, 1985-1990, it slid to a little over seven million barrels a day. Production has continued to slide slowly since then.

Viewing the human side of the equation, oil field employment peaked at 710,000 jobs in 1983 and has continued a steady slide to a 300,000 level. Well drilling hit a peak of 4,530 starts in 1981 and has continued to slump to under 1,000 rigs where it remains today. The oil industry itself sees its own future overseas. Oil companies, since 1990, have been downsizing in the United States but adding to their foreign holdings.

As a nation why have we permitted a strategic industry to shrink to these levels? Is it simply that our reserves have run dry? The reasons for this drilling decline are not due to lack of prospects; promising drilling locations are still available. Rather, the demise of the oil industry closely follows the rise of overzealous environmental regulations. While tax changes and other problems are important, the most significant concern is over the quality and shape of the regulation of the industry itself.

If an oil company wished to build a new five hundred acre petrochemical refinery, it would be faced with many different hurdles. The web of environmental rules would doom this project before it starts. Most regions would zone it out or legislate against its siting. If that didn't work the NIMBY (not in my backyard) principal would be invoked. Permitting this kind of micromanaging of our economy to destroy jobs and vital industries is economic suicide. It also creates the specter of the country being brought to its knees in a national crisis.

The economic impact of mindless overregulation can be shown in many ways. Consider the practical consequences of empowering an agency to impose fines, fees, and penalties and then retaining them for its own use. The New Jersey Department of Environmental Protection and Energy (NJDEPE) exemplifies the dangers of reposing such powers in an administrative agency.

On February 3, 1992, the NJDEPE published its new "Hazardous Waste Fee Schedule." The revenues collected under the fee schedule are all retained by the department. The revenue from that fee schedule collected for 1992 was nearly $9,000,000.

A list of increases in permit fees follows. These fees are solely for the receipt of a permit. NJDEPE provides no other service to the permit holder.

Four examples are listed below:

	1991 Old Fee	1992 New Fee	Percent Increase
1. Waste delisting Petition Review, etc.	$500.00	$ 6,500.00	1300%
2. Inspection fees, Non Commercial & SD	$500.00	$ 2,040.00	412%
3. Permit Review — Existing Facility, Land Disposal	$500.00	$58,000.00	11,600%
4. Issuance of Closure Approval w/Sampling	$500.00	$10,000.00	2,000%
w/o Sampling	$500.00	$ 6,000.00	1,200%

The thought that a governmental agency could charge (extort) such fees and publish such an extraordinary schedule is beyond belief. It is extraordinary that we have allowed this and other regulatory agencies to act in such an irresponsible manner. Such practices destroy fairness and reasonableness as well as the economic viability of many businesses.

On Wednesday, August 18, 1992, a group of New Jersey businessmen held a conference to discuss this issue. They spoke to a panel of legislators in Milltown, New Jersey. A few memorable comments were made at that August meeting. Recalling comments of some participants will readily show the economic impact of errant regulation.

> "The state has a reputation that is undeniable of being hostile to business." Jim Morford of the New Jersey State Chamber of Commerce told the legislators, among whom was state Senate President Donald DiFrancesco (R-Union).

> "Thirty-four percent of our members say if they had a catastrophic loss, they would relocate outside New Jersey...."

New Jersey Hazardous Waste Fee Schedule

Fee Category	1991 Prior Fee	1992 New Fee	Fee Category	1991 Prior Fee	1992 New Fee
Waste classifications (WC) (See N.J.A.C. 7:26 4A.3(d) for listing of categories)	$250.00 $350.00 $500.00	$ 500.00 $1,000.00 $1,500.00	Permit Application Fees (Land Disposal Facility) Storage Facility Incineration Facility (w/trial burn) Incineration Facility (w/trial burn)	$84,000.00 $23,000.00 $65,000.00 $40,000.00	$77,000.00 $38,000.00 $83,000.00 $54,000.00
Sampling Plan Review in Support of WC	$200.00	$1,000.00			
Waste Delisting Petition Review Development, Monitoring & Review of Sampling Plan	$500.00 $500.00	$6,500.00 $1,000.00	Permit Review Existing Facility Land Disposal Facility Storage Facility Incineration (w/trial burn) Incineration w/o trial burn)	$ 500.00 $ 500.00 $ 500.00 $ 500.00	$58,000.00 $11,600.00 $73,000.00 $44,000.00
Development & Publication of NJR Notice	$500.00	$6,400.00			
Generator Annual Reporting Fees 1.33-10 tons 10-100 tons 100-150 tons over 150 tons	$200.00 $300.00 $400.00 n/a	$ 125.00 $ 180.00 $ 300.00 $ 400.00	Issuance of Closure Approval w/soil sampling w/o soil sampling Review of Existing Facility Changes	$ 500.00 $ 500.00 n/a	$10,000.00 $ 6,000.00 $ 3,000.00
Facility Annual Reporting Fees	$500.00	$ 800.00	Review of Ownership Changes	n/a	$ 3,000.00
Inspection Fees Major Hazardous Waste Facility Non-major commercial TSD Non-commercial TSD Generator Transporter	$500.00 $500.00 $500.00 $500.00	Unchanged $ 960.00 $2,040.00 $1,370.00 $1,370.00	Permit Modifications Minor Major RD&D Permit Review	n/a n/a n/a	$ 1,750.00 $ 3,500.00 $38,000.00
Closure Delisting	n/a n/a	$1,100.00 $ 600.00	Generator Accumulation in Tanks Review	n/a	$ 1,200.00
Compliance (inspections)	n/a	$ 700.00	Treatability Studies Review	n/a	$ 600.00

Source: New Jersey Department of Environmental Protection and Energy, Trenton, NJ, February 3, 1992.

Table 1

"Millions of Americans can't realize the American dream of owning a home, and the real villain is the regulations driving up the price by 35 percent."

"Bureaucratic changes are being made to protect the physical environment at the cost of the economic environment," Morford told the legislative panel.[1]

Two other executive offered their views:
"When we go for a permit at an agency like the DEPE (state Department of Environmental Protection and Energy), we're looked at like we're the enemy. We create jobs," said Jeff Horn, representing the National Association of Industrial Office Parks.

Hal Bozarth of the state Chemical Industry Council said the ECRA (Environmental Cleanup Responsibility Act) has "driven people away from New Jersey."

While saying that "no one denies the need for clean development," Bozarth said the ECRA has "frozen expansion in urban areas" because the regulations for cleaning a site make expansion and development too expensive.

Bozarth said he knows many "horror stories" of companies that have lost millions of dollars trying to comply with the law.

Horn said the ECRA began as a three-page bill and ballooned into more than 100 pages of regulations. He suggested it be revised and possibly a fund established to help cities and property owners clean up sites that have been contaminated by chemicals.

Labor leaders also expressed concern that environmental regulations would reduce the number of jobs. They also urged the legislators to initiate infrastructure improvement projects to provide new jobs for the many unemployed workers.

"We have 40 percent unemployment, the worst I've ever seen in the business," said Pat Campbell of Operating Engineers Local 825 of Little Falls, which represents heavy-equipment operators.[2]

The New Jersey Environmental Cleanup Responsibility Act (now known as the New Jersey Industrial Site Recovery Act) originally began as a three page bill and ballooned into more than one hundred pages of regulations. Simply put, our elected legislators have lost the will to control the unelected bureaucrats. When our representatives pass a bill, language such as "regulations to be drafted as the commissioner may direct" or "regulations may be drawn by the bureau" are used. In today's world that is the same as having a cookie jar guarded by a hungry four-year-old.

As free citizens, we vote for our legislators, both state and federal. But when they pass laws in a frivolous manner, they abdicate their obligation to us and hand over the legislative responsibility to nonelected bureaucrats. As we saw in the New Jersey permit fee example, the nonelected bureaucrats care little about their impact on the "Liberty Crisis;" They care about their agency and their fees.

Let us turn away from the state level for a moment and look at federal regulations. Keep in mind that "the power to tax is the power to destroy," but the power to regulate closely follows that axiom.

In 1993 the *United States Code of Federal Regulations* (United States Government Printing office) contained a little less than seventy thousand pages of rules. There were more than five thousand individual regulations covered, for an average of fourteen pages each. The cost of these rules was a staggering challenge for business in terms of dollars and in terms of their ability to comprehend and comply.

The cost of compliance with regulations was estimated at four hundred billion dollars in 1991.[3] Since then, Congress has been enacting new laws every year, especially in relation to the environment. According to estimates, the "Clean Air Act," which became effective in 1992, will cost business over $25 billion per year throughout this decade. This act is only one of many new laws already enacted or proposed whose costs have not yet fully impacted jobs, business, or our economy.

The growth of regulation of business closely parallels the diminution of jobs in many sectors of the economy. In the recession year of 1992 four economic facts deserve attention:

1. During 1992 there were permanent losses reported by the United States Labor Department of 30-40,000 manufacturing jobs per month.
2. Retailers hired fewer employees for the 1991 holiday season than 1990. The drop was large — less than half the average of the previous decade.
3. In the early 1990s large increases showed up in the number of individuals who were termed long-term jobless. In government jargon these were called "Discouraged Workers!"
4. In January 1992 it was reported by the Agriculture Department that "a record twenty-five million Americans, almost one in ten, received food stamps."[4]

Against this depressing background one now knows the "who, what, when, and where," but we do not fully understand "why."

Part of the answer is certainly the explosion of complex regulations on a national and state basis. Every regulation or law has a cost and an effect. If you were to raise the minimum wage to $10 per hour, you might raise the standard of living of low-paid employees. But you would only help those who *remain employed*. Others would lose their jobs because many employers couldn't afford (or wouldn't pay) $10 per hour for employees to sweep the floor, wash the dishes, or to clean the windows.

In a 1993 study of hospital costs in the United States, it was found that $232 billion or about $.25 on every dollar spent for health care went for administrative costs. The study further revealed that the percentage of administrative costs was nearly two-and-one-half times the amount spent in Canada in the same category of expenses. In Canada, where the system is run by the government, the administrative costs are around $.10 on every dollar spent on health care. Could it be that excessive rules, regulations, and requirements required by government are the culprits? A study conducted by Dr. Steffie Woolhandler, Dr. David Hummelstein, and James P. Lewantin, was published in the August 1993 *New England Journal of Medicine.* "Dr. Woolhandler said that the analysis was designed to help health care reformers determine whether hospital administration represented an obese bureaucracy gobbling up billions of dollars."[5]

The study concluded that while Canada utilizes a state-run program, it was able to streamline the regulatory and paperwork aspects of its health care system. Strangulation of health care by bureaucracy seems to be an American problem. Our desire for complex rules and regulations and our mutual mistrust are often the sources of our overregulation.

Overregulation intrudes on our liberty, our well-being, our economy, and even our psyche. Endless rules sap the energy of a person or a business; destroys incentive, and substantially reduces funds available for research and expansion.

Nothing shows the imbalance of productive behavior to its corresponding regulatory burden more than certain employment statistics during the recessionary period of the early 1990s. In 1992, while nonfarm payrolls were shrinking, the United States Government increased its employment at federal agencies by almost seven percent. The private sector had lost approximately 800,000 jobs in 1992, and nearly double that amount between 1990-1992.

One place where a direct correlation of regulation to economic activity is evident is in the regulation of the banking industry. Too many constraints reduce the ability of a bank to make loans. This, in turn, impedes economic growth and causes economic dislocation.

At a meeting of lending institutions in Washington, D.C., as reported in *The Star Ledger,* Mr. Robert Cox, Chairman of the American Bankers Association, put the problem of overregulation clearly and simply.

> Many of the regulations installed as a result of these new laws clearly overstep the line between regulation of the banking industry and micromanaging the business.
>
> The clear message to banks from both Congress and the regulators has been "make no mistakes in lending."
>
> One might speculate that the banking industry, subject to literally dozens and dozens of new regulations, may have become too risk-adverse for the good of the economy.
>
> It is the relentless pounding of layer after layer of new regulations that has eroded the ability, and, in some cases, the willingness of banks to provide the credit necessary to move our economy forward.
>
> And it is not just bankers that feel the impact of excessive regulation and micromanagement by examiners. Bank customers are very much affected by the growing regulatory burden.
>
> As an example, he pointed out that a homeseeker must fill out forty-five forms just to apply for a FHA mortgage loan.
>
> Banks are increasingly asking their small business customers to provide reams of documentation, file more

statements, increase capital and collateral, and offer personal guarantees for loans and lines of credit that have been performing for years.

It is important to recognize that while tighter requirements may squeeze some risk out of bank loan portfolios, they also squeeze many otherwise creditworthy borrowers out of the loans they need to grow and expand.

We need to change the banking environment in order to allow banks to take prudent risks on business loans. Taking risks on business is a banker's trade, and red tape is getting in the way of even low-risk lending.

Often red tape stunts a banker's ability to use his judgement, eliminating the opportunity for loans based on past performance and character.[6]

One of the reasons given for downsizing of American manufacturers is more stringent federal and state environmental regulations. Being terminated from your job is one thing, but it becomes salt in the wound of a former employee to learn that one of the chief contributors to cost control problems is the Environmental Protection Agency, who during the 1991 recession registered a whopping 7.4 percent gain in its staffing. "Between January 1990 and December 1991, EPA's work force grew to 18,262 from 16,999."[7] At the same time, due to the economic downturn, private companies were laying off and restructuring.

What do we get in return for this massive increase in federal regulation? Do we achieve the regulatory goals and downgrade business? Or, do we achieve regulatory goals and upgrade business?

The negativity of the regulatory mindset requires our attention. When building a new factory or expanding an existing one, for example, a developer/owner is required to file an "Environmental Impact Statement." In essence, he is required to predict the impact on the environment of his proposed project. To be fair an impact analysis should take into account numerous factors and then weigh them in order to approve or disapprove the project. Why not include three other questions that would improve the chances of a fair outcome?

1. What is the impact of the proposed project on jobs?
2. What is the impact of the proposed project on the economy?
3. What is the impact of the proposed project on one's constitutional rights (such as property, due process, etc.)

If these questions were asked, we could weigh the spotted owl against loggers and perhaps do justice to both.

The huge addition of regulatory jobs at a time when the private economy is shrinking becomes a self-fulfilling philosophy. As you add regulators, they add paperwork, which adds cost to business. If business can't pass on that cost, it shrinks the size of business, which can be defined as "fewer workers."

As business resources are allocated toward unproductive regulatory responses, the national economy experiences a corresponding reaction. While these events, in the short run, can go unheeded, in the long run they are significant. While regulation must maintain a balance with liberty, it also must balance the economy.

Another side of overregulation is the loss of jobs, higher consumer prices, more inflation, and reduction of economic expansion. While most rules and regulations have good initial rationales, in many cases the negatives occur as the regulations evolve.

In football, for example, because of the increasing injuries of professional football quarterbacks, there have been more and more rules to safeguard that position. But what if there was a rule that he could no longer be tackled *the moment* he releases the ball? If a lineman did sack him at that moment, the opposing team would be penalized twenty-five yards. This new rule would differ only slightly from present rules. However, its affect would be major. That small rule change alone could affect the outcome of nearly every football game. The intention of the new rule would have been simply to protect the physical well-being of the league's quarterbacks. But the game itself would change dramatically and in a negative way.

Like the football example, government regulation over the past thirty years has exceeded a reasonable balance. Good intentions have produced negative results. When does rule making reach the point of reversing its intent? Some say that we have reached that point, while others say we have not.

Many regulations have highly idealistic goals — particularly environmental regulations.

> "Environmental regulatory interventions have long been seen as a costless way of advancing desirable social goals," said Fred Smith, president of the Washington-based Competitive Enterprise Institute. "The experience of the last two decades, however, indicates that the hidden cost of environmental regulations, both economic and in terms of stifling innovations, is large and growing." [8]

The problem with all types of regulation is, how do we measure their effect? If it takes a year to obtain a building permit, what is the economic affect? If a developer withdraws from a project due to excessive requirements, how do you calculate the loss? One unfortunate aspect of environmental overregulation is that businesses are often forced to take unreported sidesteps. If the rules are too tough in California, for example, business picks up and leaves the state. It goes to where it is more welcome, either another state or country. When the regulatory process is adversarial, as it is in the present-day United States, then both the economy and the environment may be injured at the same time. If business moves to another more permissive country, the economic effect is clear, and the impact on the overall environment may be worse if the new jurisdiction has more lenient environmental requirements.

Escaping a jurisdiction to avoid excess paperwork is only possible if escape is an appropriate avenue. Economic activity nationwide is not affected if a company moves from Ohio to Nevada. But employment is another thing entirely. If hiring is made onerous by excessive mandates, paperwork, or taxation, then employment will suffer as a result.

Let us look at the reality of the simplest job creation possible, the addition of one full-time employee to a one person business. Instead of encouraging this basic and productive activity our rule makers discourage it.

The moment that the one person business expands by one employee, he is thrust into the realm of massive paperwork. Depending on the state in which the business is located, the owner will be required (by the addition of one employee), to prepare and file between thirty to forty different forms. In addition, most of these forms require a check attached.

To enumerate just a few of the required documents, there are: the W-4 (employee deductions); the W-2 (annual income); the W-3 (summary of W-2s), the 941 (quarterly report), the necessary state forms, and so on.

While the tax forms may be necessary, the paperwork can discourage the formation of and growth of small business. Until a business becomes large enough to be able to utilize a personnel department, its owners must produce much of this paperwork itself or hire a service to do so.

Excessive paperwork places the entrepreneur in the overly burdensome position of running his business and complying with lots of regulations. In essence, it discourages employment growth. This is exactly the opposite effect that was intended or desired by legislators. It is a bureaucratic effect. It is similar to a computer virus. It just keeps invading the system.

We have become not merely less tolerant of business and development, we have become downright intolerant. This philosophy curbs business innovation, entrepreneurial risk, and economic progress. The bureaucrats, in order to protect us against risk-taking, no matter how speculative or inconsequential, have devised a regulatory framework that stops certain economic advances in its tracks.

This country achieved greatness because we were a nation of risk takers. From the settling of the West to the development of a modern transportation network, we took risks that resulted in economic progress. Rivers, canals, and wagons gave way to railroads. Americans have created the greatest opportunities for the greatest number of people through individual initiative. When we, through risk takers such as Henry Ford and Walter Chrysler, provided gasoline-powered vehicles for individual transport, we enabled individuals to move with unparalleled freedom. Years later, during the Eisenhower administration, we began a massive interstate highway program, which was completed during the second half of the twentieth century.

Could any of this happen under present-day regulations? The answer is clearly, no! Route 80 would only get a few miles from the George Washington Bridge before it encountered wetland regulations and all other environmental restraints that would stop it for decades. As it continued west through Pennsylvania and Ohio, it would likewise not be able to cross mountains, marshes, or forests. An East-West railroad would also take decades to obtain permits to span streams, utilize tunnels, or cross lakes and wetlands. Certain trees could not be cut and sensitive wildlife areas could not be disturbed. The Endangered Species Act would add decades of litigation and rancor to any project larger than the construction of a backyard basketball court.

Do you know any insurance company that would sell liability coverage to the Wright Brothers or even Thomas Edison? Edison's laboratory (a noted hodgepodge) would have been shut down by OSHA; or if he passed that inspection, he would have been stopped by his own insurer as an excessive liability risk.

The results of this heavy-handedness is that new innovations are choked off before they see the light of day. This has been particularly true in the design and manufacture of aircraft. Boeing, for example, is strong enough financially to handle most current legal and liability expenses, but brilliant designers and small manufacturers are doomed to failure from the outset. One of the most gifted inventors and designers is Burt Rutan. He has designed and developed revolutionary man-powered flight vehicles, but is most famous for his engineering success as the guiding light behind the NASA spacecraft "Voyager."

After Voyager, Burt Rutan entered the private aircraft business in the mid-1980s. Unfortunately, though his designs were revolutionary, the "Long E-Z," the "Vari-Viggen," and the "Vari-Eze," he was forced to quit the business in 1985. All of these planes passed consumer muster. The Rutan company designed and sold them to customers in kit form, complete with plans and instructions. The home airplane builder would use Burt's design, but would supply the materials, himself. Unfortunately, Burt's potential liability in the event a plane constructed from his plans crashed so scared Rutan's corporate attorneys that he was advised to pull the designs from the market and withdraw from the business. Even though his designs were marketable and saleable, potential liability shut him down.

In fact, the entire general aviation industry has been devastated by the runaway liability system that seems attached to the manufacture of light aircraft. For example, a single engine Piper Cub manufactured in 1955 (forty years ago) can be the subject of lawsuits brought in 1995 regarding parts, safety, or alleged defects.

Even if the plane had been owner-altered, resold several times, or mistreated, under many American product liability laws the responsibility still remains with the manufacturer even after four decades of usage.

The result of this open-ended liability is that nearly every single engine plane manufacturer has been driven out of business. Creativity, new designs, and forward thinking have been squashed in the process. The legal equivalent of a free lunch has devastated this business as well as many others.

It is interesting to note the result of industry pricing of airplanes during the same time period in relation to the liability explosion in our courtrooms. Twenty years ago the smallest general aviation plane (a single engine Cessna) sold for approximately $30,000. Today's models, while larger, are in the $250,000 range. During the same twenty years, automobile prices nearly quadrupled, while the C.P.I. went up less than three times. The difference in the prices of private aircraft has been due to firms being driven out of business, the cost of product liability insurance, and self-defense.

Our society has become so concerned with assessing blame, with filling out papers and stifling the doers, that we no longer care to balance reasonable risk against reward. Did you know that the crank on the Model T Ford sometimes reversed and broke numerous arms? It was such a prevalent form of accident that, if an individual had a broken arm in the 1920s, it was humorously assumed that a "Model T did it." But progress has its costs, and we must pay some price for forward motion. Wholesale stifling of inventiveness is nonsense.

While a broken arm is not a pleasant experience and product design should be safe, where would we be as a society if Henry

Ford refused to manufacture Model T's because of potential liability claims? Today, there are many Henry Fords creating new ideas and dreaming up new products. But the Fords and the Rutans are faced with numerous roadblocks to the successful development and marketing of these products. Personal injury lawyers, paperwork, regulations and bureaucrats have taken collective aim at inventors and entrepreneurs. As a result, society as a whole is suffering the consequences.

Our thought processes are rooted in negativity. Too often we say "you can't do that," not "here's how you do it." We believe that our responsibility is to make things safe by blocking innovation and innovators.

If only this negative process were single-layered. To the Edisons of modern day, there is a second barrage. The regulators first cast a web of paperwork and approval delays that can slow or even discourage creativity. The effects of this initial harassment are to raise costs, stretch one's venture capital, and delay the innovation itself. But the story hardly ends there. Should a new product make it through the first phase of our negative system, like Rutan's airplanes, they are welcomed in the marketplace and assailed by a second negative. Not by competition, but by lawyers, lawsuits, and an absurd concept of liability.

Coal fired electric generating plants, for example, are favored over nuclear by regulators. Yet, deaths related to mining accidents and occupational diseases linked to mining are a thousand times greater than those related to American nuclear power plants. Meanwhile, the nuclear electric generating industry has been brought to a stop due to aggressive regulations and disinformation promulgated by various groups, using the fear of nuclear energy to consolidate their own power and agendas; an attendant public outcry followed. The important thing to ask ourselves: Is the outcry related to sincere opposition to nuclear power or is it symptomatic of a society that no longer tolerates responsible risks?

Ask yourself if anyone other than the largest pharmaceutical companies could develop and market a modern day drug? While smaller biotech companies have been successful, they have required massive public and private funding to accomplish their endeavors. The cost, time, and legal requirements have almost eliminated small companies from the process. The unbelievable development processes have become marathon tests, which can only be survived by the largest and richest pharmaceutical companies.

In this anti-creative environment, what happens to today's Fords, Rutans, Edisons, Franklins, Whitneys, and Singers? Unfortunately, they go the way of Rutan's airplanes and the Piper Cub.

But inhibiting creativity hurts more than the entrepreneurs. The lost opportunities affect all of us. Previous to 1992, California had developed an anti-business bias. In a 1991 survey, Southern California Edison Company reported that over sixty percent of the companies moving out of California did so because of "government and environmental regulations."[9] Specifically, furniture industry employment dropped by just under thirty percent in Southern California between 1988-1991, and total manufacturing employment declined by over ten percent during the same period. At the same time aerospace and supportive technological industries were hard hit by a decline in defense spending.

Prior to the riots, Los Angeles had developed a huge inventory of vacant buildings and closed factories, and unemployment was reported to be three to four points higher than the national average of seven percent. Unemployment and economic deprivation was, in part, a direct result of the excessive regulation of the business community. The loss of furniture and metal fabrication jobs, for example, could be laid directly at the doorsteps of the regulators since many of the companies had closed because of their inability to meet environmental rules relating to clean air and clean water.

In south-central Los Angeles there had been more than one generation subjected to poverty, welfare dependency, and lack of job opportunities. But once overzealous regulatory fever hit California, the faint glimmer of hope turned to despair. Jobs were nearly nonexistent for certain categories of workers, and vacant buildings dotted the landscape. The jobs lost were those that would have benefited people from the riot-torn area.

After the riots, many solutions were offered. Then HUD Secretary, Jack Kemp, proposed "to create zones in which investment would be exempt from capital gains taxation as one method of reversing the loss. The editors of *The (Wall Street) Journal* would supplement that by [advocating the repeal of] the minimum wage laws to stimulate employment. . . . Unfortunately, these attempts cannot succeed unless there is one further change — a relaxation of California's pervasive and oppressive regulation, and particularly its environmental regulation."[10]

Peter Ueberroth, who accepted the assignment of heading the project to rebuild south-central Los Angeles, suggested that a suspension of building code requirements and environmental regulations would ensure recovery. Can America learn from the experience? How many more south-central Los Angeleses will we have to undergo before understanding that we cannot regulate people and business into abject despair?

At one time we were a positive society. As a nation we have had a long list of triumphs, from steamboats to landing on the moon, and from the American Revolution to the victory in World War II. But in the past forty years we have become timid and fearful. We have moved from creativity and innovation to regulation. We now spawn legions of people who write warnings, issue fines, litigate

Freedom and the Economy 127

cases, and pressure for more regulation. The fearful now hold sway over the intrepid and the inventive.

Peter Huber, writing in *Forbes* magazine, put it succinctly.

> Don't experiment, don't be venturesome, don't go out on a limb. Play it safe.
>
> Creative destruction — the constant replacement of old social structures and technologies with new ones — is the key to any civilization's survival. In this sense, our enemy is within, not without. We are stifled by our own do-gooders, our law courts, our bureaucrats.[11]

In March of 1991 the last manufacturer of 35mm cameras located in the United States went bankrupt. The company is best remembered for movie cameras, 8 and 16mm, but these products had been previously discontinued. Keystone Camera, located in Clifton, New Jersey, closed its doors. At the time, Keystone had approximately five hundred manufacturing workers and two hundred in other job categories for a total employment of seven hundred. Months later, at a bankruptcy sale, the equipment was purchased by another company located in Avenel, New Jersey. That company, Concord Camera, sought to reopen the Keystone plant and employ about thirty percent of the former work force. Concord had only purchased the equipment, not the property. They wanted to lease the facility in order to manufacture a part of the product line.

However, under New Jersey's strict environmental laws, Concord would have become "jointly and severally liable without regard to fault" for Keystone's environmental problems at that facility. After reviewing the situation Concord decided not *to risk the liability* by reopening the Keystone plant and backed away from the transaction. Seven hundred people remained unemployed.

Benefit to the environment — zero. Benefit to people and the economy — zero. There was no evidence of environmental problems at the plant. Out-of-control bureaucracies often have the paradoxical effect of diminishing the lives of the people intended to be helped.

Another example of this phenomenon is the California Workers Compensation System. The state system has become so excessively bureaucratic and abused that Kemper Insurance Company reported in June 1993, that "one thousand of its customers reported that they had laid off or decided against hiring ten thousand workers because of compensation costs."[12]

Bazile Metal Service, a metal distributor, cites an example of the extreme abuse that California regulations seem to foster.

> A former employee who was earning $36,000 (per year) is saying he was terminated unjustly and is suing for $1.7 million, plus punitive damages. "How many times does $36,000 go into $1.7 million? How much is a person supposed to get?" asks Woody Wurster, who owns the company with his wife, Jeannett.[13]

An article in *The Nations Business* outlined the problem. Michael Hoy, President of Kemper Insurance Company's Western Division, is quoted:

> The system is out of control...some sectors of the medical, legal, and vocational-rehabilitation fields view workers' compensation as "a big money machine." The California Workers' Compensation Institute, an independent research organization, says that litigation costs take up 20 percent of expenditures under the compensation program.
>
> Hoy points out that California law requires that only 10 percent of a claim of disability attributed to stress be job-related. He says the compensation benefits are simply "too easy to access.[14]

Freedom and the Economy 129

The economic result of this regulatory nightmare can be expressed in job losses. In the three years previous to June 1993, it was estimated by state labor officials that one million jobs had been lost in California. The job losses in California became job gains to Nevada, Oregon, Washington, Utah, New Mexico, and Colorado. Many of these states had put up the "Business is Welcome" sign. Some, like Colorado, took the gains as a mixed blessing. Not everyone was happy about this reverse migration.

Sadly, Silicon Valley, one of the strongest technological areas in the United States, has been also affected by our regulatory morass. T. J. Rodgers, CEO of Cypress Semiconductors of San Jose, is quoted as saying that he "went offshore in 1992, [and opened] a low-tech assembly plant in Thailand that [is projected to] save $17 million in costs this year. . .wages will drop from $10 to 50 cents an hour. . . . Rodgers says he "got the Bangkok plant up and running in less time than it takes to obtain local government approval to install an awning in San Jose."[15]

In several ways California, our most populous state, has been a leading national indicator and a microcosm of what is to occur elsewhere. Many state and county agencies in California are funded through their collection of fees and fines. These collections become the source of life for the agency itself. Hence, the regulators have an incentive to assess penalties and not to referee fairly. Agency growth becomes more important than reasonableness to the regulated community. This circumstance has contributed to California's malaise and has infected other states and federal agencies who are likewise becoming "speed traps."

Our economy can only thrive, produce innovations, and increase jobs if business and citizens are treated as welcome guests. An attitude of confrontation produces nothing except disappointment for all parties. As risk taking is discouraged, the "Liberty Crisis" becomes a real threat to all of us.

Chapter 6

The Sheriff of Nottingham

"The greatest dangers to liberty lurk in insidious encroachment by men of zeal, well-meaning but without understanding."

Louis D. Brandeis
Supreme Court Justice

In 1992 the national TV news magazine "Sixty Minutes" (CBS-TV) detailed a story relating the plight of a California-based airplane charter service. Since the business was small it operated a single corporate jet aircraft, and the owner doubled as the airline's chief pilot. He had booked a passenger for a charter flight, loaded the passenger's luggage, and took off for the agreed-upon destination.

Upon arrival at the destination the passenger was arrested by federal agents for suspected drug dealings. During the arrest the passenger's luggage was confiscated, pursuant to federal seizure laws. In the locked luggage the agents found a quantity of drugs and cash purportedly derived from illicit narcotics operations. The federal agents assumed custody of the perpetrator, the luggage, the drugs, and the cash. The charter airline's sole airplane was next taken by the authorities since it was *allegedly used in a drug operation*. It was seized by Federal Government agents, although the operator, himself, was not charged with the violation of any law and was not criminally indicted. The airplane was expropriated under a federal law that permits the taking of property when it is deemed that the assets have been used in the commission of a drug-related crime. The most difficult aspect for an American to understand, is that the airplane was seized not only *prior to criminal conviction of the operator but in the absence of any indictment whatsoever.*

Few laws have declared war on traditional American values or sensibilities such as the "Property Seizure Act." Wetlands comes close, but even its draconian penalties seem benign by comparison. Sadly, the charter airline pilot's story is hardly unique. The following news item depicts ever more disturbing facets of the Property Seizure Act:

> When Carl and Mary Shelden sold their home and agreed to carry a $160,000 note, they had no idea they were about to be trapped in a government web that would cost them almost everything they owned.
>
> In 1979, the Sheldens made the mistake of selling their $289,000 house in Moraga, California, to a man later convicted under a federal law that permits the government to seize his property as the product of his ill-gotten gains.
>
> The fact that the Sheldens had nothing to do with the crimes and were the legal owners, courtesy of the unpaid mortgage, meant nothing. After a ten-year court battle, they are virtually bankrupt. They got back the house, but it was so badly damaged that it made little difference.
>
> "Everything we worked for was in that house," said Carl Shelden, 52, a disabled shoe salesman. "And this is the United States. We don't know whether we want to stay in this country anymore."
>
> The Sheldens are not unique. Authorities across the nation are coming under fire from citizens whose homes, cars, cash and other property were seized in America's War on Drugs.
>
> Prosecutors and law enforcement officials insist the program, included in the Comprehensive Crime Control Act of

1984, is helping them fight the drug war. They say the seizures hurt dealers where it counts — in the pocketbook.

"This is a very powerful law enforcement weapon," said Cary Copeland, who heads the Executive Office for Asset Forfeiture at the Justice Department in Washington. "We think it is being operated well."

But alleged abuses make big headlines. A small-town Southern sheriff seizes a Rolls-Royce from a drug dealer and uses it as his personal car. Local police in Little Compton, Rhode Island, net $3.8 million in a drug bust and outfit their cars with $1,700 video cameras and heat detection devices for a police force of seven. The owner of a sailboat loses the craft after a crew member is caught with a small amount of marijuana.[1]

Since 1985, when asset seizures came into prominence, it has been estimated that nearly $3 billion in property and cash have been taken by federal authorities. This dollar figure relates only to federal seizures. Many states have adopted similar laws patterned after the national model.

That assets can be taken under the 1985 statute before and without conviction of a crime, is, in itself, very unsettling. This apparent arbitrariness has spawned the formation of many organizations protesting these abuses. One of these is an organization called Forfeiture Endangers American Rights, (F.E.A.R.) whose mission is to combat what that group sees as rampant lawlessness on the part of the government. F.E.A.R. is attempting to alert ordinary citizens to the dangers of this prosecutorial misconduct.

Those opposed to wholesale property seizures believe that the purloined assets have been utilized as a kind of pirate's booty for extortion purposes. For example, in fiscal year 1991 the United States Justice Department distributed nearly $300 million of the property to local and state agencies under this tainted program.

This number grows every year. Obviously, state agencies who are the recipients of the unearned money are not loudly objecting to the enrichment.

But the impact on presumably innocent parties whose property has been seized is immediate and devastating. Jorge Lovato, Jr., a computer retailer, and Rey Sotelo, a motorcycle shop owner, owned adjacent businesses in Morgan Hill, California. Both men had prior drug convictions, hence their plight received little sympathy from onlookers. However, neither man was charged with a crime before or after the raid on their premises by lawmen.

In July 1993, a combined force of agents raided the Sotelo home and both men's business premises. The G-men seized records, a motorcycle, inventory, and more than $100,000 in cash. After the raid, the agents disclosed that the assets *were suspected of* being involved in criminal activities. However, neither man was ever formally charged with being involved in or related to any alleged criminal activities. After five months and substantial attorney's fees, the cash and motorcycle were returned to the owners. Why is a citizen subjected to this seizure and forced to spend enormous sums of money for the return of his property when he has done no wrong? It's a question that has no comforting answer. According to an Associated Press Wire story:

> The unbelievable aspect of property seizure is that civil forfeiture can occur when there is probable cause to believe the property was connected to a crime — a far from rigorous standard. . . . Rep. John Conyors (D. Michigan) has said that he is outraged and plans further hearings to eventually introduce legislation to change the law. The cornerstone of our system of justice is a presumption of innocence until one is proven guilty. . .the time has come to change the law.[2]

It's good to know that a congressman is "outraged," but how has such an obvious reversal of traditional American standards of fair play survived for nearly ten years? How could our elected representatives have dreamed up something so grossly violative of our Constitution and their oath to uphold it?

In the following case the aggrieved party was not totally innocent, but the government's response was so out of proportion to the offense that it is hard to be anything but outraged.

In South Fallsberg, New York, a local lawyer named Joel Proyect ran afoul of the same law as our charter pilot, Messrs. Shelden, Sotelo and Lovato. In this case, however, Mr. Proyect was well-known in the community, was active in the affairs of the county, and had an excellent record of handling indigent legal cases on a pro bono basis.

He had purchased a thirty acre farmette and built a house through his own efforts. Unfortunately, along with blueberries and vegetables, he grew some marijuana for his own use.

In August 1991, Federal Drug Agents surveyed his property by air and thereafter conducted a raid of the premises. In the state of New York growing marijuana is a misdemeanor. Mr. Proyect was charged with possession but not charged as a dealer. For unknown reasons the federal authorities decided to make an example of Proyect. They indicted and tried him under Federal law, which was more stringent than the New York Statutes. On May 29, 1992, Mr. Proyect was tried in federal court and given a sentence of five years in prison. This stiff penalty was meted out for growing pot for his own use. No claim was ever made that he resold the marijuana, or that he repackaged it, or gave it to others. Everyone, including the prosecutors involved in the case, agreed that he simply grew it for himself. All parties to the case admitted that marijuana is illegal, but no one understood why the federal prosecutors pursued the case with such energy. The five year sentence was not the sum total of the penalty. In addition to his sentence, Mr. Proyect's house and thirty acre farmette were seized by the Federal Government under the Property Seizure Act. The ostensible reason for the seizure was that the farm had been used for illicit drug operations. The government, after evicting Mr. Proyect from his house, offered to sell it back to him for $170,000!

The federal law under which Mr. Proyect was sentenced provides that growing more than one hundred plants (even for home use) nets the perpetrator a *mandatory five year prison term*. There were one hundred ten plants on Mr. Proyect's farm.

While smoking marijuana is a crime, in Mr. Proyect's case it was a victimless one. He sold it to no one, did not package it, and did not distribute it. Yet, he received a very stiff sentence and had the added indignity of the loss of his home and property. Even the federal judge who handled the case disliked the remedy and remarked at the sentencing:

> I'm very unhappy about imposing this sentence. I frankly would not impose it. If I saw any (other) that was consistent with my oath, I would impose a different sentence.[3]

In Hunterdon County, New Jersey, James Giuffre was arrested in 1990 and charged with possessing a *half ounce of cocaine*. He was then threatened with the loss of his house under the Property Forfeiture Act. In order to save his house he plea-bargained and permitted the seizure of vacant investment lots that he owned.

Approximately three months later the lots were sold at a public sale for $20,000. Mr. Giuffre had purchased them in 1988 for $174,000. After the public auction, Mr. Giuffre filed a suit in federal court seeking return of the lots. While Mr. Giuffre agreed that he "illegally and stupidly" used cocaine, he insisted that he was never a "middle-level drug dealer and did not sell cocaine to others."[4]

When arrested he had $700 of cocaine in his possession. Mr. Giuffre claimed that the prosecutor threatened him with a severe jail sentence unless he was ready and willing to sign over his land. Since he was a first-time offender, he was frightened by the thought of going to prison. Hence, he felt the best way out of the mess was to accept the offer from the authorities.

No judge had agreed to the Giuffre property forfeiture. The land was forfeited *prior* to a criminal conviction. In essence, Mr. Giuffre contends in his suit that the property was extorted from him, since criminal action was held over his head if he didn't agree to plea-bargain the deal. Worse yet, it was alleged that county officials bought the property for a fraction of its value, which further clouded the case.

Property seizures of this kind are like physical torture. The thumb screw is turned until you accept the offer, whatever it may be. The only difference is the level of pain. Property seizure, when used this way, is little different from coerced self-incrimination.

There is no instance of the Property Seizure syndrome that is as perverted to justice, sensibility, fairness, and reason as the "Scott Case." An elderly retired gentleman named Scott lived alone on a two hundred acre farm in Ventura County, California. Due to the housing growth around his farm, the property became a valuable asset.

In October, 1992 a raiding party, consisting of National Park Service Officers, the Drug Enforcement Administration, the Los Angeles Police Department, and the Los Angeles Sheriff's Department, swept down on Mr. Scott's property. While Mr. Scott was the only person there, somehow more than two dozen officers participated in the misadventure. The ostensible purpose of the raid was to seize illegally grown marijuana plants, but none was found. During the raid, Mr. Scott, who was sixty-one years old at the time, awoke and became agitated. Not realizing what was occurring he and a police officer exchanged gunfire in the excitement of the incident. Rancher Scott was killed.

Several questions arose. Why not just serve a search warrant? Why were two dozen officers needed to subdue one man?

Equally unsettling was a later finding from an impanelled grand jury that uncovered a property appraisal dated previous to the raid. This appraisal was found in the files of the officers. The written appraisal noted the recent sales in the area and reflected on the value of the Scott ranch. The grand jury further found out that the value of the Scott Ranch had also been discussed in a briefing prior to the attack of the law enforcement officers. These facts in addition that no drugs were found greatly concerned the grand jury members.

The Property Seizure Act handed to the overly aggressive raiders becomes the ultimate weapon. A valuable piece of property that is saleable can be obtained by a drug raid. In the Scott case the plan backfired because no drugs were found. But in the midst of this travesty, an innocent man was killed.

Mr. Scott was killed by government officials who took an oath to protect our property rights. The Scott case proves that the "Liberty Crisis" exists, and ill-conceived laws in the hands of unprincipled zealots leads to the extirpation of fundamental rights.

Mr. Michael Perone of Vernon, New Jersey, wrote an impassioned letter on this subject to a New Jersey newspaper. One paragraph of his letter follows:

> I do not believe that it is accurate for *The Star Ledger* to characterize forfeiture as an asset in the war against crime when it is applied to people who have not been convicted of a crime. The fact that the funds and property seized can be used by law enforcement to pay for items that the taxpayers are unwilling to pay for directly does not indicate that justice or safety is being enhanced.[5]

As Mr. Perone correctly points out, seizure of property by the government now occurs routinely without regard to guilt or innocence. Once a government starts down this road, there are future erosions of rights as nuances are added and the seizures become institutionalized. There is no objection to property seizures reasonably proportional to a proven crime. It is the *seizing of one's assets in advance of a trial and the seizing of assets far in excess of the gravity of a particular crime*, which is threatening to undermine long-held constitutional and societal standards.

In 1415 AD, the Magna Charta was issued in response to the anger of citizens over unjust and highhanded royal treatment. Nearly six hundred years later we are again confronting this type of venal arrogance. Once again presumably innocent persons can have their property taken by the state on little more than a whim without being guilty of a crime.

There is a particular trial which bears out the overbearing nature of this recent action. It occurred a few years ago.

In the 1992 "BCCI-bank fraud case" we witnessed these abuses in full splendor. We will never know whether Clark Clifford was a front man for the Bank of Credit and Commerce or not. Mr. Clifford was ill at the time, in his eighties, and never stood trial. However, his associate, Robert Altman, did stand trial. Though the BCCI case was indeed one of the largest bank frauds in American financial history, guilt or innocence should only be decided by the courts or by history's later judgment. In August of 1992 Mr. Clifford's attorneys applied to the federal court for relief, since they were unable to receive payment for their services. Clifford's assets had been frozen. While the counsellors were granted relief, neither Mr. Clifford nor Mr. Altman were given the same courtesy. Their assets remained frozen.

Both Mr. Clifford and Mr. Altman had all of their assets frozen by the Justice Department *prior to a trial, prior to a finding of guilt,* and prior to any proof linking their particular assets to the alleged crimes.

Guilt or innocence is not the issue here. Reflect on the power at the command of government to seize a defendant's assets prior to conviction. This seizure can force the defendant to petition the court for living expenses, lawyer's fees, etc., as he is being tried. A defendant becomes a supplicant, brought to his knees before conviction. He is supposedly innocent until proven guilty under our system of justice. How does he defend himself without money? How can he get a fair trial without a paid attorney? How can he survive economically during the trial and the possible appeal periods?

On September of 1993 the jury found Robert Altman innocent on all counts. Hence, viewed retrospectively, Mr. Altman, an innocent man, had been subjected to intense degradation by the prosecutorial actions. Mr. Clifford was too infirm to stand trial, and the case against him was dismissed in December, 1993.

In a strange twist of fate Mr. Altman, an accomplished trial lawyer, was able to defend himself effectively. Since he was married to actress Lynda Carter, he had access to funds to enable him to preserve his lifestyle.

The average citizen, however, is not an accomplished attorney and ordinarily cannot supply a second income while his or her assets are seized. Seizure of one's property can be a powerful force. When used in the wrong way, it can subvert the rights of the guilty and the freedom of totally innocent people. It can also coerce defendants into a situation that removes any guarantee of a fair trial. It can be coercion of the highest magnitude, because seizure attacks a cornerstone of freedom.

> Thus, all other civil and political rights — the right of basic freedom, religious worship, free speech, the right to vote, etc.

— are vitally dependent on the right to own private property. "Let the people have property," said Noah Webster, "and they will have power — a power that will forever be exerted to prevent the restriction of the press, the abolition of trial by jury, or the abridgment of any other privilege."[6]

The organization named "F.E.A.R.," has informed citizens that "prosecutors are circumventing constitutional freedoms by grabbing cars and homes remotely connected to criminal acts."[7] John Paff, its president, said:

> We're trying to get our constitutional rights asserted up front. Anyone who owns property stands to lose it under the broad discretion left to prosecutors under the forfeiture statute whether you committed a crime or not.[8]

If you are a landlord, and if one of your tenants is a drug dealer, you could find yourself in big trouble. Even if you did not know about your tenant's illegal operations, an overzealous prosecutor could seize any innocent landlord's property because of a tenant's errant behavior. Other aspects of this law also threaten fairness. Even if acquitted in criminal court, you could be charged civilly under the forfeiture statutes. Civil prosecution involves a lower standard of proof. The prosecution can dangle forfeiture in front of a suspect in exchange for a reduced jail term. This process itself is extraordinary. At the very least it threatens due process as well as the concept of "innocence until proven guilty." The prosecution has the citizen at a distinct and unfair disadvantage because of the log jams in most court systems. The government can seize one's assets, and make the victim sue for their return. Three years later, when the case comes to trial, the government will still have the person's car, which is now three years older and worth considerably less.

A little known fact is that the state and federal governments already own almost nine hundred million acres of land in the United States. Of the total of approximately two and a quarter billion acres the government owns just under forty percent of the country's expanse.

Various agencies, such as the National Park Service and The Fish and Wildlife Service, have been on a land purchasing binge. Through the year 2005, these agencies and others have authorization to purchase nearly $4 billion dollars of additional land for the public repository. In the 1990s federal government land purchases have thus far averaged over $250 million per year. Most of this money is usually spent widening national parks or wildlife preserves. But the way it has been accomplished can send shudders up and down the spines of innocent neighboring landowners.

In practice, the National Park Service eyes the land that it wants and then simply draws a map that enlarges the boundaries of the particular national park. After this new boundary is mapped out, the surrounding land owners can be pressured to sell their property to the United States for the "good of the people." In essence, this expansion is done simply by the stroke of a pen and the glint of a bureaucrat's eye. While landowners are supposed to receive fair value, that often does not happen. In addition, they may not want to sell their property, even for the noble goal of park enlargement.

In 1992 in Maine, the National Park Service wanted to enlarge its "Moosehorn National Wildlife Refuge." However, seven landowners firmly stood in the way of this proposed widening. Obtaining the five hundred additional acres that the government sought was blocked by a group of traditional, stubborn New Englanders.

One of these Maine men was Albert Cusick, whose family owned a one hundred acre parcel since 1786, three years before the ratification of the Constitution. His ancestors fought in the

Revolutionary War. Mr. Cusick's view of the National Park Services enlargement plan was understandably negative.

> The Constitution of the United States says that we can own this property, and my family has for 206 years. Then the government turns around and said they want it because they think they can manage it better. I'm no college boy, but that doesn't make any sense to me. What's happening to us just isn't right.[9]

Property seizures can take different forms, and the National Park Service can bully landowners into the sale of their property. How does a small landowner fight back against any governmental agency that has his land on a target list? If the National Park Service drew a new boundary to include your house, what would you do? In Mr. Cusick's case, the matter has not yet been finalized. However, the pressure felt by these seven families has been unrelenting and unjust. The landowners felt bullied and were not inclined to cede their land to the Government in order to enlarge a park.

You can find a strong government hand in both rural and urban settings. A particularly urban problem is "rent control." Many cities in the United States have these laws, and while the rules and regulations differ, they aim at the same target.

Government property appropriation can be more than property seizures. Overregulation, such as rent control, which renders property unusable by the owner, is a more subtle form of seizure.

New York City has a rent control ordinance that was enacted in 1943 because of the housing emergency created by World War II.

The subject of rent control is broad and could encompass many volumes. However, there is one aspect of rent control in New York City that is quite disturbing. This aspect is not just abusive to property owners, it obliterates their rights completely.

Until 1984, under the New York City Rent Control Ordinance, an owner was allowed to evict a tenant if he wished to live in his own house. Since 1984, a property owner can no longer do so. While there is one exception called "hardship," this can take up to a year to enforce and doesn't really exist as a practical matter.

Regardless of how one feels about rent control, the inability to use one's own property is clearly unacceptable to most Americans. In New York City, rent control is simply another form of property seizure used to redistribute wealth. This can be demonstrated by two recent situations.

In 1993, a husband and wife caught in the New York City Rent Control Law finally were able to extricate themselves. They were Jerry and Ellen Ziman who took their case to New York State's highest court. Their request was simply that they wished to live in their own home. Their claim was economic hardship. Their eventual victory was not a victory at all due to its cost. After a seven year legal battle, the Zimans did win the right to live in their own rent controlled home, but it was a time-consuming and expensive triumph. Most people could not pursue this long road.

Another New York City case involved the Dawson family. Mrs. Dawson purchased a house with two rent controlled units. Both units were previously occupied. It was Mrs. Dawson's desire to evict the two tenants and reside there with her two children.

The eviction ran into trouble because the two tenants had lived in the same building over twenty years. This length of tenancy interfered with the eviction process due to regulations.

The Dawsons filed suit in New York State Court on the basis of an unconstitutional "taking of property." While they did not claim economic hardship, as in the Ziman case, they did claim that they had a right to live in their own home.

Late in 1993 the court held that the Dawsons could not evict the tenants, could not use their own home, and in essence said that after *a certain number of years tenancies are permanent under the Rent Control Statute.*

Speaking of these two cases, an attorney, Sam Kazman, stated the following:

> Rent control does many things. At the urban level, it is, as Swedish economist Assar Lindbeck put it, the most efficient technique known for destroying a city short of bombing. (This point is nicely driven home in *Rent Control: Myths and Realities*, a 1981 Fraser Institute book containing photos of urban devastation — you can't tell the bombing sites from the rent control sites.) At the social level, it has turned landlords and tenants into permanently warring parties, and it has made the apartment (who gets it? who keeps it?) the defining feature of thousands of lives and relationships. (See Tama Janowitz's *Slaves of New York* for a literary treatment of this phenomenon.) At the regulatory level, it has created an unparalleled labyrinth of bureaucratic snakes and ladders; if Kafka had built a theme park, this would have been it.[10]

One of the most interesting features of New York City's rent control law is that it recently had its fifty year anniversary. Not bad for a temporary World War II emergency regulation.

A similar effect can occur through zoning or environmental restrictions. If rules are made so tough that they can't be followed or obeyed in a reasonable time, then de facto confiscation may result. The Lucas Case is an example.

David Lucas purchased two parcels of beach-front land in 1986, with the intention to build there. He wanted to build a house on one lot and to resell the other parcel. At the time the property was purchased, the two parcels did not fall within the existing South Carolina regulatory restrictions on beach-front development. Hence, neither Mr. Lucas nor his attorney saw a problem.

Shortly thereafter, South Carolina changed the applicable law and altered its *method of calculation* of the nonconstruction buffer zones available for beach development. Once the broadened calculation was made it encompassed the Lucas properties. Since the new formula made the Lucas properties unbuildable, the land became nearly worthless, economically. While the new South Carolina restrictions did not affect *houses already standing*, Mr. Lucas had not yet started building his house, so he faced a serious and expensive dilemma.

Confronted with a Hobson's Choice, Mr. Lucas chose to sue the State of South Carolina and brought an action claiming that the new law was an "unjust taking" of his property. Under the protections granted to citizens by the Fifth Amendment to the Constitution (nor shall private property be taken without just compensation), Mr. Lucas's attorney felt that his client was entitled to compensation by the state for its actions that bordered on seizure. The Lucas case worked its way through the judicial system and finally to the United States Supreme Court.

In July 1992 the Supreme Court issued its long-awaited decision. While property owners and strict constructionists had hoped for a sweeping mandate by the Court, their decision was narrow. Property rights advocates, who had been under constant attack by seizure laws and environmental rules, expected to win big when the Lucas decision was rendered. But their hope was quickly dashed when the court did not consider the sweeping effects, but only those specific to Lucas and his beach-front property. The Supreme Court held in favor of Mr. Lucas in his claim. But it did so "only where government rules deny owners all of the value of their land."[11] The court's use of the word "all" restricted the decision's application to other similar cases and created a no-win situation for other property owners who had lost less than the full value of their property but were still aggrieved.

Mr. Lucas was awarded $1.2 million dollars as compensation for an "unjust taking" by the State of South Carolina. He had originally paid $975,000 for the two parcels. Given the time, attorney's fees, and court costs, it is safe to assume that this was not a big win for Mr. Lucas, either.

James Joseph, writing in the Competitive Enterprise Institute Update, makes some interesting observations about the decision.

> Justice Scalia wrote that the "assumption that the landowner whose deprivation is one step short of complete is not entitled to compensation" is incorrect. But he continued that a 95 percent taking which is uncompensated happens all the time; he gave no hint that this was undesirable. The worst aspect of the case is that the court might not require compensation unless the state takes 100 percent of the property.
>
> Finally, the Court muddled the heretofore clear and clearly unpleasant holding of Penn Central v. New York, which declared that a total taking of part of an owner's property is acceptable if the owner still has other economically viable property. Whether this bodes ill or well remains to be seen. The Court left unclear which, if either, is a taking: no value for all of the property, or no value for all of the property that was taken even if some of the owner's other property is left intact.[12]

When the government attacks property rights, none of us is secure from its reach. There is a legitimate power that the State has and can reasonably use for taking a citizen's property. In criminal cases it should only be exercised after a conviction and after proof that the assets or proceeds were criminally derived. In civil cases it is called the power of "eminent domain." When exercised, the state is required to pay a citizen fair value for what it acquires. Whether for a park, road, or military base, the government must pay for what it takes from citizens. But it is the taking of property by the excesses of rule making powers that is the most difficult to counter and to understand.

Cases of the Lucas type often arise from causes such as the defense of endangered species and the protection of wildlife habitats such as wetlands. In the Lucas case the State of South Carolina used the politically correct words of "promotion of tourism" and the "preservation of wildlife." While these are excellent goals, the writers of the Constitution didn't view citizen's rights as secondary to other public goals. They knew that individual liberty and individual rights could be attacked by an oppressive government in many ways.

Another situation of the Lucas type should be noted. It is called "The Dolan Case." The Dolan family desired to expand their plumbing supply business in Tigard, Oregon, which is a town located near Portland. To do so they required township approval.

When they applied for a building permit, the town fathers required that they cede to the community approximately 7,500 square feet of their property. The town stated that the property was to be used for drainage and as a bicycle path. In essence, the Zoning Board told the Dolans that it would give them a building permit only if they agreed to give up a part of their land in return.

The town did not offer to pay for the property. The Dolans felt that the town's request was unfair and unlawful. Broadly construed, it could be considered a form of extortion. If the property owner does not cooperate, then he does not receive a permit. Said conversely, a property owner must pay tribute (a form of bribe) to the township as a whole, in order to obtain a legally requested permit to build.

The case entered the Oregon State Court system where the Dolans lost. The town of Tigard won round one. In 1994, the United States Supreme Court agreed to hear the case. Property rights advocates were satisfied when the U. S. Supreme Court ruled for the Dolans in June, 1994.

As a nation, we cannot permit the use of appealing causes to facilitate the trampling of the rights of our citizens. This is clearly why we have a written compact and must abide by it. If we do not defend the rights of all of our citizens, then none of us will be safe from an overreaching government. It would appear that the overzealous portion of the government's appetite has no bounds.

There is often a slim barrier between a citizen and injustice. We are defended at trial by a jury of our peers. At the same time we are assisted along the way by attorneys. Though not the most popular profession in this country, lawyers protect us against an often aggressive prosecution or an overzealous government. In today's complex world self-representation is foolhardy.

With almost limitless rules, prosecutorial excess sometimes show no boundaries. In Reno, Nevada, the federal government formally moved against two criminal defense attorneys. They were personally indicted along with their law firm, and assets were seized prior to any conviction or proof of wrongdoing.

The case occurred in August 1993. Like a Clint Eastwood movie Patrick Hallinan, one of the two attorneys, was arrested by gun-toting federal law enforcement officers at his home in a predawn raid. An associate, Jack S. Grellman, was similarly taken into custody. Both attorneys were accused of participating in "a drug smuggling and money laundering ring that involved their former clients."[13] Some members of the criminal bar believe the government's actions were in retaliation for the vigorous defense these attorneys had been providing to drug dealers.

There are several disturbing concerns about the government's case against the two men. First, the government sought to take all of the assets of the attorney's law firm. While property seizures have been aimed at drug professionals, this was the first time that a law firm of criminal defense lawyers was so targeted. The lawyers had not been convicted of any crime at the time the government made its seizure request. The message was clear to criminal lawyers — if you defend too well, we will take your business away. Would lawyers offer a stout defense if, in doing so, they would risk possible loss of their business assets or personal freedom?

Second, the case shows the government to have a huge imbalance of weaponry. If the Justice Department can threaten to seize an attorney's assets or take away his freedom, then this procedure becomes a means of extortion against lawyers as well as their clients. The theory of the provision of a fair defense collapses in the wake of this potential pre-conviction juggernaut. Intimidation of advocates is just another nail in the coffin of liberty.

The threat of the loss of property *prior to a conviction* is chilling. It can discourage the purchasing of legal services and can force him to fight a battle on two fronts. Prior to a conviction, additional pressures added to the equation place an unfair burden on an innocent party. It also denies due process and clouds the concept of a fair trial.

As a society, we have abrogated our sense of personal responsibility. Often, our actions become the next person's fault. So that the next person *shall pay for our own transgression*, we then say "let's sue them."

In Japan it is considered dishonorable to sue, so suing is not done with American frequency. That Americans have come to believe that they can sue at the drop of a hat and often be rewarded, has caused another real danger to property. It is a property seizure of another form.

In November of 1993 Derby Cycle Company of Kent, Washington, found out how absurd our liability laws have become. Derby was ordered to pay several million dollars to a man who was struck by a car while riding one of their bicycles. A quick review of a few pertinent facts in the case is in order.

1. Derby manufactured the bicycle in question with ten reflectors, which were placed in various locations on the bike. This placement is called the "all-reflector system." Derby believed that this was adequate for safe riding.

2. The retail store owner, the bicycle dealer, testified that he also thought the "all-reflector system" was adequate for safety.

3. Headlights had never been standard equipment on Derby's bicycles. They were always sold as extras.

The plaintiff had been riding home from work at night. His bicycle did not possess a light since he had not purchased one. The driver of a car did not see the bicycle and ran into it. The accident victim sustained injuries to his back and face and left him with a speech impairment. While these injuries were most unfortunate, the court decision is of interest. The court found that Derby should have equipped the bicycle with a headlight and should have placed warnings on it about riding at night.

Doesn't everyone already know that riding a bicycle at night without lights is dangerous? Are there signs on twelfth floor windows warning us that it is dangerous to jump?

While Derby was hit with a seven million dollar award, the person who was riding the bicycle bore no responsibility for his own stupid actions. If a smart lawyer can devise a product "fault," personal responsibility just evaporates.

While our laws are twisted to reward personal irresponsibility, the careful and prudent citizens are often left in the lurch. Taken to its extreme, property can often be taken from careful citizens and given to those who have shown irresponsible behavior. Such a reverse reward system makes little sense.

The Sheriff of Nottingham

The following story demonstrates how far we have come down the road of this reversed thinking process about property and who is entitled to rewards:

A 71-year-old man was mugged in a New York City subway station. During the attack he was pinned down by a 23-year-old assailant. The older man was being choked as his pockets were turned out and searched. He was threatened with death and feared for his life during the entire assault.

He had trouble getting enough air and also feared that he was being strangled. As the assailant turned angrier because after his search of the victim he produced only $30 in cash, again the victim feared for his life.

The mugging was not a single effort as another young man hovered close by, just in case added muscle was needed. Indeed a third participant was on lookout, ready to sound an alarm should anyone approach.

The victim, during the attack, let out a shrill scream, desperately crying for help as the assailant's choke hold momentarily was relaxed. The attacker quickly warned his prey, "Shut up or I'll choke you to death."[14] Fortunately, the victim's screams were heard.

Two plainclothes transit police ran to the scene upon hearing the commotion. One of them took aim at the mugger who was choking the elderly victim. The officers stated that they called to the assailant to stop. Whether the warning was actually sounded or heard was never proven. However, several shots were fired from the officer's pistol. One of the bullets hit the suspect who fell to the ground upon impact.

Later, a doctor confirmed that one bullet had severed the assailant's spinal cord. After further investigation it was learned that he had just been released from jail, having served time for an earlier strong-arm robbery.

In court, the assailant pled guilty to the mugging and was sentenced to two years in prison. While he was in prison, he secured the services of an attorney and filed a suit against the New York Transit Authority for use of excessive force.

Six years later a state court jury granted a verdict in the assailant's favor. It was a $4.3 million award for damages. But the award was not for the victim. The huge award was for the mugger who pleaded guilty to strong-armed robbery and assault. After a series of appeals, New York state's highest court upheld the astounding verdict. Eventually the case made it to the highest court in our land.

In 1993, the United States Supreme Court declined to hear arguments in the case and allowed the lower court ruling to stand.

Upon hearing the verdict the elderly victim commented for all of us when he said, "It's justice turned upside down. And it sends a terrible message to other guys that crime does pay."[15]

On Monday, December 13, 1993, the United States Supreme Court handed down a decision that imposed a tepid restraint on the use of property forfeiture laws, specifically in drug cases. In a 5-4 decision the court held that real estate linked to drug trafficking should not be seized prior to a court hearing. The court stated that the government is obligated to notify the defendant prior to seizure of such real estate. The decision in the case of, "U.S. vs. James Daniel Good Real Property," did not limit other property seizures such as boats, cars, personal property, motorcycles, and airplanes, however. The court, in its majority opinion, said that other property could still be seized under the concept of "exigent circumstances" without notifying defendants or granting them a court hearing.

The Justice Department saw the decision as only a slight modification to its current property seizure course and momentum. According to Justice Department spokesman, Carl Stern: "We will continue to use the forfeiture laws vigorously. Just because there are red lights and stop signs doesn't mean you don't drive down the street."[16]

While the decision did put a small chink in the armor of property seizure laws, it did not void them or declare them unconstitutional. It did not substantially curtail their usage and/or application. Rather, it simply imposed a small restraint. The court's decision permitted the continued drift toward the abrogation of full constitutional protection of private property rights. Since the court had an opportunity to void the whole abusive and defective process and didn't do so, the decision was very disappointing to property rights advocates. The court's decision must be interpreted as narrow, since it only covered real estate and didn't recognize the importance of the basic right of private property to all Americans. The only solution to property seizure laws is that they be repealed or declared unconstitutional, not that Band-Aids be applied to reduce their bite.

Chapter 7

Big Brother is Watching You

"The enumeration in the constitution of certain rights shall not be constructed to deny or disparage others retained by the people."

The U.S. Bill of Rights
Ninth Amendment, 1789

During my son's eighteenth year, he received a letter from the Selective Service System that requested compliance with the Draft Act. As government letters go, it was rather clear and precise. The compliance letter contained three sections, marked A, B, and C. Section A was for those required to register; section B was for those asserting an exemption claim, and section C was to be filled out by disabled individuals.

It was not the Draft Act nor the registration process that caught my attention. Rather, it was the first paragraph.

> A computer match using government files has identified you as a man who may be required to register with Selective Service, but who may not have registered. Unless determined by Selective Service to be exempt from the registration requirement, Federal law requires men to register within 30 days of their 18th birthday.[1]

Clearly, the letter was sent as a result of a government computer match, and, of course, that was my son's social security number. As everyone knows, the social security number is required to open a bank account, obtain a job, go to school, etc. Once that number is established, it is almost like a beep-emitting dog tag. Every citizen is matchable, traceable, locatable, and thus no longer safe from government matching or intervention. Once a person receives a social security number, he or she is no longer a private person!

In an Orwellian tour de force, in 1993 President Clinton unveiled his health care plan. Buried in the voluminous proposal was the creation of a national health care identity card. The proposal indicated that it would be universal, unbreakable, tamperproof, and mandatory for all Americans.

If one melds a social security number, a national identity card, and a computer, he creates a formula for mischief. When mixed together, our government can produce a tracking mechanism for all citizens.

Combining these records could produce identity, financial data, tax data, health records, births and deaths, physical movement, and much more. Not only will Big Brother be watching you, he can be only one step away from controlling you. Big Brother will then possess all the necessary tools to do so.

Powerful computers will be given information making a citizen's background accessible for any and all reasons. This kind of network begins slowly but relentlessly. When originally initiated, such programs are sold to the public by assuring citizens that the data will be used only for taxes, health care, or delinquents, etc. Once the door is opened, however, and the information properly programmed, the right to privacy or free movement can be totally obliterated. If bureaucratic meddling is not tightly contained at the beginning, then relatively unobjectionable steps like issuing a social security number and a health care card could expand to include more troubling searches never initially contemplated. Who suffers? Every citizen stands to lose. What can he lose? He potentially gives up his freedom, his persona, and his privacy.

Many programs that begin innocently and with idealistic motives, often turn sinister.

The control of pollution, for example, is no longer the reality of the environmental movement. We are now faced with permits, fines, fees, and penalties for paperwork infractions that *have no relation to the act of polluting*.

The extremes to which regulators go have been chronicled many times. But they may have reached a new low during the Summer of 1992 when a man vomited on a patch of grass in Linden, New Jersey, after taking a radioactive iodine pill. His vomit was considered a hazardous spill and had to be cleaned up accordingly. The man suffered from a thyroid condition and was given a radioactive pill at the Rahway, New Jersey, Hospital. On the way home he became sick. He notified the hospital who in turn called 1-800-N.J. CLEAN.

Under NJDEPE regulations, anyone, including the hospital, has to report a discharge of any kind, *no matter how small the amount*, or be subjected to the possibility of a heavy fine.

The Linden Police Department responded and took a radiation reading, which was determined to be minimal and not harmful to anyone. The hospital was required to send a crew to dig up that portion of grass for testimony and then had to pay for the very expensive removal to a hazardous waste facility.[2]

National computer networks have the potential for subverting rights and expanding bureaucratic excesses. The information banks go hand in hand with well-meaning, well-cloaked regulations that can be turned against us. As citizens, we have permitted rule making to become a bureaucratic art form. Once a rule is in a jar, a powerful genie can be unleashed against us. To reverse the process is difficult.

Big Brother is now interested in the fruit we buy. What could be more innocuous than a piece of fruit? There is a group called the "Nectarine Administrative Committee," commonly called the N.A.C. This United States Department of Agriculture creation has established a variety of quality controls to specify what nectarines the public can and can't purchase.

The N.A.C. developed a color matching system consisting of fourteen shades. In order for a grower to sell a nectarine legally, he must match it to a U.S.D.A. color card. The color match is unrelated to the nectarine's taste, desirability, or marketability. Further, and more importantly, it has no relation to consumer health or safety.

Since most nectarines are grown in California, the color standards are mainly applied there. As the nectarine begins to ripen, the color of the fruit changes. Hence, color coding itself is inconsistent since it depends on when the color coding is done and whether a shipment is headed five miles from the farm or one thousand miles from the farm. While consumers may think this is absurd, so does the regulated farmer.

A company located in Fresno, California, discovered how absurd the regulations could be. The *Washington Times* reported that

> Elliott Inc. lost $347,000 in 1986 alone due to standards. Elliott was the only grower producing Tom Grand nectarines — a variety popular on the East Coast that does not turn as yellow as some others. The N.A.C. prohibited Elliott from shipping its Tom Grands until they had passed the color-chip test. Elliott Inc. received many complaints about overripe fruit. In 1990, the Elliott farm alone was required to throw away almost one million nectarines.[3]

This bureaucratic excess may force farmers to double their picking crews. The increased labor costs prompts a price increase to the consumer. The consumer pays more for a nectarine, but achieves little or no benefit in return.

A group of farmers (Alliance for Equitable Marketing) has tried to halt this absurd interference in a farmer's business. In frustration, and to show the zaniness of this Department of Agriculture commission they have distributed nectarines to congressmen tagged with "banned colored fruit" labels inside. On each box the farmers had affixed a label. This box contains an illegal substance. Inside the box were a dozen succulent nectarines — nectarines banned from the nation's grocery stores because federal bureaucrats decreed they were too small (or the wrong color).[4]

Since we have permitted federal agencies to direct us without limits or oversight, what often results is sheer nonsense. Unfortunately, nonsense of this kind only serves to restrict the liberty of farmers to grow, consumers to choose, and the rest of us to be free from a frightening level of interference in our daily lives.

Big Brother showed his indifference when a fire in the borough of Bronx, New York, demolished the store of Mr. Lazar Berkovits. The fire occurred in the summer of 1992. In order to rebuild his premises he was required to obtain a New York City building permit. However, Mr. Berkovits was unable to obtain this permit because of an old street named East Tremont Avenue, which no longer existed. East Tremont Avenue no longer ran through his or any other property. It had not done so for many years, or his burned out store would have been in the middle of this fictitious road.

However, the City Building Department was certain that it did exist. As a result of the City's intransigence, it took Mr. Berkovits nearly a year to obtain the permit to rebuild his burned out store. Only through the intervention of the Bronx Borough President, Fernando Ferrer, was the permit issued one year later. Four other store owners in the strip mall reported similar delays, paperwork hassles, and inaction. This kind of mal-regulation makes no sense.

Neither does the absurd hysteria that emanates from Washington, D.C. Senator John Scott reported in his newsletter that cleaning yourself may be hazardous to your health:

> Apparently there are not enough hazards to go around. The nice folks your tax dollars pay to protect you from the dangers they define are searching for job security. Federal Environmental Protection Agency officials have launched a new study to assess the risks of — brace yourself — taking showers. Seems someone in the EPA worries people might be injured by inhaling water vapor while taking a shower.
>
> No, we didn't make it up. It's true, according to a publication called "EPA Watch."
>
> Doubtless, several bureaucrats will take home paychecks for months while the imagined hazard is studied. Unfortunately, there's probably a 50-50 chance someone in Washington will decide showers really are dangerous.
>
> Wonder if anyone at the EPA ever has studied the hazards of pouring billions of dollars into overregulation?[5]

One of the strangest stories that I have uncovered while researching this book is that of Mr. John P. White and his attempt to establish a fish farm in Puerto Rico. It was his intention to raise shrimp domestically. This story was brought to my attention by the Fairness to Land Owners Committee, (FLOC) located in Cambridge, Maryland, who has graciously permitted its retelling in full:

> John P. White has been trying since June of 1987 to obtain a "wetlands" permit from the Corps of Engineers to convert abandoned salt evaporation ponds in Puerto Rico to ponds for raising shrimp. John had estimated that the shrimp farm would have created almost 200 jobs and projected that it would infuse some $10 million a year into the U.S. economy — an economy, he states, that currently imports over $5 billion of shrimp each year.

A once successful business man, John has been battered by over-zealous government bureaucrats who irreparably damaged his name with a wild, bizarre and highly publicized raid of his farm. The bureaucrats' actions have also resulted in enormous personal and financial tragedies and made it impossible for John to meet the financial commitments on loans procured to establish his business.

Having pledged his assets as collateral for loans, a bank in Tennessee took his land and family home in Knoxville. The Puerto Rico banks took all John's heavy equipment and are threatening to take his shrimp farm property. Five lawsuits for failure to pay debts are pending against him. He has sold trailers, tanks, pumps, machinery, furniture and anything else for which he can find a buyer. He lost power at his farm when a transformer was repossessed. His telephone has just been disconnected for failure to pay overdue phone bills.

After learning of this tragedy, *The FLOC* requested pro bono assistance from Bernie Goode, an environmental engineer consultant and former Chief of Regulatory Affairs of the Corps and Stan Legro, attorney and former Assistant Administrator for Enforcement at EPA.

The property involved is in an individual area of Ponce, Puerto Rico. Bernie inspected the site (at his own expense) and concluded that it consists of mostly uplands with an area of mangrove wetlands along the shoreline.

For years Ponce Salt Industries, Inc., a subsidiary of Morton Salt, used the property as a salt refinery, with earthen holding tanks in the uplands area. Salt water was pumped into the tanks which retained it until it evaporated and the salt remaining was harvested.

When Ponce Salt stopped its salt refining operation, the PR Economic Development authority was interested in making some productive use of the barren holding tanks. They persuaded John, who was a businessman in Tennessee, to start up a shrimp farm which would create desperately needed local employment opportunities.

In 1987, John went to Puerto Rico, bought the property and established Ponce Marine Farms, Inc. (PMF). Substantial investments were made in breeder shrimp and in equipment necessary for the operation. Applications were filed for numerous federal, Commonwealth of Puerto Rico and local permits. John obtained all other necessary permits to operate the shrimp farm and satisfied all of the requirements for the issuance of a wetlands permit by the Corps.

The application for the Corps permit was filed on June 5, 1987. By letter of January 13, 1989, the Corps advised that all permit issuance requirements had been met but only required the water quality certification or waiver from the Puerto Rico Environmental Quality Board. In fact, pursuant to the applicable statute and the Corps' own regulations, a waiver had already occurred. Although all requirements were satisfied and PMF was entitled to its permit no later than January 13, 1989, the EPA has blocked the issuance.

After being advised by the Corps that they were ready to issue the permit, PMF commenced some work on the uplands area of the property to make repairs to the existing earthen holding tanks. No work was done in the wetlands along the shoreline.

On March 3, 1989, a new Corps field inspector issued an order directing that no work be done in wetlands until the permit was received. John was told by the Corps that PMF could continue to do work in the uplands area of the property but could not work in the wetlands area along the shore — to which he complied.

The Corps, having satisfied all coordination requirements with other federal governmental agencies, was prepared to issue the wetlands permit. Some EPA personnel, for whatever reason, did not want the permit to be issued. Despite failing to follow applicable procedure, EPA personnel have used various tactics to stop the issuance of the Corps permit. Although the Corps had the statutory authority to make the final decision and issue the permit, EPA personnel were seemingly unwilling to accept the fact that in this case the law gave them only an advisory role.

After having tried by other means to prevent the Corps from issuing the permit, and apparently learning that the Corps was about to issue it — which it was authorized (and indeed obligated) to do — EPA personnel commenced a so-called enforcement action on August 28, 1989, to prevent the Corps from releasing the permit. This enforcement action was without legal or factual basis — no violation had in fact occurred; and even under EPA's interpretation, all activities which had occurred were allowed by the wetlands permit which the Corps was ready to issue and which PMF had been entitled to receive prior to the occurrence of such activities.

On June 26, 1990, while John was in the process of obtaining financing for the operation from a bank in San Juan, his farm was the target of a bizarre raid by well-armed agents from more than a half dozen federal agencies from as far away as Los Angeles, Denver, New York, and Washington as well as local agents. John has identified the agents as coming from EPA, FBI, Drug Enforcement, Customs, Immigration, Department of the Interior, Commerce and the U.S. Marshall's Office.

The raid was apparently initiated and orchestrated by EPA personnel, who notified the media of their "event." Thus with search warrant in hand and brandishing firearms, the government raiders were accompanied by TV cameras and newspaper reporters. Seeing the raid on TV, the bank officials terminated the loan proceedings.

John returned immediately to find his employees lined up and guns deployed on them. Mr. Joseph Russo, an EPA criminal investigator and the apparent leader of the raid, with gun in hand interrogated John. Although extensive searches, seizures of records and interrogations of employees were carried out by the federal raiders, no violation of any law was found.

No explanation has yet been received as to the legal basis for the raid, the dramatic use of firearms and other actions by the raiders or the extensive media coverage which the feds dragged along. Nothing in the record comes anywhere close to explaining this incredible and bizarre event.

Other than harvesting of the mature shrimp, all operations including the processing plant and hatchery activities have ceased. About 25 employees and 30 contract people lost their jobs. Millions of shrimp in various stages of culture died. But of the greatest consequence, White's reputation in the community, especially the lending community, was severely and permanently damaged.

As a result of the EPA enforcement action and the chilling effect of the federal raid on the ability to obtain vital financing, it has not been possible to conduct any economically productive activity on the property.

In addition to this reputation, John has lost most of his business and personal assets. His business and he have suffered financial ruin. His last desperate hope (in 1993) is that Bernie and Stan can negotiate some resolution immediately with the federal government which might open a window for some financing before a final foreclosure eliminates his last and only asset — the land of the shrimp farm he was trying to create.[6]

On July 29, 1992, the State of Maryland achieved a notable first in America. On that date Maryland enacted a law that *required all high school students to volunteer for community service* — or not graduate from the twelfth grade. The Maryland State Board of

Education issued a ruling that required each district in the state to mandate that each student perform seventy-five hours of community service before high school graduation.

Most Americans know that the Constitution prohibits enforcing "Involuntary Servitude" upon its citizens. While there is no argument that community service is an excellent character building device, it is unlikely to achieve that goal when service is mandated. How do you compel "character development?" Can states constitutionally compel community service? If so, what are the limits? Why not require all adults to provide community service, also?

Have we as a nation lost sight of what we are really trying to protect? Our nation was founded to protect personal freedom, the right to do as one chooses. If Big Brother can enforce servitude by high school students, then how about enforcing how you think, how you act, how you draw, how you cut your hair, or shave? Is this an exaggeration? I think not. In fact, on many of today's "politically correct campuses," speech codes have already eroded first amendment rights, and "political correctness" is also introducing itself into the mundane world of haircutting.

Recently, I went for a haircut to the barber shop that has served me for over twenty years. It was a crisp, cool fall day, and there was no one else in the shop at the time. After discussing the usual list of current events, sports, and local gossip, the barber, whose name is really Charlie, told me of his plans to retire in five to six years. He said that he was looking for property near Scranton, Pennsylvania, and intended to purchase a retirement home there.

"Scranton, Pennsylvania, still has good property values for retirees. Not a lot of people there either. I'll be glad to get out of this damned business, said Charlie.

"Sounds like you're unhappy in your business; you used to like it; how has the business changed?" I asked.

"Well, I'll bet that you don't know that I can't expand this shop, hire an assistant, or move the shop across the street."

"Charlie, it's still America — why can't you do those things?"

"Well, we have a state licensing board, and they've decided that barbers like me can't have a barber shop, anymore, *because I serve men only!*"

"So what?" I asked in increased frustration.

"See, this shop is grandfathered. As long as I'm working it, don't expand it, don't move it, and don't hire an assistant, then I can operate it as before. But all the new shops now have to be unisex. They have to be able to accommodate men and women. In order to do that you need more than a barber. You need a stylist, a person to do nails — you know the whole works."

"Hold it, Charlie, you mean that if you want to open a one-man business that offers men's hair cuts only — you can't legally get a barber's license?"

"That's right, you've got it, it's illegal. When I die, my shop dies. I can't sell it, can't sublease it, it just fades away, you know, dies."

It took me a long time to recover from that conversation. I returned to my office and called the state licensing board. They confirmed what Charlie had told me. The person taking my call clearly stated that new shops operate under the applicable rules and "are now unisex, sir."

Some readers might think that unisex is the modern approach while one sex barbering is old time. But that is not the point here. While thoughtful people recognize the evils of discrimination, shouldn't a barber be able to decide whose hair he cuts?

You might ask yourself, "Maybe something good occurs by bureaucratic rules?" We have only talked about the negative occurrences. Maybe there have been rules enacted with beneficial results. But I couldn't find enough to add to this book.

In 1990, Congress passed a law entitled the "Indian Arts and Crafts Act." Although it certainly sounds like an "apple pie à la mode" issue, a purely positive piece of legislation, it was not. Should you violate this law you can be imprisoned for up to five years or be fined up to $250,000. It appears strange to have penalties for arts and crafts. Though this act is of particular import to the citizens of Arizona, New Mexico, Colorado, Idaho, and other western states, its intent, however, should concern all of us.

The Indian Arts and Crafts Act is a law to control Indian arts. The Act established the Indian Arts and Crafts Board, a part of the Department of the Interior, which was granted rule making authority. The thought process behind the law was that, in order to protect Indian art, a person must be an Indian to produce it.

As an extension to this thought process, Frederic Remington would be prohibited from sculpting cowboys because he wasn't a cowboy. John Wayne would be prohibited from playing a green beret, because he had never been in the Marines. Jules Verne would be prohibited from suggesting atomic power as a source of power for his famed submarine, because he wasn't a nuclear scientist.

At the same time, it will be difficult to prove that you are an Indian in the first place. Can you produce Indian art if you are less than fifty percent Cherokee, or more than twenty-five percent, or do you have to be full-blooded?

Many readers might just call a law like the "Indian Arts and Crafts Act" silly. While it is inane, it is also frightening. Imagine being sentenced by a court for the crime of painting and selling a picture of an Indian girl? Your crime — you were a white man, a black man, a Jew, or an Italian!

How many citizens are familiar with the operation of the NCIC system? NCIC, or the National Crime Information Computer, contains data on criminal activities. It is arranged by drivers' license number, car registration, and/or social security number.

The problem is not with the maintenance of such a data bank, since centralized information on criminals is positive. Rather, it is the protection of innocent people's rights from overreaching eyes that could become a future issue.

A police officer can pull up behind a car and request a computer check on the vehicle by license tag number. If an officer pulls a vehicle over and the driver surrenders his license to him, the policeman usually returns to his vehicle. The reason for the officer's return is that he then calls in the license I.D. number and the name listed thereon. What happens almost instantaneously is an NCIC check. The dispatcher comes back with a response that is either "Negative or Positive NCIC." In this case the license plate number provides the computer with search identifiers.

While the catching of criminals is obviously a high priority in today's lawless society, there is nevertheless, a fine line that must not be crossed in the future. With the advent of high powered miniaturized equipment, in a short time a police officer will be able to carry a miniature computer in his pocket and be able to check a person's data bank record. We are only a few steps away from having the technological ability for a policeman to say, "Sir, the gum you just tossed is littering, please identify yourself." The proposed "tamperproof" national medical identification card (complete with social security number) may have to be supplied upon request. Since everyone may have to carry a NMIC, it can be made producible upon demand, only one step beyond the current proposals. The gum disposal, or some other minor infraction could provide the excuse while NMIC provides the ability to look anyone up on the national crime computer. The tools are there. The bureaucratic tendency towards malevolent behavior is omnipresent. Why not take the single, additional step of hooking all these tools together for "government convenience." We are very close to "Big Brother" watching all of us.

Given the electronic miniaturization and computer advances of modern technology, these developments could not have come at a more inopportune time for freedom's cause. Since the 1960s, society appears to be at odds with itself. Government suspects citizens, citizens suspect government, and groups suspect other groups. Our technological advances serve to heighten the ability to eavesdrop and provide an excuse for mischief. We must not let this societal irritation provide an excuse for an assault on our civil liberties. An example of this failure to listen comes from a very unusual quarter, a law designed to allow citizens to examine inner workings of government.

The Freedom of Information Act (FOIA) was enacted into law as a barricade to the potential stonewalling of citizens by bureaucrats. It was to provide a way around "Big Brother" since it afforded the citizen access to the truth, however and wherever buried. Unfortunately, since its passage the truth can still be blurred as bureaucrats have quickly found out that they hold all the cards.

When an agency refuses an FOIA request, the citizen's only recourse is to sue in federal court. There is no quick resolution system. As we shall see in the Landano case, this pursuit can take years and years and cause great suffering.

The problem once again is that the agency withholding the information bears no individual responsibility for its own actions. By stonewalling the citizen, it is solely the citizen who bears the pain — not the agency or its representatives.

Being watched by Big Brother is one thing, having urgently needed information withheld, altered, or misdirected is clearly another, as the Landano case shows.

In August 1976, James Landano was on the way to his mother's home in Staten Island, New York, when he was pulled over by several police cars. He was subsequently charged with the murder of an off-duty police officer in an armed robbery. Even though he had an excellent alibi, he was found guilty and eventually sent to prison.

Since 1976, Landano's attorney has been uncovering leads, evidence, and sworn statements, that all pointed to James Landano's innocence, not guilt.

One of the strangest parts of the case was that the prosecutor and F.B.I. decided to withhold information from Landano's attorney, Neil Mullin. The files requested by Mullin were so heavily edited that in most cases they made no sense. Initially, Mullin felt that he could nudge the F.B.I. into acquiescence. Nudging did not work.

In order to obtain the information needed for appeal of Landano's sentence, Mullin found that he had to sue the F.B.I. to obtain the files in an uncensored condition. Making this decision Mullin sued under the F.O.I.A. in Federal District Court and won. The agency appealed. Eventually the case went to the United States Supreme Court.

The F.O.I.A. appeal was heard by the Supreme Court in February 1993. The court ruled against the bureau, in favor of Mr. Landano. At that time the F.B.I. was ordered to open its files for the purpose of giving information to support an appeal by the defense.

The F.O.I.A. took over five years. Meanwhile, Mr. Landano was in jail during the entire process. Since he had no money to pay his legal bills, his attorney and aides performed all work pro bono.

As the evidence left the hands of the prosecution, they began to see the light of day. It became obvious that important items were being kept from the defense. Documents have now been found that indicate Landano was probably not the armed robber and that the prosecution knew it — or at the very least should have known it!

In late 1993, Mr. Landano was freed on bail pending a retrial as the results of an appeal. He had been held in prison for thirteen years. Mullin's efforts to free him had been stonewalled for nine of the thirteen years. Much of this time had been spent just trying to obtain the evidence in the government files under a law that protects our rights.

Even though new facts are available for the appeal, a hearing has not yet determined just how much of the F.B.I. files will have to be disclosed under the F.O.I.A. In other words, even though the agency has lost its ability to hold back full disclosure of its files, it can still partially stonewall the process.

While a man languished in prison, the F.B.I. was able to hold back evidence from the defense. How is this possible? The answer is simple. No one in the agency bears personal responsibility for his or her actions in this case or any other case. Hence, one can hide under this shield while the citizen is exhausting his money, time (residing in prison), and *efforts just to obtain the facts*! The Kafkaesque part of this is that Mullin couldn't obtain the truth even though a law, the F.O.I.A. said he could have it *under normal circumstances*.

Eric Neisser, a law professor who has been aiding in the preparation of the appeal, put the matter in legal prospective.

> This was clearly material that was favorable to the defense. . . To withhold such exculpatory evidence from the defense seriously violates a long-standing constitutional obligation of the state.[7]
>
> Mr. Landano's seventeen year struggle for justice was successful. On Friday, February 26, 1994, an appeals court threw out the conviction of James Landano by ruling that the prosecution had violated his constitutional rights by withholding exculpatory evidence. . . We conclude that there is a

reasonable probability that the outcome of the trial would have been different had this evidence been disclosed to the defense.[8]

In essence the court held that the violations were so egregious that they warranted the reversal of the verdict.

This high-handed attitude that has been assumed by government has occurred because of lack of individual responsibility and lack of congressional oversight. It is also part of a recent phenomenon that I call the "nasty syndrome."

Do not think that the Landano case is an aberration. Under the guise of lofty goals the statue of freedom is continually chipped away by the sculptor's chisel. In 1994 Congress passed a crime bill that created a new stipulation called the "criminal gang provision." This provision, if violated, carried penalties of imprisonment for a maximum of twenty years as well as property forfeiture. It is by its nature, very, very broad.

Its aim is to reduce crime by gangs but its net may be so expansive as to include boards of directors, school parent groups, and more than five individuals joining together in any protest movement. Hitherto innocent people will be corralled in the future by this high-sounding law, if prosecutors think expansively. Since expansive thinking is nearly a sure bet, one can expect the bill to be misapplied.

The predecessor to the 1994 crime bill is known as the Racketeer-Influenced and Corrupt Organizations Act (R.I.C.O.). This was passed twenty years previous to fight organized crime.

But recently, R.I.C.O. has been brought into cases involving abortion demonstrations, franchise disputes between dealers and manufacturers, divorce decrees, and a myriad of civil cases. R.I.C.O. has been applied to so many nonracketeering cases that it has lost its effectiveness as a crime fighting tool.

In August 1993, Deputy White House Counsel, Vincent Foster, committed suicide. It was a tragedy for himself, his family, and the Clinton Administration. In a note that he left behind he bitterly complained about the nastiness and the savagery of Washington. This indictment included the establishment as well as the members of the press. A part of the note plaintively stated: "I was not meant for the spotlight of public life in Washington. Here ruining people is considered sport."[9]

The level of our national tensions, distrust and confrontation, has become more intense since the 1950s. Some of these tensions can be traced to the expansion of bureaucracy, the growth of rules and regulations, and the increasing complexities of American life since the 1950s. Some can be traced to the emergence of new societal forces. Yet, the micromanaging of society has produced an overall tension that infects the actions of individuals without their even realizing it.

Our lives have become increasingly complicated. It is no wonder that high blood pressure is endemic. Why have things become so complicated, so nasty? Marlen Fitzwater, White House spokesman under President George Bush, noted that Washington's culture has developed into "confrontation and sometimes full scale combat between Republicans and Democrats, the White House and Capitol Hill, and not the least, the news media."[10]

While confrontation has become the watchword in Washington, the elected establishment has insulated itself from us, the people who sent them to the Capitol. The comfort of pensions, perks, good salaries, large staffs, and benefits have prevailed over the concerns of the electorate. The party in control of the White House or Congress may change, but the same level of tension and complexities remain. Little change results in terms of the relationship between the government and the average citizen. The two parties, regardless of what they say, deliver similar results.

During the past four decades both parties have participated in this deception. They have passed laws that distance the people from their representatives and their government while accepting the frills, comforts, and benefits reserved for public office. It is this weakness in modern day American government that portends future difficulties for those citizens who desire to protect their individuality and freedom.

The growth of the federal government over the past forty years is now common knowledge.

- In 1930 government expenditures were 12% of the GNP.
- In 1960 government expenditures were 27% of the GNP.
- In 1990 government expenditures were 37% of the GNP.
- In 1960 the budget deficit was .08 of a percent of the GNP. In 1990 it was four percent. In the year 2000 some have predicted it will reach six percent.
- In 1950 government workers totalled six million. In 1992 the total was eighteen million.

Both political parties on both the state and federal levels have distanced themselves from the people. As the process develops, government becomes less efficient, produces more paperwork, and, as a result, breeds contempt and suspicion.

In economic terms the results inhibit our progress. Higher taxes, more regulations, longer delays, and a bad attitude harm business and affect employment. It also makes us less competitive as a nation.

The growth of Big Brother government has been permitted, not planned. The founders of our country never foresaw Departments of Housing and Urban Development, Education, or Commerce, for example. Some new areas are surely required by modern technological changes, but most are not. We have permitted these government excesses and have allowed our government to develop new weapons that could some day be turned against us.

In today's arsenal of the American government is the NCIC (National Crime Information Computer) system, the social security number, license numbers, and all kinds of modern scanning and eavesdropping equipment. Can our government be entrusted to maintain the line between liberty and control of our citizens? Or will the ever-increasing bureaucracy tighten the noose on our daily lives? Will the noteworthy idea of halting pollution only lead to increased control over the people? If so, then it's a good idea gone sour.

We started on a path to reasonable environmental protection, but then created a system of heavier fines and paperwork that were worse than the pollution itself — a victory of errant bureaucracy over rational rule making. Will this penchant, coupled with the computer and the social security number, lead us down a more devilish path in the future?

The excuses of the environment, high crime rates, or societal good provide excellent rationales for bureaucrats and elected officials who would like to plan our lives for us. We are becoming dangerously close to a police state. Milwaukee District Attorney, Mike McCann, has observed.

> That continued erosion of the protections guaranteed by the Constitution will lead society dangerously close to a police state.
>
> When one person's rights are trenched upon, everyone's rights are trenched upon, the deepest threat to civil liberties is the government. Historically that is true, but many people forget that lesson.[11]

We have already noted that America is a litigious society. Legal fees on a contingency basis tilt the scales toward frivolous lawsuits. The accuser is often provided with a lawyer who shares in the booty, but the defendant (unless poor) must pay for his defense.

If a plaintiff comes to a lawyer with an inadequate case, the lawyer might still take the case. By threatening a person or company the plaintiff's attorney could obtain a settlement prior to trial and take thirty-three percent of the settlement in fees.

A defendant must pay his attorney while facing his legal problems. In this country many people's assets are calculated by including the potential value of lawsuits even though they have not yet won. Others must spend their assets to defend against this frivolous system. Our system can bankrupt you even while you are vindicated. A recent addition to our list of bureaucratic excess has been in the area of anti-discrimination laws. A majority of Americans favor equality of access and opportunity, but a whole host of anti-discrimination laws have produced a witch's brew for bureaucrats and lawyers to brew in their cauldron.

The Knight Protective Industries is located in North Hollywood, California. The company's business consists of the sale of crime protection services. Serving homes and businesses, Knight acts as an interface between the subscriber and police by use of direct lines of communication.

In 1992 Knight dismissed a well-liked employee who suffered from occasional temper tantrums. According to the owner some of these outbursts were quite stressful to the company and the staff.

On one occasion the employee interrupted a Saturday morning meeting, which was being videotaped, by shouting intemperate outbursts. The company then felt that it could not function with this employee and terminated his employment.

The terminated employee then filed a complaint with the State of California, Department of Fair Employment. His complaint was simple and straightforward. He told the CDFE that he had been fired because he was black. Since the owner was white, a plausible case could be made for discrimination.

In its own defense, Knight Protective sent letters to the agency stating that over thirty percent of its staff was black, and that a recent payroll survey showed that blacks received wages that were equal to whites. It offered to prove these assertions to the CDFE.

The owner related that the representative of the Department of Employment suggested that the case might be solved in another fashion. Since the state representative admitted that the rules were so complicated and the situation so fraught with litigiousness, Knight was told of another path. In essence, they could alter their corporate records. Since the state agreed that these situations can be extremely complicated, perhaps lying might be the solution. Assumedly, that meant in this case and perhaps others? According to *The Wall Street Journal*:

> [The owner] says the state agent, Renee Ackel, suggested the case could be resolved by expunging the dismissal from the employee's record and indicating a voluntary resignation instead, and further said this was a common way of handling such matters. [The owner] says the state is advising him to falsify files and that doing so could subject Knight to a lawsuit if something horrendous occurred.[12]

If we have come to the point that lying is the only answer to complex regulations, then why don't we fix the underlying problem? In further discussions Ms. Ackel agreed that her agency settled cases generally for cash considerations, not always on their merits. Rules have been made so complicated that people can't be allowed to talk with each other directly. Companies are expected to lie to stay out of court. The state agency can't deal with the absurdity of its own rules either, hence, they "settle mainly for money."[13]

In December 1993, the Justice Department served the small city of Aurora, Illinois, a surprise Christmas present — a lawsuit. They found out that Aurora doesn't have any police officers in wheelchairs or any firefighters with chronic back problems. So the city was slapped with a lawsuit for discriminating against the disabled.

Common sense has completely disappeared from regulation. The Washington, D.C., ambulance service has an employee who is a carrier of Hepatitis B, an extremely infectious disease. The department kept him on, but told him he could not perform mouth-to-mouth resuscitation. But he filed a discrimination lawsuit, and Federal District Judge Joyce Green ruled that the worker was indeed covered by the Americans with Disabilities Act. In essence, the D.C. government could not prevent the infected worker from giving mouth-to-mouth resuscitation to unsuspecting, unconscious patients.

It is time to sit back and ponder what we have already lost in the past fifty years. We have continuously turned over our rights to government. We have ceded our guarantees as free citizens and have irrationally accepted peace of mind in return.

What peace of mind will we have when the edifices we have established continue to go sour, services become rationed, and citizens are continually caught in unforeseen petty complications.

Then and only then will we realize that we have created an unexpected exchange, our freedom for what in return? Then and only then can we determine whether or not "Big Brother is Watching."

Chapter 8

We Are Not Being Heard

"I am in earnest — I will not equivocate — I will not excuse — I will not retreat a single inch — and I will be heard."

William Lloyd Garrison, in
The Liberator, 1859

There are two other insidious aspects to the "Liberty Crisis." The first is that most of our legislators no longer listen to their constituents. Congress has learned to insulate itself. If vocal environmentalists gain their ear, for example, Congress has permitted that cause to drown out protections of liberty for others. While the legislators are growing more insensitive to constitutional protections, it is important to realize that most citizens aren't listening, caring, or taking inventory of what they are losing.

In the 1970s the Sperry Rand Corporation ran a memorable TV and newspaper advertising campaign, which was right on target. Its subject was simple and of a single purpose, it was — "Listen." In one of those remarkable ads, the Titanic was shown listing at sea while the announcer is heard in the background saying: "If only the Carpathia had been listening."

On July 1, 1993, a terrible incident occurred in San Francisco. An obviously disturbed individual named Gian Ferri visited the offices of Pettit and Martin, a law firm, and killed eight people while injuring six. He then committed suicide. While the act of murdering innocent people was barbarous, the aftermath was ludicrous. Rather than thoughtfully reacting to the underlying problem, the president of the California Bar Association put part of the blame for this incident on negative lawyer jokes. Harvey Saferstein said: "There's a point at which jokes are humor and acceptable and a point at which they become nothing more than hate speech."[1]

Recently, court cases have been decided where *the thought behind the crime changed the sentence*. A sentence was made stiffer in a Wisconsin case because blacks urged others to "move on white people." The crime of assault was bad enough, but punishment was meted out for the thought behind the incident. In California we were urged to add lawyers to a protected list of special thought crimes. We have already protected women, the elderly, blacks, "sexist comments" — and next — "lawyers?" Why isn't crime *itself*, a justification for punishment?

The next step may be a kind of thought police. If the idea is hard to believe, consider that some colleges in the United States have "speech codes." Perhaps criminals will have speech codes also. And lawlessness will be judged by the assailant's mental condition rather than the criminal activity. Attorneys are already creating defenses based upon the defendant's motivations.

Another serious framework of abuse has evolved because the federal and state agencies are presumed to be "experts." It is difficult to get a court to intercede in cases where the agency has exceeded its authority or acted without actual foundation. At the same time state and federal legislatures are reluctant to rein in or oversee the actions of the bureaucrats because the legislators don't have the time, interest, or background to intervene in the day-to-day regulatory affairs. It is this power vacuum that enables bureaucrats to run amok.

An example of this misplaced "expertise" occurred in the use of Los Angeles as a model for clean air standards. In 1993 the entire Northeastern United States was in the process of being ordered by the EPA to adopt the California standards. But these stringent standards were specifically designed for the worst smog in the United States. That smog was in California, not in the Northeastern States.

The geology of Los Angeles is not common to the United States in general and certainly not at all similar to the Northeastern United States. But the bureaucrats resolved that the worst case scenario of Los Angeles would be transferred to the East without regard to the different air quality and the resulting affect on the economy and jobs. The EPA is the "expert," and because Congress has abdicated its responsibility to be accountable for the power it has reposed in the EPA, that agency and others are free to impose any standards it chooses with impunity.

While this solution may appease environmentalists and make for good public relations, it is a poor solution to the underlying problem. The imposition of the California solution has forced the Northeastern states to devise schemes to comply with the EPA directives. A few states are devising regulations about car pooling and directing employers to reduce their employees' use of personal cars. Gordon Bishop, in his syndicated environmental column observed the following:

> Take the employer trip reduction program. It's a massive employment dislocation scheme that is a logistical nightmare by any bureaucrat's standard for planning and implementation.
> Mr. Carrellas (a coordinator of the National Motorists Assoc.) predicts that when "this great fraud hits the fan and with the passage of time," the trip reduction plan "will no longer be a mandated program.
> So why spend millions of dollars preparing for a program at the state level and requiring every business with more than one hundred employees to commit incalculable resources to something that is not going to make a difference in air quality?

Because bureaucracy works that way. And it's one of the reasons the working taxpayer is going broke subsidizing such governmental nonsense.

There are all kinds of technical solutions to air pollution, but government would rather tinker with human behavior and the marketplace for some irrational, politically correct reason.

While the bureaucrats pursue their unworkable programs, the real-world engineers and scientists are forging ahead with applications to burn fuels cleanly.[2]

The ordinary citizen and businessman is trapped regardless of the absurdity of the regulatory scheme. As we have said, courts generally side with an agency because the bureaucrats are the "experts." Even regulations that impinge on individual rights are not easily overturned unless they are of a flagrant nature. Equally important, the sheer cost to pursue rights and remedies in modern America is so expensive that few individuals or companies possess the resources to attempt the challenge. The balance has markedly shifted in favor of the bureaucrats, and the cards stacked against the individual citizen.

There are devices used by bureaucrats to reinvent the truth and blur distinctions between perception and reality. The reporting of job statistics is a case in point. During the 1990s, these numbers have been tilted to indicate what the bureaucrats want you to perceive, not what the facts are. When job creation figures are released, they indicate a gross number. But they fail to note that, in the 1990s, much of job creation has been in part-time employment and low-paying service jobs. These jobs offer little in the way of benefits and serve for short durations.

The 1990s have seen good paying jobs, such as in manufacturing, diminish. During the same period many low-paying franchise restaurant positions have been created. Workers in low-paying jobs can be "discouraged workers" but their plight is not reflected by the government statistics. These workers are not counted in determining unemployment figures. It is bad enough to be underemployed and discouraged, but it is both untruthful and insulting not to reflect this problem in the government statistics.

In the changing 1990s the odds are that many families were formerly one-wage-earner units. Now a household may have one full-time and one part-time job or even two part-time jobs. In addition, many individuals who are counted as self-employed are actually listed that way because they were unable to find other jobs. The percentage of unemployed Americans is not really those actually out of work. It is those out of work who fit the government's definition of "joblessness." This approach is now called "spin;" in the 1950s it would have been called "manipulation of facts." Prior to that the word "lying" would have been an acceptable synonym. If an executive officer of a public company took such a cavalier attitude toward facts relating to his company, he would likely become the target of a Securities and Exchange Commission proceeding as well as countless shareholders' suits.

With this distortion how can we believe the reported information? The skewing is to the side that the government wants you to believe, i.e., fewer unemployed rather than more. When you combine spin, bureaucracy, and "cooking the books," you come up with an attempt at societal mind control. The use of government statistics is only one example.

In the Spring of 1992, I was asked to testify before the New Jersey Senate Environmental Committee on the Environmental Clean-Up Responsibility Act (ECRA), which had become an impossible burden on the citizens of New Jersey. The hearing room was packed with over one hundred people from all walks of life. In the front row, however, were the Assistant Commissioner of the NJDEPE, an ECRA management official, and a secretary.

We Are Not Being Heard

The DEPE presence was made known to the people gathered to testify.

The Chairman of the Committee, Senator Henry MacNamara (R., Bergen County) allowed thirty to forty minutes for each of the seven testifiers. After each individual gave his presentation, all with suggestions for legislative improvement, the senators were given an opportunity to question each of the presenters. When all seven were finished, the Assistant DEPE Commissioner was given ten minutes to rebut (in this case, negate) each of the presenters point of view. In essence he was the expert cleanup batter before the Committee.

At the end of the day, the Assistant DEPE Commissioner was given another thirty minutes to rebut the collective testimony, which had been negative to his agency. He had the final word on the subject. Seven citizens gave up their time to share their negative experiences with the senators. They presented their suggestions in the hope that this would help in correcting the abuses that they contended were caused by the DEPE itself. However, these complaints were then subjected to rebuttal by the agency. But the testifiers were not given the right to respond.

An older couple who had driven a long distance to Trenton was seated next to me, prepared to speak of their negative ECRA experiences. When they saw the DEPE representatives at the meeting, they quickly realized they were being placed in a vulnerable position. They could not voice their complaints unless they were willing to have their case affected by their views. They were placed in the whistle blowers position without protections. The very people they wished to register complaints about were seated in the first row, taking careful notes. At the end of this testimony the agency could refute it all.

The elderly couple asked me, "How can we relate our situation to the committee? Our case is still alive, and we are sure that our business will suffer retribution if we speak out." I could not offer advice or refute their statement. So they declined to speak.

After the hearing I sought out and located the committee chairman to register my complaint. Simply put, I was annoyed about citizens not being heard due to the latticework of the meeting. "How can citizens tell you what their honest experiences are when the agency being complained about is given the "cleanup position" in the debate?" The chairman gave an interesting answer. "The New Jersey sunshine law prevents our meeting with citizens privately," he said. "How do you find the truth?" I rejoined. "That's the only way we can do it," said Senator MacNamara.

The story of that legislative experience lives in my consciousness. The recollection is very important, not because of the specific bill and/or its purported reform, but because of the flagrant abuse of the process itself. Supposed protections designated to defend citizens were turned around to harm those whom they were designed to protect.

As that reform bill emerged, however, it became evident that the bill was written by the New Jersey Department of Environmental Protection and Energy ("NJDEPE"), the agency that was responsible for the regulatory overkill, which had substantially destroyed New Jersey's manufacturing economy. This agency had always opposed any ECRA reform. Its sponsorship of the bill was an omen that should have been heeded by business groups. It wasn't. Under the agency's aegis, the proposed bill codified the most unfair and oppressive aspects of the existing law and regulations. In other words, it made the previous rules the proposed law. Nonetheless, during hearings before the Senate Environmental Committee, it became obvious that a bill proposing ECRA reform would be passed. At the committee hearings the business community delineated numerous deficiencies inherent in the proposed bill, but the Senate committee stood fast and changed very little.

Pseudo reform lumbered along, since it was a safe issue, and the bill passed the Senate in May, 1993 without a nay vote. Shortly thereafter, the bill moved to the Assembly Policy & Rules Committee where the debate was again spirited. While the Policy and Rules Chairman permitted all voices to be heard, again, substantive change never materialized. The reform bill moved to the floor of the Assembly in June, 1993 and passed 76-3. Governor Florio signed it into law on June 16, 1993. While it was billed as reform, a closer look shows that it is more of the same nonsense.

New Jerseyans had been treated to a flanking maneuver. Various groups were led to believe that reform was imminent and hence supported the proposed bill. But as it turned out, few politicians were courageous enough to endorse realistic change just prior to an election. The weak-kneed effort represented by the bill produced instead a reform package that consisted for the most part of an extensive codification of pre-existing rules, regulations, definitions, and rulings that had been gathered from ECRA's inception in 1983 through the passage of the reform bill in 1993. Indeed, the revised cleanup law, now entitled the Industrial Site Recovery Act ("ISRA"), actually made the cleanup process more cumbersome, more detailed, more costly (in filing fees, etc.), more time consuming, and potentially more anti-business.

The name change mentioned above is perhaps the most substantive feature of the reform bill and represents an Orwellian tour de force in which the legislators apparently felt that by changing the name you ameliorate the problem.

In short, ISRA was nothing more than a clever public relations ploy that New Jersey's political leadership determined had to be passed previous to the November, 1993 elections. Both parties agreed that the bill had to be positioned so that both parties could take credit for reform without interfering with their Fall election campaigns. Fearing the inevitable flak from the well-financed and well-organized environmental lobbies, the political leadership chose to run rather than confront the difficulties of real reform.

In this case and others an agency was able to control the legislative process from behind the scenes, while the elected legislators bought into the entire procedure. Who runs our democracy? Apparently, it is not our elected representatives who turn to the unelected bureaucrats for the answers. From such a scenario, one might ask, "is change really possible?"

Change is possible if we as citizens make it a high priority. Chapter 11 of this book proposes solutions to this dilemma, but they will not be easy. Our regulatory agencies have become so insulated, so secure, so powerful, that elected representatives literally pale before them. I had a conversation about twelve years ago with a regional Defense Department official regarding the processing of some papers. The President of the United States had ordered certain changes. In so many words the official told me that, "he wasn't going to comply with it."

I remember telling the official, "The parameters are quite clearly written in the executive order from the President of the United States. It appears to me that the Defense Department has no choice and must comply."

He answered, "You are correct, but in this regional office we have chosen to look the other way."

"How's that?" I asked somewhat bewildered.

"Well, look at it our way. I have been here sixteen years, and this is my fourth president. If every time a political change was made, and if we listened, we would have to alter the consistency of what we do here. We can't do that. So, we don't listen to a lot of these things and stay consistent in our policies. It's only the top speaking, anyway, it's not the level where things actually occur in government."

I was bewildered.

He added, "presidents come and presidents go, but I will be here for fourteen more years until my retirement. Do you understand me now?"

I remember realizing at that moment that people who held the power to choke liberty were people whose faces I didn't recognize; they had names I didn't know. Those behind-the-scene operators had succeeded in constructing a frightening backdrop for the rest of us. They had found a way to create a power base that was out of our control, partially because it was hidden from view.

I spent over seven years studying political science and realized that what I had been taught in college about government no longer existed. Perhaps it never existed. I felt as though I had been mugged on a darkened street corner. How arrogant is the arrogance of power?

I am sure that not many people know, or care, that both the Democrat and Republican Parties are *required by law* to be listed at the top of the ballots on an election ballot. After that listing, generally the county clerk (or appropriate official) determines the order of the remaining candidates. It does not sound like much, but this simple requirement is enough to solidify the power base of the two party system. Where is it written that there should only be two political parties? Our founders didn't proclaim this to be a fact of American political life. No mention is made of this in the Constitution or the Bill of Rights. The parties, in their own self-interest to protect their fiefdoms, have implemented this defense mechanism.

The power that this requirement gives to the two entrenched parties is enormous. Prominent placement is a major aid to reelection. If you don't believe that location is all important, open your telephone book to the Yellow Pages and turn to the category of house movers. Observe the companies crowding the top lines: "AB Movers, "Acme Movers," "AAA Movers" etc. These companies fight for space, for view all over the country. Ask your supermarket manager about the fight for shelf space in the soft drink and bread categories. You will, after your own short investigation, see why this is so important, yet subliminal.

The two major parties have maintained this hold on power, which shifts between them. The torch is passed with each bearer reaping the reward. Members of Congress of both parties receive $133,000 per year in salary. The House Speaker and five other top leadership positions are paid much more. Over one thousand of the Congressional aides are in the $80,000 salary category. The budget of Congress, estimated at $2.7 billion in 1994, can be thought of as $5 million per member. That is the average cost.

The two parties have nearly guaranteed their continued but intermittent succession. Examine the case of the 1992 Ross Perot challenge. There were state ballots where it was extremely difficult to find his name. Adding to Perot's problem was the rule that other Republican and Democrat candidates, such as those running for the Senate, were entitled to a column of their own. Hence, even though the Perot forces collected nearly twenty percent of the final vote, they were, in some cases, harder to find than the Socialist Workers Party. This is not an endorsement of Perot's effort; it is a statement of the uphill battle required for someone outside of the two major parties to be heard!

In some states the law requires that *after positioning the Republicans and the Democrats*, the remaining parties draw lots for ballot positions from a hat. In other states placement is determined by the county clerk. In either case, since the minor parties are treated differently than the two major parties, ballot placement aids entrenchment in power.

The arrogance of power has evolved in a similar way. In 1989, after succeeding Jim Wright of Texas, House Speaker Thomas S. Foley began to increase the physical size of his office. First, he enlarged his office to include outside public hallways. The question of legality never was raised. As the Speaker, he was unchallenged in this grab of a public hallway. He then installed a shower and exercise area in the expanded space. Next to his suite was an area known as the Rayburn Room, which was a gallery open to the general public. The public entrance to this area was closed and it was then annexed by building an entrance to it, which became reachable only through Speaker Foley's office. This effort was also unchallenged. He then expelled the "House Document Office" from its facilities so that additional office space could be aggregated for the Speaker's sole usage.

Meanwhile, on the floor below, twenty-five seats were eliminated in the House Restaurant so that a wall could be built separating that area from the remaining section. This new area was annexed by the Speaker to become his *second dining room*. Further, it was then redecorated at taxpayers' expense. Again, due to the enormous power of the Speaker, no one was brave enough to protest these actions.

Once the restaurant grab was completed, Speaker Foley then placed under construction a two-floor suite of offices to accommodate the growing Speaker's staff. This enlarged area included a full kitchen and eating area for the sole use of his staff. Of course, marble floors were installed in the connecting elevators. Probably this was required to make the trip more comfortable!

Recall that the 1988-1991 period were years of difficult economic conditions in America. It was a time when the average citizen was sacrificing and working to retain his home or job. The average American was cutting back. Let us examine the costs of just some of the Speaker's luxuries that were installed in the expanded suites:

- approximately $40,000 for lighting and carpeting

- approximately $314,000 for the completion of the 2 story suite
- approximately $72,500 for an oriental rug for the annexed Rayburn Room
- approximately $20,000 for the installation of marble floors in 3 elevators that transported people to the enlarged suites.[3]

The above list is not complete since the total costs are hard to obtain because of overlapping budgets.

This is not merely another example of government waste. It is more significant that our government no longer cares to set an example, does not listen to the citizens, and has simply lost touch with the people it governs. Our elected officials have set themselves up as a new class, a kind of royalty. Speakers of the House, whether Democrat or Republican, are indeed royalty with full royal prerogatives and have insulated themselves against potential protest.

Is Speaker Foley's office expansion an aberration? I think not. Were this a book on government waste, we could fill many more chapters. It is not, but it is a book on the arrogance of power and how it has corrupted our lives. Here is an example of disdain that even supercedes the insolence of Tom Foley to the taxpayers.

> While federal courthouses are being built at an average cost of $230 per foot, versus $100 for a state courthouse, the ultimate prize is reserved for a new Washington, D.C. super edifice. It is called the International Center for Trade and Technology. The center is located near Capitol Hill and it is one of the most expensive designs for any building of its type, anywhere in the United States.
>
> The General Services Administration (G.S.A.), has recently admitted the final cost will be just under $700 million for this one edifice. This amount excludes items in the original

design, such as swimming pools, movie theaters, and top-flight restaurants, which were recently dropped due to public embarrassment.

Imagine the impact that $700 million could have if used for good causes such as homelessness, education, or AIDS research?

The arrogance of the trade building was commented on by Peter Sep of the National Taxpayers Union. He said, "It is a monument to the fiscal stupidity of our federal construction policy."[4]

It is hard to disagree with Mr. Sepp.

The compact with constituents has evaporated when tested in reality. Honesty, their oaths, their promises, are all treated lightly.

All congressmen are sworn to "uphold and defend the Constitution of the United States of America." They take an oath; they swear to uphold our societal covenant as the basis for their endeavors. Does it mean anything to the operation of our government?

In August of 1993 Congress voted on the budget and tax bill submitted by President Clinton. It passed on August 6, 1993, by two votes in the House and by a tie breaker in the Senate. The extra ballot was supplied by Vice President Al Gore. A salient point of that bill was a provision that the taxes would be retroactive to January 1, 1993. That date was actually *prior* to Bill Clinton being sworn in as President. It was also prior to the new Congress being in session. That portion of the bill was in direct violation of the constitutional prohibition against "*ex post facto* laws," which are laws made after the fact.

This prohibition is found in the Constitution, section 9, in which our founders stated that "no. . .*ex post facto* law shall be passed" by Congress. Our founders had been through the travail of tyranny that came from the ability of a king to impose punishment for acts done prior to the date they were prohibited by law. Hence, our founders felt strongly that citizens should not be judged retroactively. They were clear on this issue and did not equivocate by using words like "sometimes," or "occasionally." They used the word "no."

In the Clinton tax bill, liability for taxes is made retroactive to a period before the law was passed. This is a clear violation of constitutional principals.

There have been several court cases on this issue. In the 1878 decision of "Burgess vs. Salmon," the court upheld this constitutional principal. More recently, in a 1927 case "Nicols vs. Coolidge," the Supreme Court voided a retroactive tax on estates. More recently in 1981, the Supreme Court held in the "U.S. vs. Darusmont" that tax legislation could be dated as *to when it was proposed in the House or Senate* on the theory that everyone was on notice. In 1984, in "Gray Co. vs. Pension Board Guaranty Corp.," the Supreme Court again held that the *ex post facto* date began when the specific legislation was proposed in Congress. The notice provision apparently was a key factor to the deciding justices.

Whether one agrees or disagrees with the Supreme Court's definition of *"Ex post Facto"* there had been a legal interpretation of this issue at the time of the passage of the 1993 Tax Act. Congress should not have passed legislation that pre-dated the introduction of the legislation in one of the chambers. This issue had already been decided in several Supreme Court cases.

The introduction of the tax and budget bill in Congress was April 8, 1993. Hence, using the court's guidelines, the retroactive date should not have preceded April 8. It should not have been January 1, 1993, since the new president was not even sworn in until January 20, 1993.

The bill voted on by our legislators violated their oaths of office. One cannot uphold the Constitution by passing unconstitutional laws. The majority of the members of both houses are lawyers. Hence, they knew what they had done and what had occurred.

If our elected officials have no respect for our laws, why should the citizens? In an article in *The Wall Street Journal*, Stephen C. Glazier, an attorney, wrote:

> The larger issue here, though, is not economic or legal — it is political. This type of unconstitutional legislation is the norm that will continue until the current majority of Congress is removed. Self-satisfied incumbents in Washington might like to take a look at the current draft of the new Russian constitution. That document's own Article 57 states that "laws introducing new taxes. . .are not retroactive." It seems that, in this instance, Boris Yeltsin may have more respect for the U.S. Constitution than the majority of our own House of Representatives.[5]

If our lawmakers don't have to obey the law, then respect for the law is greatly diminished. Although all Republicans voted against the tax bill and only Democrats voted for it, the issue raised is not partisan. Neither party has shown itself to be a paragon of virtue when it comes to listening to its constituents. In this sense, we have thus become a morally bankrupt nation.

An example of our moral bankruptcy was evident during the NAFTA (North American Free Trade Agreement) debates in November 1993. When NAFTA looked as if it would not pass the House, the Clinton administration went into high gear. They brought in Richard Daley from Chicago to spearhead White House efforts for passage. About two weeks before the vote, President Clinton adopted a new strategy; he would promise anything to purchase the pro-NAFTA votes from undeclared congressmen.

It is alleged that he gave special benefits to Florida agricultural groups to gain those House members. In Representative Eddie

Johnson's (D. Texas) district he agreed to have the government purchase two more C-17 Air Force planes and secured his vote by doing so. More money for developing minority business opportunities was agreed to so that Representative Floyd Flake (D. N.Y.) could sign on. Canadian wheat subsidy action was taken to pick up four farm state representatives. Two North Carolina representatives bargained for a reduction in the proposed seventy-five cents a pack increase in the tobacco tax. He picked up two votes there. It is reported that roads, airports, and water projects were promised for the securing of pro-NAFTA votes. Pork barrel politicians worked overtime. While many people may believe that it was just politics as usual, there is something wrong with that argument. First, the taxpayers' money, which was being traded for votes, doesn't belong to the President or the Congressmen. It belongs to the citizens. Trading someone else's property for a desired benefit would be a crime if done in the private sector. Secondly, this shameless approach to government is without ethics, morality, or limits. It is not an appropriate use of the discretion given to elected representatives by the people, but rather is simply a feeding frenzy directed at the people's assets.

After the passage of the tax bill in the House, the former Mayor of New York City, Ed Koch, was quoted on WABC (August 6, 1993) on his "Talk to the Mayor" radio program as saying: "When I was a congressman, before being Mayor of New York City, I was in this type of situation many times. Even though I think the tax bill is wrong and poorly conceived, I would have voted for it to protect the presidency."

Mayor Koch's statement is revealing and deserves careful attention. What he has said is what many congressmen still believe. They are not there to serve their constituency or the Constitution. They view their role as protecting the infrastructure of government. The Speaker must protect the "Speakership," the Congress protects the "Presidency" and the courts protect the experts (the bureaucrats). The *people* are left out of the equation. Power is a corrupting, all-encompassing influence permeating all layers of government. Congress views its role as the protection of its own rights, privileges, and prerogatives. The people provide the economic power but are not coequals. This self-serving indifference to the greater good has contributed to a kind of national moral bankruptcy.

We should write our congressman, write the Speaker of the House, or write our senator. Maybe an avalanche of letters would make our elected representatives "listen" to the citizens who are outraged by these actions.

But don't count on that as a solution! Congress receives approximately two hundred million letters per year. Many letters can't even be counted let alone personally answered. Perhaps you think your letter will get through and you will get an answer. Unfortunately, congressmen have found a way to lead us to believe they are responsive to our concerns by using computers to store and answer letters by the category of inquiry. These high tech gadgets personalize letters and look like a personal response. The letter was probably written by a staffer and stored in the computer *well before you wrote your letter.*

When a letter is received and answered, it just becomes a statistic. Ellen Miller, Director of the Center for Responsive Politics, states: "I think it's pretty clear that individual voter opinions don't really count for much anymore. Those who really matter are cash constituencies, those who pay the campaign bills."[6]

In 1993, as a member of a business organization, I was chairman of a committee working for change in certain governmental pension-related regulations. We had worked for several years and had finally produced a bill that was being debated. The fight was long and hard. The results were, as usual, a compromise and hence unsatisfactory to nearly everyone.

We endeavored to enlist the aid of representatives and senators and wrote letters in earnest. The letters went unanswered, until suddenly, one long-sought answer appeared. I was in my office when one of our committee members called to tell me that he had received a four page detailed letter from the senator's office. "Four pages?" I asked. "Four pages," he answered, "Let me fax it to you." He did so.

I spent about twenty minutes digesting this four page single-spaced response. It was tightly written and, although I disagreed with many of its conclusions, we had finally received an answer. It appeared to address our previously stated arguments and objectives for pension reform.

About ten days later, I attended a meeting of another (non-related) regulatory reform committee. That group had been experiencing the same difficulty in communicating with the same senator. I announced triumphantly that one of our members had finally received a detailed response from the senator's office. No sooner had I finished that statement when four members reached into their briefcases and also pulled out letters. They, too, had received four page single-spaced responses. Yes, they were all the same. The long explanation was a carefully prepared computer form letter. Close examination of the letters showed that two of the four letters had discreet paragraph variations. One of the member's letters included an altered first paragraph that included a request to "vote for me." Another letter had a different final paragraph. The computers mix and match abilities provided fertile ground for changes. The computer solved the problem of an honest constituent response.

The senator eventually answered me, also. But my answer was completely different. Even though our group was clearly on the negative side of the issue, my answer was only one page. Yes, it too, was a form letter. After years of being a prominent antagonist to this senator, one of his aides became confused. The computer's generated answer thanked me for supporting his efforts!

After this incident, I conducted a survey of state and federal legislators whom I knew and found that all used personalized form letters. Most form letters were prepared well in advance by aides. They were prepared about various subjects and legislation being proposed, with alterable inserts, and stored for future issuance. Most of the elected officials with whom I spoke were proud of their computers. They told me they could answer quantities of letters with ease. It was all done by their aides.

One legislator told me that the responses were numbered so that an aide only had to write, #1, #2, or #3, on the constituent's letter and the answer was conformed. He never saw most of them. In many cases the signatures were placed on the letter by a signing (pen) machine.

Our system has developed cracks. The primary one is that we have lost touch with our elected representatives. Or, they have lost touch with us. Not only are our individual complaints and problems not answered, they are treated in a cynical and dismissive manner.

Are our representatives listening? I doubt it.

Representative government has become a sham. What is important to an elected representative is the number of letters received and answered. But representing our specific views is not important. The citizen legislator on horseback riding to Washington or to Albany to represent the interests of his constituents, attending a session and returning home to report to the people — is gone. Our government is no longer ours. It belongs to faceless unelected aides operating mindless computers. And we have permitted this to happen.

Chapter 9

Helping Others

"The strength of the Constitution lies entirely in the determination of each citizen to defend it."

Albert Einstein

America was colonized and settled through the mutual cooperation of the settlers. As Americans moved west, neighbors helped each other building homes, barns, and fences. Barn raisings were a festive occasion, with a celebration party concluding a day of hard work. In small towns charity was dispensed in the community through the churches, by concerned citizens, or private organizations. Citizens knew their neighbors and often depended on them for survival.

For varied reasons there has been a change from neighborliness towards alienation and isolation. As recently as World War II, I can remember riding to work with my father who operated a small business in Newark, New Jersey. He owned a 1941 blue, four-door Chevrolet sedan. As we drove to Newark, if there was inclement weather, my father would pick up people at bus stops and take them down Clinton Avenue to the downtown business district. At no time was I taught to fear a Black, Chinese, or White stranger whom he randomly picked up enroute. In these years there was never an incident other than the expression of "thank you." My father was simply helping someone who needed a ride to work.

Of course, the largest gap is between the ordinary citizens and our new elected ruling class. Once ensconced in their ornate

Helping Others

chambers they seem unable to recall from "whence they came." If for one minute you do not believe that we have a governing class in America, then you are not reading recent history.

I attended school with a childhood friend named, Tony. His family moved to New Jersey from outside of Denver, Colorado, when Tony was in the eighth grade. Tony told me that his mother missed one thing in New Jersey that she used to do when their family lived in Colorado. She had always left drinks, sandwiches, and baked goods on their Colorado porch so that prospectors and drifters going past their house would have something to eat if they were hungry. The family never was in fear of a break-in or of their hospitality being abused. It was simply her idea to aid a passersby if help was required. Tony told me that on numerous occasions there were notes or even little trinkets left upon their return trip. In one instance a small gold nugget was left for his mother by a returning prospector.

These stories are simple reminders of a national desire to help one another that we once possessed as a people. This instinct has been blunted by both anonymity and the loss of community responsibility and control in the aftermath of an intrusive and monolithic presence of government in our everyday lives. It has been stripped away from us by rules, regulations, procedures, and governmental attitudes. It is easier to accept the premise that the government will provide and that Washington will be the answer to all of our problems, big and small. Social Security, disability, unemployment compensation, and welfare are society's way to provide income for the unfortunate. But the unintended effects are that community and neighborhood involvement have become the casualties of this process.

In Oriental society, it is a duty of a father to support his children for as long as necessary. If a son had sufficient money, the father would not have the pleasure and honorable duty to keep supporting his son.

About ten years ago, I was drawn into a case involving a young child. He had been born with hydrocephalis. As I later learned, this condition results from an abnormal increase in the amount of cerebrospinal fluid within the cranial cavity. It is accompanied by an enlargement of the skull resulting in a corresponding atrophy of the brain. The child's parents could not afford the cost of the required medical care. To keep the child alive and pain free was expensive, but they tried very hard.

The child's father ate breakfast in the same rural coffee shop that I stopped at every morning. Several of us in the restaurant began to talk about the child's plight. Soon this conversation escalated into action. We wanted to help the family since we all felt drawn to this young child's unfortunate condition.

From a germ of an idea the conception grew. We formed a committee to enlist all sorts of aid, from raising cash to obtaining medical supplies. A large Maryland-based manufacturer of bandages (who has always declined to be identified) donated a box of necessary supplies every month. We received the material through the company's New York City advertising and marketing division. It kept coming as long as we agreed not to identify the source or that it was being donated. Of course, we kept the secret.

A local newspaper, also trying to help, suggested that the family file for some kind of federal assistance. One of the members of our breakfast group was a lawyer who offered his services. He agreed to perform all necessary paperwork on a pro-bono basis. He helped the family file for a government grant. Within six months the family began to receive much needed government assistance for the child's care at home.

At that moment the collective effort felt beautiful; the community had helped, the government had helped, and the family was able to keep the child in its home. While all of us knew that the life span of the baby was quite limited, at least he could be with a loving family for as many days as he had left on earth.

Shortly thereafter, the sands shifted. One day my office phone rang. The caller, one of the members of our breakfast group said, "Mr. Siminoff, we are going to have a meeting tomorrow; there's trouble with the baby."

I attended the meeting. It turned out that the trouble was related to the government assistance, not to the community involvement. The government had asserted in a letter that the agency technically erred in providing assistance to the family. In re-examining the case they learned that the father had a moderately paid job, and the baby was not being treated in a hospital. These factors were two critical elements in their determination. In other words, the family might have to give up their personal supervision of the child in order to provide his medical care. The government believed that he should be placed in a hospital, at much greater cost to taxpayers and without the personal interaction of his desperate mother. Persons unknown to the child should care for him *because that was the rule*. To care for the child in a hospital setting would have been about six times the cost of home care and be without the love and comfort of a normal mother-son relationship.

Our little group met and rehashed the issue thoroughly. It was our unified and adamant decision that the parents should keep the child. We chose to fight alongside of the father and mother. Four of us decided to accompany the mother to the district headquarters of the Social Security Administration. We were granted an audience with the district director and presented our case.

After all the facts were rehashed with the district director, whose face I can still visualize more than ten years later, she said: "It really doesn't matter what you say. The rules are the rules! The only way we can assist the family is if either the father quits his job, is impoverished, or if the baby is given up for public nursing care at an institution. We can no longer provide assistance for the child at home since the family is not insolvent."

I will always recall the essence of my reply, which was, "Madam, what you are saying is that as long as the paperwork is correct, you don't care if the child lives or dies. You are not here to help the child or the family, but to be one hundred percent sure that the file is properly closed."

"Mr. Siminoff, that's all we can do," said the director. "The rules are the rules. I have told you that here today and in letters to you, personally." Fortunately, for everyone, including himself, the child died a few weeks thereafter.

The incident clearly demonstrated that, while people may try to help other people, bureaucrats are not really involved in the process — only the movement of papers. Help is not part of their agenda; it is only making the paperwork right. To bureaucrats people are just numbers, blurred faces, or files. They are not people.

In October 1992 the Internal Revenue Service published a rule change, which in government parlance is called "a clarification." This clarification stated that the I.R.S. had decided *not to allow hardship exclusions* on withdrawals from pension plans and IRA's. In those cases when a person needed an emergency withdrawal, he could be faced with a penalty to do so.

Most early withdrawals from pension plans and IRA's are motivated by medical or personal emergencies. An IRS spokesperson said that the agency really wanted to grant this exclusion but felt it could no longer do so. No reasons were forthcoming.

The net result was that a person who incurred a medical emergency would have to withdraw the money from his retirement account and pay tax and a ten percent penalty at the same time. There seemed to be little thought that a medical emergency was not the time to hit a taxpayer with a withdrawal penalty. If asked, an agency spokesperson would probably say, "a rule is a rule."

A relevant story appeared in an emergency medical magazine called "Jems." It was entitled "Quiet! Testing in Progress." It related an incident that occurred in 1993:

> Do not open your test booklet until told to do so. You will have three hours to complete this portion of the test. Please hold all seizures and heart attacks until after the examination so as not to disturb those around you.
>
> During a California Bar Association examination in late February, only a few students in the room full of aspiring lawyers stopped to help a fellow test-taker who stopped breathing while suffering an epileptic seizure.
>
> According to California Bar Association spokesman Jerome Braun, five of the 500 test-takers put down their exams to help the fallen man, administering CPR while test proctors went to call for help. A paramedic who was taking the test did not stop to render assistance.
>
> Then, after paramedics arrived and transported the patient, the five good Samaritans were denied extra time to take their tests — despite the 40 minutes they missed while aiding the victim.
>
> Braun said the test proctors were correct in not giving the students more time because it was difficult to determine who actually was disturbed by the event. "When a disruption occurs and is definable, we take that into account," he said. "If the power had gone out for 10 minutes, that would be easy. Everyone would get 10 extra minutes. There were 500 people in the room when this incident occurred, and [proctors] could not tell who had been disrupted."
>
> Braun said the bar plans to bring in a psychometric expert to determine how people were affected and help establish appropriate adjustments for grading the exams. In addition, he

said, the exams of the five people who were directly involved in helping the seizure victim will be graded both with and without the section of the test they were taking when the incident occurred and given the higher of the two scores.

Yet John Leslie of North Hollywood, Calif., one of the good Samaritans, said an exam proctor told him he would be given extra time to finish and didn't feel that the grading adjustment would help him.

"I was told not to worry and that I would have more time," Leslie said. "But then [the proctor] said she was mistaken."

While test results were not available at press time, Leslie said he expects to pass and has not given much thought to an appeal.

As for the seizure victim, he survived — but not without raising some serious moral issues which, we hope, will not be easy for the legal community to forget.[1]

Unfortunately, the above speaks entirely for itself.

In 1992 Pennsylvania passed a new law related to its statewide Emergency Medical Service system. Following this enactment rules were promulgated that required ambulance crews to sign to a dispatch radio within a specified time or that unit would be cancelled and another corps dispatched. From a purely theoretical standpoint it seemed like an acceptable idea.

From a practical point of view it was tantamount to ridiculous. In large cities like Philadelphia, Pittsburgh, or Harrisburg, where paid crews await a call, this plan might work fine. But many areas of Pennsylvania are quite rural where the emergency teams are ordinarily staffed by volunteers. The volunteers are trained as EMT's (Emergency Medical Technicians) and/or American Red Cross First Responders but are unpaid. They are dispatched from their home or business by pagers or plectrons. In many rural counties it is more than ten minutes from an ambulance corp member's location to his or her station. Hence, in practical terms the rule could not be followed.

In Monroe County, Pennsylvania, the new statute required the following rule: "Upon receipt of an emergency call the ambulance crew chief is to call the dispatcher and say 'I acknowledge the call and am enroute to the building.' Once at the building the crew would assemble and then proceed to the call. The first member who reached the building would call dispatch and state, over the radio: 'Acknowledging call, awaiting crew.' When the crew assembled they would go 10-8 (proceed to scene of the emergency)."

Should the volunteer crew be unable to assemble from home to the ambulance location within ten minutes, then the next station would be dispatched. The next station, however, could be located from fifteen to thirty minutes away.

Since the object of this exercise is supposedly directed toward a public policy of delivering the best emergency patient care, how does a mandatory ten minute rule work in practice? It doesn't.

1. The rules deal with people who volunteer their services. These individuals are generally dedicated and don't need a spur under their collar to function appropriately.
2. The rule is potentially dangerous to the crews. By pushing people to respond faster while driving their personal cars, accidents will surely be one result.
3. Many volunteers became angry by the promulgation of those rules and just felt "I can't do it anymore, and I will not renew my certification." (It requires more than 150 hours of education to stay an EMT — these are unpaid training hours.)
4. The practical aspects of calling out another corps after a ten minute lapse simply creates another problem, that is, a new twenty to thirty minute response time (from the more distant station).

Here is a microcosmic example of what is wrong with bureaucratic overregulation of American life. Dedicated, unpaid volunteers, unsung heroes do the best they can because "it's their calling." If we ask ourselves why a person volunteers as an ambulance attendant or as a fireman, the answer does not encompass goofing off on the way to a call!

How does this system function in the real world? On Sunday evening, September 5, 1993, an incident occurred in Monroe County, Pennsylvania. A sixty year old female patron was attending the German Fest at the Edelweiss Restaurant in Pocono Lake, Pennsylvania. She inexplicably collapsed while dancing, and an ambulance was called to the scene by onlookers.

Ambulance Station Seven was the nearest emergency unit and was requested to respond by the Monroe County police dispatcher. The assigned crew of volunteers was summoned over their home-alert systems. About three minutes later, a second request was put over the pagers. About five minutes after the second request, or eight minutes into the call, the driver answered:

> "Monroe County Control, this is ambulance number seven-o-one.
>
> "Seven-o-one."
>
> "Monroe County, driver is acknowledging call and awaiting a crew."
>
> "Ten four, seven-o-one, you have a sixty year old female who was unconscious. She is now conscious but is disoriented. We have been informed that she has a history of brain surgery. According to her husband, approximately one year previous she was in the hospital for this problem. She is now conscious but is having seizure activity."
>
> "Acknowledged, Monroe County."

Helping Others

Two more minutes passed.

> "Monroe County Control, this is seven-o-one." "Seven-o-one."
>
> "Monroe County, can you set the tones for an EMT?" (To complete the crew)
>
> "Negative, seven-o-one. That is negative."
>
> "Ten-four."

"Seven-o-one" over the radio came another voice, but it was not that of the dispatcher.

> "Seven-o-one, bye."
>
> "Seven-o-one, an EMT is going to the scene, you can roll the rig. I will meet you there."
>
> "Monroe County, this is seven-o-one."
>
> "Seven-o-one."
>
> "Seven-o-one is ten — eight [enroute] to the scene.
>
> "Monroe County, this is seven-o-one, we have arrived at the scene." (Four minutes later)

It may not be readily evident, but what is wrong with this picture is that the rules being enforced by the Monroe County dispatch system are the problem not the solution. Let's review the call.

A. First emergency call is sent over the pagers and volunteers alerted.
B. The volunteers are given three minutes to acknowledge the call.
C. Second call, if not acknowledged, goes over the system in three minutes.
D. The ambulance is given ten minutes to leave for the scene.

E. If the initial station does not leave, the next station, regardless of the distance away, is called out.

This particular call was saved, and maybe too, the patient. But it was by a lucky break. The EMT answering over the radio was a squad officer with a hand-held radio, which ordinary crew members do not have. If the EMT had not been an officer and did not have a hand-held radio, then seven-o-one would have been cancelled and an adjacent rig dispatched. The nearest next town was Mount Pocono, Pennsylvania, with an ambulance building about twelve miles from the scene. If the rules were effected, their response time would have been about twenty minutes longer.

The driver of ambulance seven-o-one had asked Monroe County Dispatch to page for an EMT to complete the crew. Monroe County had refused ("Negative, seven-o-one"). The dispatcher said she couldn't do that. Why? Simply because it was the rule, based on the Pennsylvania statute.

A patient with a history of a past brain operation could be in serious difficulty. The patient may have been suffering from a possible brain aneurysm. Every minute counts. This could have been a true life and death situation.

Seven-o-one, the initial ambulance dispatched, was stationed about three to five minutes from the scene; it was the very best chance for the patient's survival. Hence, it made common sense to page out for an EMT, complete the crew, and get the patient to the hospital — without bureaucratic games of chance.

Use of the protocol would have taken twenty more minutes than the common sense answer of "Yes, I will tone out for an EMT to help you." In a life and death situation, should games or protocol be played? Is the patient more important than the rules?

The patient in this case was probably saved because an EMT squad officer had a hand-held two-way radio and could alert the rig of her availability. Otherwise, the petty rules would have resulted in an additional twenty precious life-threatening minutes and, perhaps, the endangerment of the patient's life.

Any ambulance volunteer is always doing his or her best to save lives. He is a committed citizen and doesn't need protocol inflexibilities to doom his goodness of heart. By enforcing inflexible rules the patient is disregarded, and the rules take on a life of their own. Even the common sense of the dispatcher is removed from the field of play.

Could bureaucratic interference be one example of why volunteerism is disappearing from the American scene? Better results for society *will not* occur because a rule requires a volunteer EMT to speed faster to a call that he already was responding to out of civic responsibility.

There is no greater calling than desiring to assist another human being — without recompense. The State of Pennsylvania doesn't see it that way. Pennsylvania is only an illustration of the problem. The truth is that many Americans no longer see it that way either. We tend to view problems as "other people's problems" not ours. If someone has a desire to help another out of the goodness of his heart, we must suspect him, give him rules, and make his travail difficult.

Emergency Medical Technicians are taught under a federal guideline with licenses granted by each state. The courses are nearly alike, except in certain areas where additional requirements are added. Maine stresses water safety, for example, Colorado includes mountain rescue training.

This author is a licensed EMT. I volunteer my time on two first aid squads. For a number of years I have volunteered in Pennsylvania during summer vacations since a resort area (where I owned a house) needed help in July and August. My regular certification was out-of-state, hence I was granted "reciprocity" (a right to volunteer my services).

In 1993 the reciprocity rules changed. Pennsylvania's bureaucrats decided that my state's recertification process did not fit their own criteria. So they denied me the right to volunteer my services in Pennsylvania unless I would agree to schedule a Pennsylvania Practical Skills Examination. If passed, I would then be scheduled to take the Pennsylvania State Written Exam. Once the tests were completed I could then send my reciprocity application to the Department of Health in Harrisburg, Pennsylvania, for action.

The test locations were from fifty to one hundred miles from my out-of-state residence, and the extra preparation would have been time-consuming. I felt dejected and insulted that my licensed volunteer services could no longer help save a life in Pennsylvania. I, as a matter of principle, refused to play the bureaucratic game. It was too much to ask — study more, take more tests — to volunteer for two months. It made no sense.

But, I don't give up easily and thought about it more and more. My wife and I plotted a way around the state's medical bureaucracy. We believed it to be foolproof. I had an American Red Cross CPR certificate, so I could serve as a driver on the squad. My wife had impressive credentials. She is a Registered Nurse, and holds instructor certifications for teaching EMT, Red Cross First Responder, and CPR courses. Considering that she taught the Basic EMT Course at a state certified Fire and Police Academy, we believed she would certainly be granted reciprocity. Hence, we could ride the ambulance as a family (our son is an EMT also) and volunteer our services as before.

So, we filed a reciprocity application for my wife with the "Northeastern Pennsylvania Medical Services Council," and waited. Within three weeks my wife received a form letter stating that reciprocity would not be granted to her since "Pennsylvania does not recognize certification based on recertification through CEU's (Continuing Education Credits)."[2]

In addition, Pennsylvania's form letter was incorrect since her recertification was not granted through C.E.U.s, but rather because she taught a state approved basic EMT course at the Fire Academy. They just must have gotten it wrong, or so we thought. Obviously, the form letter must have been incorrect.

Since this was a form letter and still undaunted, we wrote a two-page letter explaining my wife's impressive credentials and indicating our desire to volunteer to help Pennsylvania at no charge to their citizens. We clearly pointed out that my wife teaches (one to two courses per year) the Basic Emergency Medical Technicians Course as scheduled in the United States Department of Transportation Manual, dated 1991, which is the bible for training in the United States. The letter was sent with a revised reciprocity request, and we awaited an answer.

Within a few weeks a second form letter was received. It once again rejected her application. It then dawned on us that we had not found a way around the bureaucracy.

Attempting one final appeal, my wife called Allentown, Pennsylvania, and spoke with the area Council Director. She explained that her certifications were ten times that required on any ambulance in the United States, and that my training was years above that of paramedic and even above Medevac attendants, and not derived from C.E.U.s.

"Yes, I know, I am familiar with your case," was the answer.

"Then, you do understand."

"Yes, I do understand your first and second reciprocity request."

"Well, then are you aware of the shortage of daytime volunteer ambulance attendants in Monroe County? Especially in the summer when my husband, son, and I help out?"

"Yes, I know we're short."

"Well, then, when will you approve my reciprocity application?"

"I can't. I can't because the rule says you have to take the basic course, not teach the basic course. The rule's the rule — I can't change it. The only solution to resolve your case is that you go to Harrisburg and appeal."

"I live nearly two hundred miles from Harrisburg. You are asking me to go to Harrisburg so that I can volunteer for two months in the summer? I will not do it; it's downright insulting."

"Then there's nothing I can do, the rule's the rule."

So, it was. Pennsylvania's petty rules had removed three volunteer EMT's from their highways. They said that we could still stop as good Samaritans, but could not be dispatched as part of an ambulance crew. The rules had held, but any person needing medical assistance might just bleed a little longer.

At that time Monroe County had about forty "out-of-staters" who also had volunteered their service. I spoke to several. Many said the same thing, "the hell with it." I never found out how many of the "out-of-staters" quit, but I've always believed it was the majority of them.

Who lost? Just the ordinary citizens who needed help. The bureaucrats still had their jobs. They had succeeded in setting up complicated rules that proved they could place their own testing procedures above that of surrounding states. The bureaucrats lost nothing at all. But the people lost another round!

It's not just Pennsylvania bureaucrats. The FDA (United States Food, & Drug Administration) is also specifically chartered to "help others." But it has taken this charge so broadly that in 1993 it stated its intention of determining what we eat and how individuals should determine their own nutritional intake.

It determined to do this by lowering the potency levels of vitamins to the levels found in foods. By doing this, the agency could interpret higher levels of vitamins and minerals to be classified as

Helping Others

unsafe food additives. Hence, by this sleight of hand technique, the agency might be able to require a medical doctor's prescription for those desiring to take vitamins and minerals as supplements, and at a far higher cost than at present.

As the health food industry fought back, ordinary citizens signed petitions and agreed to help in the battle to ingest what they choose. The outcry became so broad that Senator Hatch (R-UT) and Congressman Richardson (D-NM) introduced legislation that would amend the Federal Food, Drug and Cosmetic Act in a positive way. Senate Bill S.784 and House Bill H.R. 1709, both titled the "Dietary Supplement, Health and Education Act of 1993," would help to prevent overly restrictive government regulations that currently threaten individual health, food, and supplement choices. This proposed law would preserve the citizen's right to have access to dietary supplements and information about the benefits dietary supplements provide. Among other things, it would establish:

1. A broader definition of "dietary supplement," to include herbs and other supplements.
2. That dietary supplements would not be classified as drugs.
3. That dietary supplements would not be classified as food additives.
4. That truthful/scientifically based information about dietary supplements would be permitted.
5. That the FDA would have no prior restraint authority on truthful labeling or vitamin supplement advertising.

Why does an American citizen need a law (S.784 or H.R. 1709) to permit him to choose a vitamin or supplement of his choice? Why does an American citizen need a law that prevents the FDA from classifying vitamins and supplements as drugs? Why is a law required to permit "free speech" regarding truthful information about supplements?

The F.D.A. is a good example of a federal agency that has lost its way. Its goals have been confused with self-aggrandizement, similar to other federal agencies. A quick review of some facts about the F.D.A. will make it apparent that something is indeed amiss:

- The current number of employees is approximately nine thousand, which is six times higher than thirty years previous.
- Very few drug companies complain about the agency publicly, but they do so privately. "Whistle blowers" may be subjected to delays and harassment tactics.
- Thirty years ago it took about seven years to develop and obtain approval for a new drug. Today, the time lag has nearly doubled.
- A recent study of Tufts University...showed that 80% of drugs approved by the F.D.A. between 1987 and 1989 were available earlier in other countries by an average of about six years.[3]

The results are disheartening for the citizens of America, although not for the bureaucrats causing the problems. The net results are higher costs for drug development, longer time to achieve success, and the retarding of scientific research. All of these have negative consequences.

According to the same Tufts University survey, "it costs an average of $231 million to develop each drug approved in the 1980s."[4] That enormous cost, coupled with the $100,000 drug application fee, have squeezed out small companies and independent scientists while minimizing competition. Is it proper public policy for an agency to (in essence) decide that only large companies willing to spend $200 million and wait fourteen years should find promising pharmaceuticals for America? That is the result of their policies.

Somehow, under the guise of "helping others" we have permitted agencies to take away our rights to do so. We then require laws to get them back.

We have lost our way on the path. We have succumbed to the "calfpaths" of our minds and no longer think clearly as a society. We have permitted faceless experts to take over the thinking process for us.

Agencies have grown like monsters, with tentacles into nearly everything we do. We have let them interfere with individual choices and civic concern in the belief that somehow they are better equipped than we to run our lives. Why have we let all this happen?

Chapter 10

The Liberty Index

"These are the times that try men's souls. The summer soldier, and the sunshine patriot will, in this crisis, shrink from the service of their country. Tyranny, like hell, is not easly conquered."

Thomas Paine
The American Crisis
1776

"What is the Constitution?" Justice William Paterson inquired in a Supreme Court opinion of 1795. "It is the form of government, delineated by the mighty hand of the people in which certain first principles of fundamental law are established."[1]

While these established principles have held for nearly two centuries, they have been eroded during the past two decades.

There were good reasons why the Constitution was produced as an instrument of limitations on government and a statement on protected rights. The framers were fearful of tyrannical and abusive governments. They forbade *"ex post facto"* laws, or laws passed after an act was committed, which then made that act illegal and the actor subject to punishment.

The Fourteenth Amendment says that "no person shall be deprived of life, liberty, or property, without due process of law," a message often unheeded by Congress. Property rights have been assailed by our legislators, nearly without letup for the past thirty to forty years.

The Liberty Index

Madison and Hamilton were both distrustful of governmental power and cognizant of the need to safeguard individual rights. As they wrote in the Federalist (No. 22), rights had to be balanced against "interested and overbearing majorities" in order to establish and maintain a free government. Unfettered majority rule was rejected since it did not provide adequate security for individuals, rights, minorities, property, and enumerated privileges.

The first ten amendments or the Bill of Rights were proposed in 1789 so that the people and the individual states could be assured of security against encroachment by an overbearing or overzealous federal government.

The debate over the Constitution was largely pro- and anti-federalist. The three authors of "The Federalist" papers were Alexander Hamilton, James Madison and John Jay who had three major concerns that caused them to issue a strong endorsement for the fledgling Constitution:

1. Glaring defects in the loose structure of the Articles of Confederation.
2. The need to protect the divergent interests of farmers, shippers, storekeepers, etc., in a new and growing America.
3. The need to protect the propertied minority from the unpropertied majority. With chaos in the countryside, property rights needed protection.

Hamilton and Madison believed that the fundamental weakness of the fledgling government would result from human nature. They agreed with Thomas Hobbes who believed that "man was potentially an evil creature, whose passion and appetites needed restraining."

In the Federalist Papers Number 51 Hamilton asked: "If men were angels, no government would be necessary." He believed that the basic cause of trouble was economic inequality. His forecast was visionary since it has become a permanent, unrelenting problem. Madison and Hamilton urged us to recognize the legitimate existence of the passion of the majority, but control it by legal, counterweighted means.

While our founders magnificently crafted the Constitution, they could not foresee the erosion that would be caused by Congress, the courts, bureaucracies, and by factionalism two centuries later. Certain inherent safeguards of the Constitution have been breached because Americans are now too far removed from the abuses of the English monarchy, abuses which gave rise to the Bill of Rights. Americans are insensitive to many of the current abuses because they are either too subtle or do not directly affect citizens in ways that are apparent to them. Further, many of today's Americans believe that the problems that prompted the creation of the Constitution were unique to the eighteenth century. However, that is decidedly not so. People have acted the same throughout history; only the surroundings change. Greed, envy, and lust for power are still with us.

The important question for today is how has this document fared over the years? Have we succeeded in protecting our liberties, our collective freedom, and our rights as deeded to us by our founders? As we have already seen, we have not done very well at all. With our tacit consent, rights have been eroded, limited, or entirely extinguished.

Growth of government has gone hand-in-hand with the diminution of individual rights. During the last thirty years, the need to reduce the size of, limit, or change government has been recognized by presidents and other leaders. In the past six administrations there has been at least a recognition of the problem and a resolve to do something about it. Some examples are worth noting.

In Lyndon Johnson's administration, a strategy was developed called the "Programming Planning and Budgeting Systems Plan."

Its objective was to use modern management techniques to change government, to reduce costs, and to improve service to the citizenry. But it failed to deliver material results.

Richard Nixon attempted to introduce "Management by Objectives." It did not play well with the bureaucracy.

Jimmy Carter introduced "Zero Based Budgeting." He was impressed by the simplicity of this process to reallocate resources. He believed he could use his engineering background to achieve more efficiency. But it similarly went nowhere.

The Grace Commission was appointed by President Reagan and was officially titled "The Private Sector Survey on Cost Control." The Grace Commission produced a report showing governmental inefficiencies, waste, and even negligence. Its recommendations are still valid a decade later. As compelling an indictment of government mismanagement as it was, the Grace Report did not revolutionize or change government.

Not to be left behind, President Bush called his approach "Right Sizing Government." His aim was to reduce the size of government and get it under better executive branch control. Vice President Quayle headed the effort and many suggestions were produced. Few were enacted, however, and once again entrenched government won while efforts to alter it lost.

In September 1993, President Clinton and Vice President Gore, with great fanfare, announced their plan to "target the bloated bureaucracy." President Clinton stated that he would make government work better and cost less. The Clinton-Gore program was called "The National Performance Review." In November 1993 an official of the Congressional Budget Office was quoted on an ABC News program that the "Government Reform and Savings Act of 1993" would not work. He projected that the plan would be ninety-two percent less effective than the administration's forecast.

While the success of the Clinton-Gore plan is yet to be determined and will require four years to measure, its prospects look poor. Since 1964, beginning with President Johnson, all attempts to corral the bloated beast have failed miserably. The reason for the lack of success in controlling government growth has been the unwillingness of Americans to face the real problem.

The attendant impact on individual rights can be charted on the "Liberty Index" below. With the use of bar charts, the degree of impact on each constitutional right is graphically depicted. The bar charts are rated one to ten. A ten represents the right as originally promulgated and understood in 1789. A one indicates a very serious erosion of that right. Over time, *no rights have been more vigorously protected* than when granted. In other words we *have never been able to improve on our freedoms* after their granting. Freedoms are there to remove — not to improve. They have been tempered with, curtailed, or altered. The highest scores cluster around the most recent constitutional amendments. The lowest scores are, unfortunately, given to those rights that our founders held in the highest esteem, such as "private property."

Much of the erosion has been caused by Congress because of its inattention to controlling bureaucratic rules and regulations. On balance, more damage to our Constitutional guarantees has been done by the bureaucrats than by Congress itself. But it is a close contest who should be blamed the most. At the same time we must accept much of the blame ourselves — we allowed it to happen.

The following is a subjective interpretation of our rights (our constitutional bases) as seen today, versus the perceived goals of our founders. Since it represents an opinion more than a scientific analysis, agreement or disagreement rests solely with the reader. The important point, however, is that the problem be recognized.

The Liberty Index

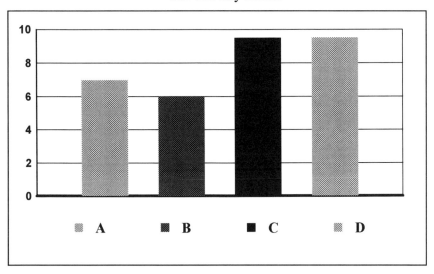

A. *U.S. Constitution, Article I — Legislative Powers Section 1-8.* Congress has altered the founders objectives with respect to its "compensation and privileges."
B. *U.S. Constitution, Article I — Legislative Powers Section 9-10.* Congress has passed *ex post facto* legislation in the areas of the environment, taxation (the Tax and Budget Act of 1993), and debased the currency at odds with the founders intentions (see Section 10-Par. I).
C. *U.S. Constitution, Article II — Executive Powers, Election and Qualification of the President.* This section while altered by time has not been eroded.
D. *U.S. Constitution, Article III — Judicial Powers and Tenure of Office.* Generally altered by time and decisions, but not changed materially.

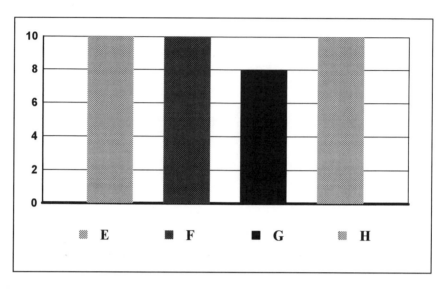

E. *U.S. Constitution, Article IV — Faith and Credit Among States.* Unchanged.
F. *U.S. Constitution, Article V — Amendment of the Constitution.* Unchanged.
G. *U.S. Constitution, Article VI — Debts, Supremacy and Oath.* Many of our elected representatives ignore their constitutional oaths in the lawmaking process.
H. *U.S. Constitution, Article VII — Ratification.* Unchanged.

The Bill of Rights, Amendments #1 - #10

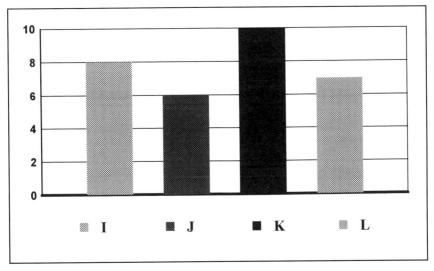

I. *U.S. Constitution, Amendment I — Freedom of Worship, Speech, Press and Assembly.* This is still close to our founders ideals. Some areas such as freedom of the press are abridged. In modern media licensing, such as found in the realms of T.V. and radio, abuses of this have occurred.

J. *U.S. Constitution, Amendment II — Right to Keep and Bear Arms.* States such as New Jersey, California, and Massachusetts as well as cities like New York City have limited this right. Our founders viewed this as a requirement to enable the people to form into a militia and protect themselves against unjust government.

K. *U.S. Constitution, Amendment III — Quartering of Troops.* This has remained within the context of the founding fathers.

L. *U.S. Constitution, Amendment IV — Right Against Unreasonable Search and Seizures.* This has been altered in many ways. Property seizure laws found in Chapter 6 illustrate the problem.

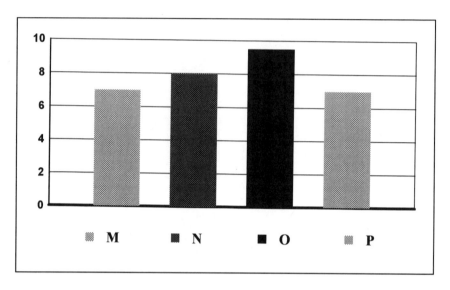

M. *U.S. Constitution, Amendment V — Grand Jury, Rights of Accused Persons, Due Process and Just Compensation.* This section has also been abused. Double jeopardy is violated constantly by the duplicate use of state and federal trials. Due process and just compensation are equally violated.

N. *U.S. Constitution, Amendment VI — Trial by Jury.* Intact, although curtailed in the jury selection process, and speedy trial in certain jurisdictions.

O. *U.S. Constitution, Amendment VII — Rights to Suit in Common Law.* Slightly eroded, but generally intact.

P. *U.S. Constitution, Amendment VIII — Prohibition Against Cruel and Unusual Punishment.* Property seizures, pre- and post-trial, and excessive fines imposed by agencies, especially those related to the environment, have altered this section, which remains otherwise intact.

The Liberty Index

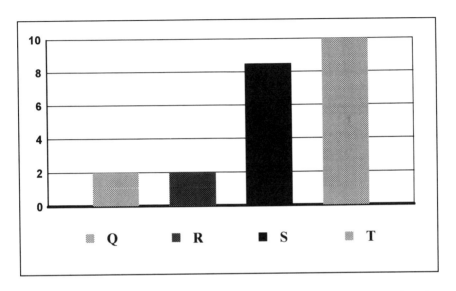

Q. *U.S. Constitution, Amendment IX — Rights Retained by the People.* The federal government has continually assumed rights supposedly reserved for the people. Few rights are now still reserved for the people. [Rate this a near failure or a "2."]

R. *U.S. Constitution, Amendment X — Powers Reserved for the States.* The federal government has continually assumed power over the states. It is currently a fictional grant.

S. *U.S. Constitution, Amendment XI — The Federal Judiciary Curbed in Relation to the States.* This is still in near juxtaposition to the original intent.

T. *U.S. Constitution, Amendment XII — Changes in the Procedure of Electing the President.* Intact.

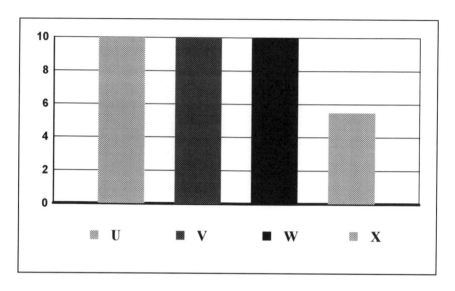

U. *U.S. Constitution, Amendment XIII — Abolition of Slavery.* The prohibition still endures as to slavery.

V. *U.S. Constitution, Amendment XIV — Citizens of the United States Defined, Privileges and Immunities.* Relatively unchanged.

W. *U.S. Constitution, Amendment XV — Negro Suffrage Granted.* Unchanged.

X. *U.S. Constitution, Amendment XVI — Income Tax.* The intent of this Amendment has been eroded continuously. The initial purpose of this amendment was lost decades ago.

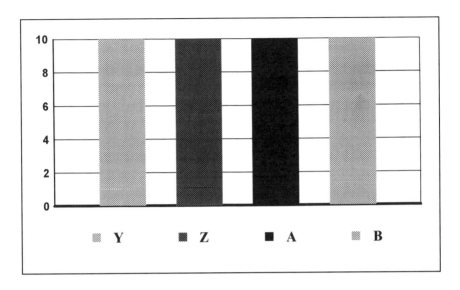

Y. *U.S. Constitution, Amendment XVII — Election of Senators by Popular Vote.* Unchanged.
(Eighteenth Amendment was repealed.)
Z. *U.S. Constitution, Amendment XIX — Women Suffrage.* Unchanged.
A. *U.S. Constitution, Amendment XX — Terms of President and Congress.* Unchanged.
B. *U.S. Constitution, Amendment XXI — Repeal of XVIII Amendment.* Unchanged.

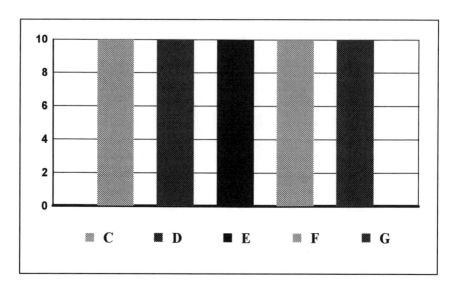

C. *U.S. Constitution, Amendment XXII — Tenure of President Limited to 2 Terms.* Unchanged.
D. *U.S. Constitution, Amendment XXIII — Right to Vote in Presidential Election and District of Columbia Residents.* Unchanged.
E. *U.S. Constitution, Amendment XXIV — Poll Tax Eliminated.* Unchanged.
F. *U.S. Constitution, Amendment XXV — Presidential Succession in the Case of Disability.* Unchanged.
G. *U.S. Constitution, Amendment XXVI — Voting Age at 18 Years for Federal and State Elections.* Unchanged.

Now that we have reviewed the problems in both essay and graphic forms, let's proceed to some proposed solutions. Gaining lost liberty will not be easy, but it is possible.

Chapter 11

Conclusion

I pledge allegiance to the flag of the United States of America, and to the republic for which it stands one nation under God with liberty and justice for all.

The Flag Salute

The United States Government has veered off course. We have permitted government to enter our lives without accountability and without rationale. The problem of an all-pervasive government must be revisited, reviewed, and re-evaluated. Government is debasing liberty as well as crippling the entrepreneurial spirit of most Americans. Creativity is being smothered. Paperwork and regulatory strangulation have become a reason for business failures and uncompleted projects. Jobs are being exported. As a result, our standard of living has dropped for ourselves and perhaps for our children. Our population is suffering from the suffocation of forms, tax returns, census data, and lengthy documents. Our lives and souls have thus been smothered. Bureaucracy, a living, breathing entity, has caused more harm than good.

Our elected officials have joined with our bureaucrats in an unholy alliance. They have told us hundreds of lies, made hundreds of broken promises, and yet are not held accountable for their actions. "Facts" require "spin" before they can be communicated to citizens. Reports are written in "Newspeak" so as to avoid communicating anything or holding anyone accountable. Legislators and bureaucrats, unfettered with the yoke of accountability, advance personal or social agendas at the expense of a hapless public who have little understanding of the manipulation and the abuse of power at their expense.

The 1993 movie, "Lorenzo's Oil" relates a true story about a family trying to save their son. Lorenzo is afflicted with Schilders Disease, a metabolic disorder occurring mainly in boys. It is characterized by atrophy, cerebral demyelination, and usually results in death within one to five years. Lorenzo's father and mother pored through books in the library, did calculations of their own, and performed in-depth medical research. Miraculously, they found a promising treatment for their son's disease.

But bureaucracy frustrated their efforts. Lorenzo's parents faced the intractability of the ALD Foundation. The rules had to be obeyed. In the background was that, should a cure be found, the ALD Association would be out of business. There would be no need for the group if Lorenzo's disease were to be eliminated. Of course, there are dozens of barriers to nondoctors searching for cures. The barriers often inhibit and discourage these efforts and could postpone the cure. Only because of the dogged determination on the part of Lorenzo's parents was their battle won.

But how many battles are lost and buried in the faceless bureaucracies that we have erected? Once a bureau is established it rarely dies. In New Jersey the responsibilities of a state bureau was to seek out "discrimination in the statutes." The Bureau was established prior to the 1970s when a plethora of anti-discrimination laws came into being. But the bureau lives on with a director and seven people. They quietly changed their own focus to education. Now they give out anti-discrimination materials — even though it was not their mandate. They have found a way to stay in business.

Sam Walton, the founder of Wal-Mart Stores, had an approach to business that eventually created a sixty billion dollar enterprise.

Conclusion 231

The canny merchant from Arkansas was able to establish a company and build it to more than two thousand stores by following one basic rule. In talks around the nation Walton emphasized that he would *never permit the growth of a Wal-Mart bureaucracy*. The company retained a folksy culture. Sam drove his pickup truck around the country visiting new stores until his death on April 5, 1992.

His anti-bureaucratic bias produced a number of axioms that were developed to keep the company's eye on its original mission. He wanted change to occur on a daily basis. He wanted store managers to run their own store and to innovate. Walton constantly forged ahead with experimentation.

Wal-Mart employees are not punished if they try and fail. Walton spent his life rooting out bureaucratic thinking. By not permitting bureaucratic fuzzy-headedness, Walton created one of America's great financial stories of the twentieth century. Sam's legacy is a managerial approach that is as pertinent to government as it is to business. Many of these principles are embodied in the proposals discussed below.

Here are some specific recommendations to restore our democracy and get back the rights that we have allowed to be taken from us.

Term Limits

Term limits is an idea whose time has come. Congressional service has become a profession — it was never intended to be one. It was never anticipated that being a senator or congressman would be a virtual lifetime job.

Our founders' idea of a citizen legislator is still valid. By creating a "profession" of Congress, we have encouraged a division between the elected officials and the people. Our elected representatives must be aligned with the community they serve. If our representatives understood that their service was to be for a limited term of years, they might again view their role as public servants rather than as a Mandarin class with more concern for the emoluments of office than for good government.

Congress is the root of many of our suffocating problems. Since the 1950s Congress has evolved into a bureaucracy that is larger and more impenetrable than that of any federal agency. The rationale behind many Congressional initiatives is self-perpetration of its own near royalty status and of its organizational structure. Congressmen see Washington as an opportunity to achieve status, riches, and power, all of which are as antagonistic to democratic rule in the 1990s as they were in the 1790s. Many Congressmen no longer care about their constituents other than as the vehicle to be re-elected to their good salary, their good benefits, and their perks.

If elected representatives were limited to four years and Senators to six years, self-aggrandizement would be seriously curtailed. Once elected, there would be little reason for raising money, making promises to special interest groups, or preparing for the next election. There would be less influence over an elected member's vote. His vote would be his own and not controlled by the party hierarchy or a political contributor. The risk of duplicity would be lessened, and votes based on conscience would be more prevalent.

Since both political parties share in the booty, it makes little difference, from an ethical perspective, which one is in power. Both parties have fooled us. Like a professional wrestling match, there is much sound and fury but little substance. So let the people respond by removing the Hollywood set. Let us strip the stage bare.

In the elections of 1993, the voters in New York City and the state of Maine sent a clear message. They voted for term limits in a clear, unmistakable manner. Perhaps this is an omen of things to come. Let us send people to Washington who fairly represent the diverse interests of their constituents and who will, in good conscience, try to balance those interests for the common good. Let's take the greed and avarice out of Washington by sending a different kind of person. Limit terms and a different kind of political animal may well appear.

Reduce Emoluments

Since the 1950s the financial and fringe benefits of being a Congressman have grown enormously.

While Congressmen should be entitled to a salary, medical benefits, and necessary office and staff expenses, there is no reason for a special speaker's pension or *any pension at all*, if he or she is only there for four years or six years.

To serve in Congress is an honor and a public service. If a person doesn't want to serve his country, he shouldn't run for office. Emoluments should not be the reason to provide such service.

Congressional Exemptions

The lives of ordinary citizens have been made difficult. Government regulations and forms are confusing and all-encompassing. Americans have been overwhelmed by complicated tax laws, suffocating regulations, and the enormous paperwork necessary to conform to the regulations. This has changed our society and has made us interface with each other through forms, not personal contact.

But there is a route out of the problem; just get elected to Congress. Congress has regularly exempted itself from its own laws. While we are subject to wage and hour regulations and discrimination statutes, Congress is not. And it has chosen to exempt itself from a whole host of other laws that the ordinary citizens must wearily obey.

A good example of congressional disdain for the average citizen occurred in October of 1993. The national health care debate had just begun in earnest. The Clinton Administration was pushing hard, while other forces were arraying against certain aspects of the reform.

The national press reported that the Senate, in a quietly passed resolution, excused themselves, in advance, from enrollment in the proposed health care plan before even seeing it. In other words, whatever plan would be passed and whatever limitations that inhere in such plan will not be good enough for or acceptable to the demigods of Congress. This arrogance is another brick in the palace of congressional hypocrisy. Congress must be made to obey the same laws as everyone else.

Personal Responsibility

Congressmen and bureaucrats are protected from suit by ordinary citizens unless they do something horrendous — like murder.

One of the world's leading welfare states is New Zealand. In its 1993 World Competitiveness Report, the World Economic Forum, a Swiss organization, rated New Zealand number one for its "quality of government policies." The report cites that all of New Zealand's top civil servants are on fixed term contracts linked to their own individual performance. Imagine a government employee being judged by his own performance? What a novel idea!

Wallace R. Wirths put the problem clearly:

> The answer lies in making our non-elected officials responsible to those we elect to govern our Republic. And to accomplish this, our elected federal and state officials must not only manage and supervise our huge bureaucracies constantly, but must take full responsibility for the actions of our bureaucrats

and for the myriad of complex regulations they so prolifically promulgate under the myriad of laws our legislators pass. In the case of the executive branch, our president has no choice other than to delegate control of the giant bureaucracy to the various cabinet members, military leaders, advisors, and department heads whom he appoints. These men, known as the "Administration," must be the rulers of our nation. Their bureaucrats must be the managers but not the ones who make strategic, broad policy decisions.[1]

In the United States federal bureaucrats are free to impose their wills on citizens and even deprive them of their rights, but incur no personal responsibility for doing so. Property seizures, as we have seen, can be a clear violation of citizen's rights. Yet, the officials enforcing these draconian measures bear no responsibility for their actions. Washingtonians, as well as state officials, must be accountable just like the rest of us.

Size of Government

The federal government must be reduced in size by at least twenty percent in its overall size, employee staffs, and agencies. At first blush, twenty percent may seem too large. It isn't.

In business there is an old axiom: "The Twenty Percent Rule." Generally speaking, it means that in any business:

1. Twenty percent of the employees produce most of the sales and profits.
2. Twenty percent of the customers produce most of the business.
3. Twenty percent of a company's product line usually produces most of the profit margins.
4. Twenty percent of the employees and products are not really required by the business.

The axiom will work in downsizing government. We know by the twenty percent rule that there is probably one-fifth of the employees that obtained their jobs through patronage or are not required. Hence, much of the suggested cutback will affect very little of everyday government services.

When there are less people to do a job, there will be less mindless proposals for senseless permits, forms, and documents. Fewer people means government must concentrate on the important issues. Fewer employees spend less dollars.

Will the government voluntarily agree to restructure or downsize itself? Probably not. Will the citizens take back the control of their lives so as to enforce meaningful change? The answer to that question is uncertain.

In the late eighteenth century less than ten percent of the colonists actively supported George Washington at any one time. But a determined minority can make a difference. It did in 1776, and the revolutionary forces were a minority.

If you need a call to action, then think about the three hundred congressional committees with staff members approaching four thousand persons. Think about 535 members of Congress with an army of over 11,000 assistants. That's a ratio of 23 to 1. A government body that has grown this large turns into a self-perpetuating monster. It is too large and too interested in its own prerogatives to be in touch with the citizens at large. Government by the people and for the people has become government by the governors and for the governors.

The federal government has evolved like a large formerly successful company that has forgotten the basis of its success and has begun to grow aimlessly. When a business faces this dilemma, it must restructure, close factories, shut departments, and reduce staff size. The only other alternative is to fail.

The U.S. Government must do likewise. It must go back to the basics. Elected officials are not sent to Washington to become rich. Bureaucrats should be paid adequately, but not endowed with unchecked power or be permitted to insulate themselves from us.

Reduce our Deficit

Fiscally, our country cannot survive if budget deficits continue. The Federal debt cannot go from four trillion to five trillion to six trillion. The reason should be obvious. Even though we "owe the money to ourselves" the private sector eventually will be crowded out of the monetary equation, and the imbalance will cause disastrous economic and political consequences for the coming generations.

Fiscal and personal responsibility begins with the willingness to cut and cap programs. It requires efficiencies that we seemingly have not cared about, and a reduction in entitlement programs.

The deficit can be reduced if the size of government is reduced. Priorities are: cost cutting first, size reduction second, and deficit reduction third. The result will be less interference in our lives as well as a stronger country. Let's reduce the deficit.

Reduction of Paperwork and Regulations

A review of permits, forms, filings, fees, etc. must be conducted with the goal of reducing all but the most important paperwork. All petty annoyances must be eliminated.

We have already seen that federal rules and regulations require over 60,000 pages. If one wanted to follow every one he could not. No sports contest or business situation could function with such a vast web of rules. It just wouldn't work. We have accepted oppressive regulation because we have renounced common sense.

Prior to the promulgation of new regulations, appropriate scientific testing must be undertaken. Many regulations have been passed based on hype and hysteria rather than scientific analysis. We must research problems first and proceed cautiously.

Paperwork that is unnecessary must be expunged. Each agency should have an ombudsman who reviews the proposed form and has the power to simplify or eliminate them. This job cannot be performed by a committee. A committee forestalls an answer because it shields individual responsibility. The "let's not get involved" syndrome is perfect for committee membership. Committees don't solve problems; an action-oriented individual does. Let that person be on an incentive contract to make it happen. The incentive will be paid for eliminating unnecessary requirements — not dreaming new ones up.

An adjudication mechanism that is quick, fair, inexpensive, and available to ordinary citizens must be found that can unblock traffic when necessary. An arbitration could solve many paperwork problems. Our court system, which generally sides with the government "experts," puts the citizen at a disadvantage. The present judicial system is too costly and too time-consuming to be utilized by the average citizen in a simple dispute with regulators.

Unless overbearing paperwork requirements are reduced or eliminated, the energy and determination of both individuals and business will be sapped. Forward movement must be substituted for paper pushing.

Bureaucratic Latitude

After reading most of this book you may be taken aback by this suggestion. But it is a very important one. Many of the problems that we have faced have been caused by the stridency of our own rules. Our government is angry with its people and it shows. But the rule makers, the bureaus, also have unwittingly been caught in their own trap. While it is a trap of their own making, together we must create a solution or suffer further harm.

Several years ago I underwent a personal income tax audit covering a three year period. During the audit, which turned out to be innocuous, it was discovered that I had inadvertently placed income in a wrong year. I had received a check around Christmas but didn't deposit it until January 3rd. No 1099 was received. The auditor said that she would have to move the income from the first year and place it in the second year.

"Mr. Siminoff, that is the rule I must follow."

"Why do we have to do that, when the income tax rates are the same, unless there's to be a penalty?" I asked.

"No there won't be a penalty; I imagine that the tax will be the same that you paid."

"Why don't you just note it in your file and state that there is no change in tax, instead of spending all this time and rewriting two tax forms just to adjust the years?"

"I wish I could do that but the rule is the rule. I don't have the authority to do it any other way."

So we spent approximately two to three hours making up two new tax returns without any change in tax resulting from the misplaced income. In the process, however, a mathematical error was uncovered which resulted in an overall refund for me.

The process showed a serious, deep flaw that, if corrected, might help to reverse our collective regulatory deterioration. The answer to many of these problems are simple, logical and require only the application of common sense. Officials working for government agencies must have some latitude to make judgements that bend the rules if the outcome is beneficial to all parties. In business there is a standard that trustees and directors follow called the "Prudent Man Rule." It generally means that one's actions (by hindsight) were performed correctly if a prudent person would have done the same thing under the same circumstances.

Government must likewise adopt a prudent man rule. If this rule were in use, then the federal tax auditor could have said to me, "I will write a memo and explain that no change will occur, so we do not have to go through the waste of time and rewrite two tax returns."

That approach would have saved time and money, not just in my case but in thousands of cases.

Many of the obstacles we have erected are created by ourselves. Getting past our own stupidity would solve many of the issues on a practical basis. If the bureaucracies could unbundle their rules so that a practical and prudent solution could be found, then time, expense, and rancor could be eliminated.

Form Letter Reform and the Truth

The computer and the form letter are at the root of this next problem. Together they have caused much deception. As I have pointed out, when a constituent receives an answer to an inquiry to an elected representative, it is most probably a form letter written well before the constituent wrote his inquiry.

This particular use of the computer is more insidious than the ordinary computer-generated notice with which we are familiar. Form letters from our elected officials are deceitful and can cause more problems than they solve by isolating the representative from the concerns and attitudes of his or her constituents.

The form letters of our elected representatives don't really provide an answer to our questions; a research assistant's advance

Conclusion

work does. A clerk can choose one of four or five answers adjusting the response to the inquirer's circumstance. The writer may be getting the proverbial brush-off, not an answer to his problem from an elected representative who has taken an oath to represent him. Many people *think that they have been answered and that their voice has been heard*, but the only thing that happened was that their inquiry was given a number that was entered for statistical purposes.

Form letters have broken the circuitry of democratic communication and have built a hypocritical wall, behind which facelessness can hide.

The solution to this problem is the restoration of candor. The missing modern day word is "truth." It's a collateral solution to the elimination of the modern government word "spin." The truth does not require alterations, spin, or obfuscation.

If an elected (or nonelected) official answers your inquiry by choosing a form letter as an appropriate method, it should state on top in bold type:

> This is a form letter. Your letter was not read by Senator Smith due to the pressure of time. It was prepared by an assistant, whose name is John Jones.

If the answer was chosen from one of several possible replies it should state: "This is a form letter chosen from one of four replies."

If it is a form letter from an agency such as the IRS, it should clearly indicate that, if it does not fit your case precisely, you may contact a *named individual who will correct it*. That individual's name and phone number should be clearly indicated. If an elected official receives so much mail on an issue that he cannot respond, then send out a letter and say so. Tell the truth!

Candor can be restored to government if form letters are labelled for what they are. If not, the democratic process is violated.

Balance Impact Statements

By now most Americans know what an "Environmental Impact Statement" is. If a project is to be proposed by a builder, then engineers, architects, and developers must prepare a complicated booklet outlining the impact of a project to endangered species, wetlands, air, and water. This requirement extends to residential and commercial roads, airports, and government buildings.

Our preoccupation with the environment has blinded us to other problems. I am not suggesting that we build an oil refinery in the middle of a reservoir; but that there are other areas of concern that command equal weight. Two important areas are (1) the economy and jobs, and (2) personal freedom as related to our constitutional protections.

Utilizing only the environmental impact statement produces an unbalanced equation. Any law, rule, or regulation should be required to weigh several important interests, such as (1) Environmental Impact, (2) Economic Impact (Jobs), and (3) Constitutional Impact (Citizen's Rights).

To be considered along with an environmental impact statement is that there is no balance or restraining mechanism given to the passing of a law that appears beneficial but whose economic impact is major.

To examine one side of an issue inspires actions that may not stand up to a factual challenge. We have all heard that the earth's ozone layer is being depleted and the harmful effects of CFCs

Conclusion   243

(chlorofluoro carbons). But we have only heard one side of the controversy. Did you know that:

- A single volcanic eruption can put more chlorine in the atmosphere than a full year's industrial production of CFC?
- Over three million tons of chlorine are sent into the atmosphere each year from ocean vegetation, alone?
- Burning wood emits chlorine?
- As sea water evaporates, hundreds of million of tons of chlorine enter the atmosphere, naturally?

When you weigh these factors, it becomes obvious that man has not altered the balance of nature. In fact:

> When the likely amount of chlorine from CFCs in the stratosphere is compared to natural sources, it is not clear that CFC production is sufficient to significantly affect the concentration levels of stratosphere chlorine. The fact that large amounts of chlorine are in the stratosphere, and have been there for billions of years, indicates that it is part of a normal equilibrium. There is no evidence that this equilibrium has been upset by the trace presence of CFCs.[2]

It is less important which side of a controversy appeals to us, but that science and balance are required in the rule making process. To do otherwise may cause one-sidedness, dislocation, and heavy-handedness.

The imposition of rules, regulations, and massive paperwork tends to curtail any activity, even if the intent was not to do so. Environmental impact statements have had this effect on road construction, airport building, basic research, port dredging, etc. Balance must be achieved for fairness and justice to prevail.

If both sides of an equation were given equal weight at the outset, then an environmental impact statement would not become a subtle way of curtailing positive activities.

I have used the word "subtle" because rights can be curtailed or even eliminated *without visible signs of the loss*. It was in the 1920s, for example, when the federal radio broadcast law came into being. The law is little thought of today because passage of time has tended to institutionalize its effect. Congress then determined that the freedom of the press was not a generic term, but a specific one. A sleight of hand was performed with limited opposition since the regulation sounded on target because of the new emerging technology. It was determined that radio (and now television) were press freedoms that had to be licensed. Whereas freedom of the press (newspapers, magazines, news letters, etc.) is constitutionally established, the then new medium of radio and the modern medium of television were not considered of the same genre.

Except for modern delivery and techniques, there is no difference between opinions that are written in the press, read aloud over radio, or read from a teleprompter on television. Yet, Congress was able to pass a licensing law by orchestrating the need to regulate the total number of channels in the airwaves. While that reasoning may have been correct, the constitutional problem becomes serious, not when we assign registered channels, but when we renew existing broadcast licenses.

A station can lose its license if it does not comply with FCC rules and regulations. The interpretation of these regulations can influence the broadcast content of a station. Therefore, it becomes a fair question whether the licensing system has become a subtle way of controlling opinion.

Why isn't the Constitution considered before the laws are written? Our legislators give so little consideration to the Constitution that laws are passed with the attitude of "let someone challenge it in the courts." But it is far too difficult to remove something that has become institutionalized and far too expensive to get your day in court.

Restore Power to the States and the People

If Jefferson and Madison were alive today, they would point to the Tenth Amendment to the Constitution — the "separation of powers" doctrine. States were supposed to have become the repository of powers not delegated to the federal government. What happened in practice was nearly the reverse. The federal government took most of the powers and left relatively little to the states.

The federal government can do many things well. We have proven our defense and military capabilities. We have proven our space technology. But defense and space technology are concerns of national importance and scope. This is not the case where the federal government attempts to micromanage regional and local concerns. When Washington imposes rules, they are called "mandates," and the states must comply.

On May 20, 1993, the "Motor Vehicle Act" was signed into law. Its intent was to make voter registration easier by providing appropriate facilities at state motor vehicle agencies. One might say this is a good idea, but the states will be required to spend over one hundred million dollars to get the job done. Unfortunately, they were given no federal dollars to do it.

The Advisory Committee on Intergovernmental Relations (a federal office) stated in a 1993 report that there were one hundred mandates from Washington to the states in the period 1980-1990. From 1940-1950 there were less than twenty. During the first 150 years of our democracy (1789-1939) there were few such mandates.

At the National Governors Conference in 1993, an official of the Ohio Department of Environmental Resources reported that his state was mandated to test Ohio water for more than fifty pesticides. The mandated test proved to be rather silly, though expensive, since less than ten substances were known to exist in Ohio's waters. Ohio, nevertheless, had to obey the mandate.

In a hearing before the Senate Committee on Governmental Affairs in November, 1993 four senators, not part of the committee, testified to the costs and harm occasioned by federal mandates. There are about 172 federal mandates with which local governments are obliged to comply. Senator Moseley-Braun (D-IL) pointed out that the "city of Chicago spends over $160 million per year to comply with just 50 of them and spends $27 million annually on paperwork associated with federal mandates and regulations."

Senator Gregg (R-NH) told of the town of Lancaster (population 3486) that collects $1.4 million in revenues each year. But complying with the new Safe Drinking Water Act alone will cost $2 million. Another senator told of a small town where new safe drinking water regulations would cost each user $6000 per year. A local official said, "We will have the cleanest water in the country and the dumbest kids." The mayor of Philadelphia, Edgar G. Rendell, cited five instances in which the EPA has made substantial errors in estimating costs to local governments of its regulations. The EPA estimated that the costs of preparing storm water permits for Philadelphia would be $76,681. The actual costs were $916,950.

Rendell noted a proposed $500 million tertiary water treatment plant for Philadelphia. Tucson, Arizona, a desert community in which waterways are dry most of the year, must spend millions to monitor pollutants in nonexistent water in dry stream beds. Under the Safe Drinking Water Act, cities must monitor at least 133 specified pollutants. One of them is

Conclusion

a pesticide that was used only on pineapples in Hawaii and has been banned for 15 years.[3]

The mandate problem, like the overregulation problem, began to plague us in the 1960s. Its roots can be traced to the New Deal, but it really took hold with the centralization of our federal government during the past thirty to forty years.

The process must be reversed and returned to the founding fathers' concept of state control of local affairs. In many instances, Washington is simply too remote to deal effectively with these local issues.

Years ago welfare and relief was offered to local citizens by churches or townspeople. It was provided largely by volunteers. Caring was a community affair. By letting "Washington Do It" we have removed the community, volunteerism, and the private human act of caring from the equation. We have made it cold and calculating instead of warm and feeling.

The power of caring for people should be brought back as close to the populace as it can. It should be administered by the towns, counties, and states where people live. The current distancing process has led to many societal negatives. It has increased complexity and denied us the simplicity and warmth of local caring.

Columnist Gordon Bishop put it very well:

> Something happened (to us) in the '60s that changed the attitude and values. . . .
> Americans must get back to the basic quality of life values that made the '40s and '50s a safe and decent time in which to live and raise a family.[4]

We have lost our closeness with each other. Reliance on a cold, unfeeling federal government is just one of the causes. Such reliance must be reversed.

Property rights are no longer respected in rules, regulations, laws or even court decisions. Part of this disrespect for property rights can be placed at the doorsteps of environmentalists, bureaucrats, our elected representatives, and our national problem of litigiousness.

However, respect for property rights is at the cornerstone of our constitutional system. Property seizure laws must be reformed.

> Forfeiture money has allowed cities to buy squad cars, radar detectors, and other equipment. Scary, but true: Since 1985, the federal government has seized private assets worth more than $2.6 billion in over 170,000 seizures. Nearly half that was "kicked back" to over 3,000 state and local agencies since 1986.[5]

Abuse of property rights, our court system and errant litigation has become a way of life.

The Negativity of Litigiousness

Our Congress is largely populated by lawyers, so this proposal will be the hardest to implement. But let us face that our litigation system is simply out of control. Justice is a game played by lawyers, permissive judges, and a system that is often simply a means of redistributing wealth.

Three come to mind: (1) malpractice, (2) suing at the drop of a hat, and (3) contingency fees. Americans have come to believe that if they have a problem, someone else is probably at fault. We have become a nation that does not want to accept individual or collective responsibility for our own actions. "It's someone else's fault," is the mantra repeated endlessly by a self-centered, overly indulged nation of whiners who have enthusiastically embraced the national sport of scapegoating.

Conclusion

Recall the story about Bert Rutan and his terrific line of airplane kits that were so good he couldn't sell them. Lawsuits and litigation have literally grounded the small aircraft industry. Even if a plane is twenty years old and has been modified by the owner, the original manufacturer can be held responsible and sued. The game is deep pockets, not justice, and while it enriches attorneys in the process, the system does nothing to encourage the modernization of our general aviation fleet. It does nothing to encourage innovation or promote fairness in commerce or society.

In 1978, production of small planes, called general aviation by the industry, totalled nearly 18,000 units. Fifteen years later, killed mostly by legal liability forces, the total output of small planes was under one thousand units, or a decrease of almost ninety-five percent. The industry is in tatters. Importantly, this is only one example of the result of unrestrained litigation.

The big losers included Cessna Aircraft of Wichita, Kansas, Piper Aircraft of Vero Beach, Florida, and Beech Aircraft, also of Wichita. The employees who lost their jobs also lost.

Indeed, except for the lawyers, we all lose. Because of the dearth in production of new small planes, the general aviation fleet has aged dramatically. Moreover, sales of new aircraft are, of course, affected by price. Prices have increased significantly because of litigation and the open-ended product liability of the plane makers. This has further suppressed sales.

The problem is so serious that Congress has tried to solve this problem on several occasions during the 1980s and 1990s. But the trial lawyers, who have a disproportionate influence in Congress, managed to derail the reform.

Our current system makes those with assets, as well as the doers and the professionals, easy targets for unfair legal assaults. When a patient is taken to the hospital, he is subjected to a battery of tests. But he may only need one such test. Fear of lawsuits makes a large part of the practice of medicine defensive. It raises costs, increases time spent, and enervates the spirit.

Suing at the drop of a hat is a sign of a dysfunctional society. Instead of working out our problems, many people feel that they have to take every problem to court. This is often inappropriate and unfair to the person being sued. The suits have clogged our justice system and damaged our collective ethos.

Contingency fees, which are not permitted in many European nations, may promote abuses. Attorneys may take cases on a percentage basis where the target is well-heeled and where a settlement may be the sole value of the case.

Another suggestion that could be implemented together with or in lieu of eliminating contingency fees is the "loser pays principle." The person who loses a suit would be forced to pay both the winner and losers legal fees under this concept. Either of these reforms would make it more difficult to sue over frivolous matters. The key is to reduce the use of the legal system in cases that are often unfair to "deep pockets" who are often willing to settle rather than continue to incur legal fees and the disruption that occurs during the litigation process.

In a citizen-vs.-government dispute, such as a property seizure case, the system must be changed to make justice accessible, affordable, and fast to an aggrieved party. In short, our legal system must be reformed so that we act like human beings toward each other and not like gunfighters.

The Power Is Still Ours — Let's Take It Back

A friend from Minnesota shared a vacation with me and related the following story. Within the story is the essence of our survival as a free nation. Since the story is taken from the records of grand

Conclusion 251

jury deliberations, names of all parties have been changed as well as certain facts.

An assistant prosecutor, who was an aspiring young attorney, presented the case to Alan's grand jury. The case alleged rape and carnal abuse of a fifteen year old girl named Sue by an eighteen year old male named Ted.

Sue, a sophomore in high school, had taken the day off from school and was home alone in her family's second floor apartment. The apartment was located above a delicatessen on a main street of a quiet suburban community. Ted also played hookey from school on the same day. He was a senior and arrived on that same day at Sue's apartment "asking to be let in." Since she was acquainted with him, she opened the door and allowed him entrance. Allegedly, Ted then committed the rape and carnal abuse. The girl's screams were not heard in the deli downstairs. Approximately thirty days after the incident occurred, Ted was charged with the crime and arrested by the police on a complaint sworn out by the victim's father.

The grand jury on which Alan was seated heard the case and was asked to return an indictment against the eighteen year old boy. They listened intently to the testimony, which was mainly a plea by the Assistant District Attorney and a monologue by Sue, the victim. After the case was presented, the grand jury was left to its deliberations. In her address to the panel the young assistant prosecutor, named Rachel, importuned that it was an open and shut case and requested the return of a "true bill" or an indictment by the jury.

Alan was seated in the rear along with two other male members who had been mumbling back and forth that the case seemed to have too many holes in it. He had questioned Rachel who seemed to answer the questions inadequately. His doubts lingered.

Alan was one of those Americans who took his grand jury responsibility seriously and had done considerable reading about his rights and privileges as a grand juror. He had galvanized the jury during a previous case. That disagreement with the prosecutor's office had earned him and the jury the reputation of a nonrubber stamp panel. Alan had learned that, by the request of one juror, the foreman could be requested to excuse the prosecutor from the room. Something told him that there was more to this case than what had been disclosed. He raised his hand:

"Madam Foreman, I request that the prosecutor leave the room so that the jury can deliberate privately."

"That's not necessary, this is an open and shut case," intoned Rachel.

"I don't think it is," replied Alan. "I again request that the prosecutor leave the room so that I may talk to the jurors."

"Alan, your request is understood. Rachel, please give us some time to ourselves," requested the foreman.

Rachel left with an angry look plastered on her face, but Alan said nothing further. When she cleared the room, Alan asked for and received permission to address the jury members.

"This case has a number of troubling aspects. First, why did the complaint take thirty days to be filed? Second, how did Ted know that Sue was playing hookey and was home on a school day? Third, why were her screams unheard, the apartment is right over a delicatessen? Fourth, did you all see the complainant; she looks eighteen years old herself?"

"I agree, the case smells fishy," said a male juror.

"Madam Foreman, I would like to recall the complainant and be permitted to ask her some of the same questions that I have posed to the jury. More needs to be done before we vote, regardless of the prosecutor's assertions."

"How does the jury feel about that?" asked the foreman.

A sizeable majority raised their hands. Both Sue and Rachel were then asked to return to the jury room. Rachel was told that

Alan would ask the questions. She instantly became furious. Alan and the jury stood their ground. Alan was given the floor.

"Young lady, I am troubled by this case and have a few questions for you," began Alan.

"Yes, Sir."

"Why did you stay home that day from school?"

"I was not feeling well," replied Sue.

"How did Ted know that you were home and not feeling well? He played hookey also."

"I told him."

"I thought he was just an acquaintance? That is what you said before, isn't it?"

"Yes, but I knew him better than that."

"Were you boyfriend and girlfriend?"

"Yes, you might say that."

"How long?"

"For two years," replied a now tearful Sue.

"Two years, so this was a planned meeting between the two of you, wasn't it?"

"Yes."

"Had you had sexual relations with him prior to this occasion?"

"Yes."

"So, it sounds like you planned to have relations on this date. You both took off from school on the same day to meet when no one was home — is that right?"

"Yes," replied a now sobbing Sue.

"Then why did you sign this complaint?"

"I didn't want to."

"Why did you?"

"My father found out."

"What did he find out?"

"He suspected that we were having sex."

"So?"

"He said that if I didn't charge Ted with rape, he would beat the crap out of me."

"So that's why the charge was filed a month later?"

"Yes."

"Did you ever hear of perjury?"

"Yes."

"Look, you did the wrong thing. You lied to us. Did you lie to the prosecutor, also?"

"She was a woman and was more sympathetic than you are. She didn't ask all these questions, like you did."

"Okay, young lady, please leave the room, but wait outside."

When Sue had left the room Alan sat down. Rachel stood up and addressed the jury. She said:

"Okay, maybe the rape charge is wrong but the carnal abuse still fits. Why don't you vote a true bill for carnal abuse?"

"There's no case here," shouted Alan.

"This is a boyfriend-girlfriend situation compounded by an irate father," said a woman juror.

Alan once again requested that Rachel leave the room. By this time her face was reddened.

After a few minutes the jury deliberated and voted not to indict the eighteen year old senior. They agreed that to do so would be a gross miscarriage of justice. Rachel returned to the room and lectured the jury. She said this was a "runaway" jury, and *was now outside of her control.*

The next day Rachel's boss, the D.A., came down, and he too addressed the jury. He informed them that a few sensitive cases would be shifted to an alternate jury.

Evidently, although unsaid, that would be punishment for upholding the Constitution and standing up to the prosecutors. The system was designed so that a grand jury could do what Alan's jury did. It was not designed to be a playground for ambitious prosecutors. However, as citizens, we have in many instances ceded this indictment power to prosecutors without a fight and without the inquiry that we are obligated to conduct.

In this case, the jury prevailed in its will. Alan told me that of the two hundred cases they heard, they argued with the prosecutor in over twenty-five percent. Of that number more than half of those charged were not indicted. In one case Alan admitted to making an error, but smiled and said, "forty-four to one is not bad."

After they were dismissed from service, the prosecutor eventually told Alan's jury that his office has "trouble with about one in ten juries." Nine out of ten docilely accede to most of the state's requests. The Constitution did not intend it to be that way and it does not have to be that way. We have permitted it to evolve away from the concept of the founders of our nation.

Alan and I talked about his experience at length. Both he and I agreed that his Minnesota experience was a microcosm of one of our national problems. Americans have become so mesmerized by the supposed expertise of authority figures that they have forgotten their own responsibilities. A citizen/juror's responsibility is to question authority, to protect the innocent, and not to submit because they are told to do so.

If Americans showed the kind of resolve that Alan's jury demonstrated, we could restore the respect for and protection of individual rights, which were the hallmark of our nation. There would be no "Liberty Crisis."

Our founding fathers created the grand jury system as part of the constitutional bulwark to protect citizens against abuse by government. They gave enormous power to the jurors. But as citizens, we seldom invoke it.

In Triumph, Idaho, a strange phenomenon recently occurred. The townspeople told the Federal EPA that they didn't want them to bulldoze their town. They wanted to keep it just the way it was.

Triumph is an ex-mining town with just a little over fifty residents. It is beautiful but has been markedly influenced by years of mining operations. The EPA said the residues of the mining operation are dangerous — the townspeople say they are not. Further, the residents insisted that they haven't experienced any illnesses or side effects and don't expect any in the future.

The EPA's designation of the town as an environmental problem site has caused concerns to the entire population. Banks look askance at mortgages, and real estate agents say houses are unsalable. Who wants to own property in an EPA problem area?

The EPA has insisted that the residents have an environmental problem, but numerous blood and urine tests have indicated no unusual concentrations of toxic substances. The general population seems to be as healthy as other cross sections of similar communities. The town's water has been tested regularly and appears as safe as any other aquifer in like areas.

The townspeople have held meetings and have decided that it's their town and they want it to remain unchanged. Citizens have stood their ground and have fought back against the threatened juggernaut.

Once a site is listed in the Superfund Category, as is Triumph, the EPA pursues its claim. In face of this, the townspeople have remained equally adamant. They have tried to mobilize their congressmen as well as state officials to help keep Triumph just as it is. They like it and have hung a sign, "No bulldozers wanted!"

The citizens of Triumph are standing firm, as one unit, to keep the EPA out of their paradise. There is yet no reported resolution, but Triumph's fight proves that organized citizens can confront a larger government force such as the EPA.

Conclusion

A courageous lady named Peggy Reigle, who resides in Cambridge, Maryland, also decided to fight back. Cambridge is located on the Western Shores of the Delmarva Peninsula. Peggy became irate about the many violations of property rights by environmental laws. She believed that many rules were simply unjust takings. Peggy formed a group called the "Fairness to Landowners Committee," or FLOC for short, that is trying to reverse this trend.

Relying solely on volunteers, FLOC has grown to fifteen thousand members. They have aired their stories on CBS and NBC network news shows and in numerous newspapers including *The Wall Street Journal, New York Times,* and the *Philadelphia Inquirer.*

They have publicized stories and have fought back individually and together. Congressmen and state officials are beginning to listen. Peggy Reigle's group shows that change can be effected. You, we, all of us can fight back. We can be like Peggy or join groups such as FLOC.

All of us must become activists. We can take back our rights, and the operation of our country. If we get involved, if we speak out, if we are not easily squelched, we can do it. By submitting to the control of others, without a fight, we simply give up our rights. It only takes a few good men and women to begin the process. Other like-minded, good citizens will follow.

Perhaps you can't write a book, or an Op-Ed piece. But you can write a letter to the editor or to your congressman. Perhaps you can't form an organization like Peggy Reigle did, but you can join an organization.

The taking back of America's lost freedoms will be hard. It can be done. We have no choice but to participate, unless we wish to see our heritage disappear.

Over two hundred years ago Thomas Paine said during our first "Liberty Crisis" that "the sunshine patriot will, in this crisis, shrink from the service of their country. Tyranny, like hell, is not easily conquered." He was right on both counts.

Once again we must reach far inside our American character and take back what we have lost. It can be done if we do it together.

Appendix I

Glossary of Superfund Terms

CERCLA — the Comprehensive Environmental Response, Compensation and Liability Act; the original Superfund law, signed into law in 1980.

SARA — the Superfund Amendments and Reauthorization Act of 1986, passed by Congress to reauthorize CERCLA.

NPL — National Priorities List; the master list of Superfund sites, as identified by the U.S. Environmental Protection Agency (EPA).

PRP — potentially responsible party; the name given to any party that may have generated, transported, or disposed of waste at a Superfund site, or that may have owned or operated a site and can be held liable for cleanup costs.

Superfund "Trust Fund" — the actual trust fund created by Congress, from which the name "Superfund" comes. The trust fund is financed by taxes on businesses and is used for the cleanup of those sites where PRPs cannot be identified, commonly known as "orphan" sites. It is also used for emergency cleanup actions at sites.

Retroactive Liability — any PRP can be held liable for waste with which it is associated, regardless of when it occurred.

Joint and Several Liability — any single PRP can be forced to pay the whole cost of cleanup at a site, regardless of its specific contribution to a site.

Strict Liability — a PRP does not have to have done anything illegal or wrong to be held liable at a site.

Settlement — a legal, binding agreement with the government and/or private parties to pay or take action at a Superfund site.

"De Minimis" — a relatively small contributor, as determined by EPA, based on the quantity and toxicity of waste contributed to a particular site.

NBAR — Non-Binding Preliminary Allocation of Responsibility; created by Congress as part of SARA, its purpose is to help the government make quick, preliminary determinations of liability in order to speed the settlement process.

Remediation — actual cleanup activity at a site.

RI/FS — Remedial Investigation and Feasibility Study; the thorough investigation which helps determine the extent of contamination and the most appropriate cleanup remedy for a site.

ROD — Record of Decision; the actual cleanup remedy plan and costs for a site.

Consent Decree — settlement between EPA and the PRPs as to the assignment of allocation of responsibility, submitted for court approval.

Transaction Costs — fees to lawyers, consultants, steering committees, and other non-cleanup related activities associated with establishing Superfund liability.

Appendix I 261

Enforcement — EPA's policy of forcing PRPs to comply with Superfund liability standards and fund cleanup.

Section 106 Order — an administrative order issued by EPA demanding that PRPs take immediate cleanup actions or risk substantial financial penalty; a 106 order is based on the presumption that the site poses a serious threat to the environment and, therefore, requires an emergency response.

Third-Party Contribution Suit — a suit by one PRP against another, to help defray the costs which they have agreed to pay the government.

Appendix II

Regulations and the Price Per Life

In 1991 the Federal Office of Management and Budget attempted to forecast costs of safety regulations on the basis of "lives saved per dollar spent" to achieve the result. While the analysis was theoretical and computer generated, it nevertheless did offer a guideline and hence is useful in general terms. Below are listed most of the OMB results:

Regulation/Standard	Estimated Cost Per Potential Avoided Death Per Millions of Dollars
Ban on unvented space heaters	$ 0.1
Aircraft cabin fire protection	0.1
Auto passive restraint/seat belt	0.1
Trihalomethane drinking water	0.2
Aircraft floor emergency lighting	0.6
Concrete and masonry construction	0.6
Ban on flammable children's sleepwear	0.8
Grain dust explosion prevention	2.8
Rear seat auto lap/shoulder belts	3.2
Ethylene debromide drinking-water	5.7
Asbestos exposure limit	8.3
Benzene exposure limit	8.9
Standards for electrical equipment in coal mines	9.2
Arsenic emission standards for glass plants	13.5
Ethylene oxide exposure limit	20.5
Hazardous waste listing for petroleum-refining sludge	27.6
Acrylonitrile exposure limit	51.5
Asbestos exposure limit	74.9
Arsenic exposure limit	106.9
Asbestos ban	110.7
1,2-Dichloropropane limits in drinking water	653.0
Hazardous waste land-disposal ban	4,190.4
Formaldehyde exposure limit	82,201.8
Standard for altrazine/alachlor in drinking water	92,069.7
Hazardous waste listing for wood preserving chemicals	5,700,000.0

Appendix III

Current Cancer Risk Assessment
May Harm Health
(Linear Extrapolation From High Doses in Animal Experiments
To Low Doses For Humans Is Scientifically Invalid)

Draft Statement Presented to the
International Center for a Scientific Ecology
Paris, France, May 10, 1993
B.N. Ames *et al.*

(1) The major causes of human cancer are becoming better known: smoking, unbalanced diets, chronic infections, and genetic factors. In addition, occupational exposures might cause a few percent of human cancer and exposure to the sun is another minor contributor. Pollution appears to account for less than 1% of human cancer; yet public concern and resource allocation for chemical pollution are very high, in good part because of animal cancer tests.

(2) Animal cancer tests, which are done at the maximum tolerated dose (MTD), are being misinterpreted to mean that low doses of synthetic chemicals and industrial pollutants are relevant to human cancer. Half of all chemicals tested, whether synthetic or natural, are carcinogenic to rodents. A plausible explanation for the high frequency of positive results is that testing at the MTD frequently can cause chronic cell killing and consequent cell replacement, a risk factor for cancer that can be limited to high doses. Ignoring this greatly exaggerates risks.

(3) In any case, the vast bulk of chemicals ingested by humans is natural. For example, 99.99% of the pesticides we eat are naturally present in plants to ward off insects and other predators. Half of these natural pesticides tested at the MTD are rodent carcinogens. Reducing our exposure to the 0.01% that are synthetic dietary pesticides, whether to individual chemicals or to mixtures, is enormously expensive and will not reduce cancer rates. On the contrary, fruits and vegetables are our most effective dietary cancer fighters and making them more expensive by reducing synthetic pesticide use will increase cancer. Humans also ingest large numbers of natural chemicals from cooking food. Over a thousand chemicals have been reported in roast coffee: more than half of those tested are rodent carcinogens.

(4) The reason we can eat the tremendous variety of natural chemical "rodent carcinogens" in our food is that animals and humans are extremely well protected by many general defense enzymes, most of which are inducible (i.e., whenever a defense enzyme is in use, more of it is made). The enzymes are equally effective against natural and synthetic reactive chemicals. One does not expect, nor does one find, a general difference between synthetic and natural chemicals in ability to cause cancer in high dose rodent tests.

(5) Risk should be estimated using a weight-of-evidence approach, not by a blanket worst-case rule. A high proportion of rodent carcinogens is likely to have a threshold dose below which no pathological effect is observed. Scientists must determine mechanisms of carcinogenesis for each substance and revise acceptable dose levels as understanding advances.

(6) The idea that there is an epidemic of human cancer caused by synthetic industrial chemicals is false. The steady rise in life

expectancy in the developed countries provides evidence of this error. Linear extrapolation from the maximum tolerated dose in rodents to low level exposure in humans has led to grossly exaggerated mortality forecasts. Such extrapolations cannot be verified by epidemiology. Furthermore, relying on such extrapolations for synthetic chemicals while ignoring the enormous natural background, leads to an imbalanced perception of hazard and allocation of resources. It is the progress of scientific research and technology that will continue to lengthen human life expectancy.

(7) Zero exposure to rodent carcinogens cannot be achieved. Major advances in analytical techniques enable the detection of extremely low concentrations of all substances, of both natural and manmade origins, often a million times smaller than thirty years ago. Low levels of rodent carcinogens of natural origin are ubiquitous in the environment. It is thus impossible to obtain conditions totally free of exposure to rodent carcinogens or to background radiation.

(8) Risks compete with risks: society must distinguish between significant and trivial risks. Regulating trivial risks or exposure to substances erroneously inferred to cause cancer at low doses, can harm health by diverting resources from programs that could be effective in protecting the health of the public. Moreover, wealth creates health; poor people have much shorter life expectancy than wealthy people. When money and resources are wasted on trivial problems society's wealth and hence health is harmed.

NOTES

Chapter 1

1. Paul J. Lim, "Bungee Jumpings Unencumbered Cord Gets Tangled," *The Wall Street Journal*, August 11, 1992.
2. H. R. Perot, "United We Stand," (New York: *Hyperion Books*, 1992).
3. *The Observer-Tribune*, Chester, NJ, "Leaves Roll into Lake, brings Fine to Homeowner," November 9, 1989.
4. Donald D. Etler, "Nightmare in Iowa," *News From The FLOC*, February 1993. Reprinted by permission of the Fairness to Landowners Committee, Cambridge, MD, 21613.
5. Jimmy Hayes, "Danger, Bureaucrats At Work," *The Readers Digest*, December 1991, p. 113-116.
6. Ibid.
7. Ibid.
8. Editorial, "Wetlands," *The Wall Street Journal*, March 25, 1992.
9. Shanley & Fisher, *Environmental Law Briefs*, Morristown, NJ, Editorial, August 1993, p. 3.
10. Editorial, "Wetlands," *The Wall Street Journal*, March 25, 1992.
11. "Endangered Humans and Other Species," *News From The FLOC*, August 1993. Reprinted by permisision from the Fairness to Landowners Committee, Cambridge, MD, 21613.
12. "The Verdict Is In," *Investors Business Daily*, February 13, 1992, p. 10.

13. "Forgotten Civil Rights," *The Wall Street Journal*, August 14, 1992, p. A10.
14. Peter C. Everett, "Regulations Freeze Out Desperate Job Seekers," Letter to *The Wall Street Journal*, June 17, 1992.
15. Patricia Sullivan, "Crackdown," *The Star Ledger*, Newark, NJ, January 14, 1992, p. 1.
16. B.N. Ames and L.S. Gold, "Chemical Carcinogenesis: Too Many Rodent Carcinogens," *Proceedings of National Academy of Science, U.S.A.*, 87, (1990), 7772-7776.
17. B.N. Ames, Letter to Author, University of California at Berkeley, September 20, 1993.
18. Linda Molnar, "Changes in an Environmental Law Draw Mixed Reviews from Business," *The New York Times*, October 24, 1993, Sect. 13, p. 1.
19. Murray Weidenbaun, "The Pentagon's Fruitcake Rules," *The New York Times*, January 5, 1992.
20. Martin Gross, *The Government Racket* (New York: Bantam Books, 1992), p. 46.
21. Brian Murray, "Harding Sued by Developer over Stalled Permit," *The Star Ledger*, December 16, 1992, p. 42.
22. Kent Jeffreys, "Politics Makes a Mess of the Environment," *Intellectual Ammunition, The Heartland Institute*, Palatine, IL, September/October 1993.
23. Margaret Ann Reigle, "National Biological Survey Debate," *FLOC*, November 1993. Reprinted by permission from the Fairness to Landowners Committee, Cambridge, MD, 21613.
24. Reprinted from "The Bill of Rights, 200 Years, 200 Facts," Copyright, Philip Morris Management Corp., 1990, p. 15.
25. Meg Nugent, "Family Planners Unhappily Comply with Gag," *The Star Ledger*, October 1, 1992.
26. Diana Jean Schemo, "Gotti Lawyer is Convicted of Contempt," *The New York Times*, January 8, 1994, p. 25.

Chapter 2

1. James Madison, "Notes of Debate in the Federal Convention of 1787," (Athens, OH: *Ohio University Press*, 1984), p. 214.

Chapter 3

1. Jay Romano, "Easing the Glut of Legislative Bills," *The New York Times*, January 5, 1992, Sect. 12, p. 1.
2. Margaret Ann Reigle, "Family and Friends Gather to Welcome Home Bill Ellen," *FLOC*, July 1993. Reprinted by permission from the Fairness to Landowners Committee, Cambridge, MD, 21613.
3. "Weathering the Regulators," *Time Magazine*, February 17, 1992, p. 17.
4. Commonwealth of Pennsylvania, Pennsylvania Fish Commission, Harrisburg, PA, "Summary," 1992.
5. Ibid, p. 4.
6. Ibid, p. 4.
7. "Adding Insult to Injury," *The Star Ledger*, August 24, 1992.
8. Editorial, "Disabling America," *The Wall Street Journal*, July 24, 1992.
9. Paula Heeschen, "Disabilities Act Puts County Library in Bind," *Pocono Record*, Stroudsburg, PA, August 22, 1992.

Chapter 4

1. Gordon L. Crovitz, "Florida's Unconstitutional Return to Swampland," *The Wall Street Journal*, April 1, 1992.
2. Edward Bove, "Pouring $100,000 Down a Hole," *The Daily Record*, Morristown, NJ, January 19, 1992.

3. Ibid.
4. "What's Wrong with Superfund," National Paint and Coatings Association, Washington, DC.
5. Jim Florio, "Budget Quackery Mode—Mess of Cleanup Law," *The Record*, April 21, 1994, p. B-7.
6. Darrell Smith, "Wetlands, Confusion and Conflict," *The Farm Journal*, June/July 1991, p. 28.
7. Rich Henderson, "Is California 40% Wetlands," *The Wall Street Journal*, October 3, 1991.
8. Nicholas Veronis, "DEPE Hears Contrasting Views on Cooling Tower for Bayway Refinery," *The Star Ledger*, December 8, 1992, p. 54.
9. Ibid.
10. Keith Schneider, "How a Rebellion over Environmental Rules Grew from a Patch of Weeds," *The New York Times*, March 24, 1993, p. A-16. Copyright 1993, by The New York Times Company, reprinted by permission.
11. Jones-Blair Company, "NPCA, Improving Superfund," National Paint and Coatings Association, Washington, DC.
12. "Study Finds 33% of Cleanup Funds for Toxic Sites is Paid to Lawyers," *The Star Ledger*, November 5, 1993.
13. Ibid.
14. J. Scott Orr, "Cleaning Up Superfund," *The Star Ledger*, February 11, 1994, p. 25.
15. Bruce N. Ames and Lois Swirsky Gold, "Chemical Carcinogenesis: Too Many Rodent Carcinogens," Division of Biochemistry, University of California, Berkeley, CA, October 1990.
16. Jonathan M. Moses, "Trustees May be Liable for Costs of Pollution Clean Up, Judge Says," *The Wall Street Journal*, March 9, 1993, copyright Dow Jones & Company, Inc. All rights reserved worldwide.

17. "Environmental Liability Versus the Corporate Veil," Newsletter of the law firm of Wolff & Samson, Roseland, NJ, Vol. 4, No. 4, (Winter 1991), p. 2.
18. Ibid, p. 3.
19. Gordon Bishop, "Better Allocation of Governments Scarce Resources," *The Star Ledger*, September 29, 1993.
20. John J. Huryk, Letter, "To Whom It May Concern," dated July 14, 1993.
21. Michael Strizki, Letter to the Author, dated September 21, 1993.

Chapter 5

1. Tom Hayden, "Labor Leaders Say Glut of Rules Forces Firms out of State," *The Star Ledger*, August 19, 1992.
2. Ibid.
3. Center for the Study of American Business, "Study," St. Louis, MO, Washington University, 1992.
4. "Record 25 Million People on Food Stamp Roles," *The New York Times*, March 29, 1992.
5. John Whitlow, "Bureaucracy, Salaries Consume 25% of Hospital Bills Nationwide," *The Star Ledger*, August 5, 1993.
6. Alexander Milch, "Banker Says Over-Regulation Burdens Nation," *The Star Ledger*, February 28, 1993, Sect. III, p. 5.
7. David Littmann, "The Cost of Regulation, Counted in Jobs," *The Wall Street Journal*, April 21, 1992.
8. Michael Fumento, "The Hidden Cost of Regulation" *Investors Business Daily*, March 9, 1992, p. 1. Reprinted by permission of *Investors Business Daily, Inc.*
9. John S. DeMott, "California's Economic Crisis," *The Nations Business*, July 1993, p. 16. Quoted by permission *The Nations Business*, July 1993, copyright 1993, U.S. Chamber of Commerce.

10. Philip K. Verleger, "Clean Air Regulations and the L.A. Riots," *The Wall Street Journal*, June 5, 1993.
11. Peter Huber, "Who Will Protect Us from our Protectors," Forbes, July 13, 1987. Excerpted by permission of *Forbes Magazine*, July 13, 1987.
12. John S. DeMott, "California's Economic Crisis," *The Nations Business*, July 1993, p. 16. Quoted by permission *The Nations Business*, July 1993, copyright 1993, U.S. Chamber of Commerce.
13. Ibid.
14. Ibid.
15. Ibid.

Chapter 6

1. "Law Agencies Under Fire on Property Seizures," *Associated Press*, Wire story dated February 14, 1993. Reprinted by permission of the *Associated Press*.
2. Ibid.
3. Michael Winerip, "Tend a Garden, Pay the Price," *The New York Times*, July 12, 1992, p. 25.
4. Jon Nordheimer, "Seizure of Assets by an Aggressive Drug Fighter Raises Eyebrows," *The New York Times*, August 2, 1992, p. 37.
5. Michael Perone, "Forfeiting Too Much and From Too Few," Letter to the Editor, *The Star Ledger*, December 12, 1992, p. 26.
6. "Lose Your Property, Lose Your Freedom," Pacific Legal Foundation, *FLOC*, December/January 1994. Reprinted by permission from Fairness to Landowners Committee, Cambridge, MD, 21613.

7. Brian T. Murray, "Group Takes Aim at Police Seizure of Property," *The Sunday Star Ledger*, May 31, 1992.
8. Ibid.
9. Keith Schneider, "Families See Park Plan as Threat to the Land," *The New York Times*, August 2, 1992, p. 21. Copyright 1992, by the New York Times Company, reprinted by permission.
10. Sam Kazman, "Home, Not Alone," Competitive Enterprise Institute, Update, January 1994, p. 1.
11. Paul M. Barrett, "Supreme Court Supports Right of Landowner," *The Wall Street Journal*, July 1, 1992.
12. James Joseph, "Lucas Leaves Everybody Hanging," *The Competitive Enterprise Institute Update*, Washington, DC, July 1992, p. 6.
13. Wade Lambert, "Unusual Seizure Upsets Defense Lawyers," *The Wall Street Journal*, August 3, 1993, p. B5.
14. Editorial, "Justice for Whom?" *The Star Ledger*, December 2, 1993, p. 20.
15. Ibid.
16. Paul M. Barrett, "Justices Impose New Curbs on Use of Forfeiture Laws," *The Wall Street Journal*, December 14, 1993, p. B.10.

Chapter 7

1. Robert W. Gambino, Director Selective Service System, letter dated December 4, 1992.
2. Jack Elliot, "The DEPE has Gone Wild Says the Mayor of Linden," *New Jersey Business Advocate*, July 1992.
3. James Bovard, "Putting Nectarines in their Cuds," *The Washington Times*, Washington, DC, October 1, 1991.
4. Ibid.

5. News from Senator John P. Scott, Lyndhurst, NJ, May 12, 1993.
6. Charles C. Jowaiszas, "Bizarre Raid in Puerto Rico," *FLOC*, February 1993. Reprinted by permission from the Fairness to Landowners Committee, Cambridge, MD, 21613.
7. Robert Crum, "Justice Reserved," *Rutgers Magazine*, New Brunswick, NJ, Winter 1993, p. 22.
8. Guy Sterling, "Landano Gains Victory in Long Quest," *The Star Ledger*, February 26, 1994, p. 1.
9. R.W. Apple, Jr., "A Measure of Savagery," *The New York Times*, August 13, 1993, p. 1.
10. Ibid.
11. Kathryn Kahler, "Civil Liberties Caught in Drug War Crossfire," *The Star Ledger*, March 27, 1993, Sect. 3, p. 1.
12. Editorial, "Hiring Hell," *The Wall Street Journal*, March 9, 1993.
13. Ibid.

Chapter 8

1. Richard Cohen, "How Long Will America Continue to Regulate Everything—Except for Guns?" *The Philadelphia Inquirer*, July 10, 1993.
2. Gordon Bishop, "One Size Fits All Clean Air Rules," *The Star Ledger*, September 8, 1993.
3. "Critics Question Foley's Artsy, Expensive Capitol Renovations," *The Star Ledger*, January 28, 1992, p. 8.
4. Dean Foust, "Lost in Space, Uncle Sam's Crazy Building Spree," *Business Week*, February 14, 1994, p. 62.
5. Stephen C. Glazier, "Tax Bill: Retroactive Unconstitutional," *The Wall Street Journal*, August 5, 1993.

6. Miles Benson, "Congress Using Taxpayer Money to Ignore Voice from Home," *The Star Ledger*, February 3, 1992.

Chapter 9

1. "Quiet, Testing in Progress," *Jems* Magazine, Carlsbad, CA, June 1993, p. 82. Reprinted with permission of *Jems*, copyright June 1993, Jems Communications, P.O. Box 2789, Carlsbad, CA, 92018.
2. Mary F. Windisch, Eastern Pennsylvania Emergency Medical Services Council, Allentown, PA, July 2, 1993, letter to the author.
3. Peter Brimelow and Leslie Spencer, "Food and Drug Politics," *Forbes Magazine*, November 22, 1993, p. 115. Excerpted by permission of Forbes Magazine, (c) Forbes, Inc., 1993.
4. Ibid.

Chapter 10

1. Colliers Encyclopedia, "Constitution of the United States," 1988, p. 235.

Chapter 11

1. Wallace R. Wirths, "Democracy, The Myth, The Reality," *Media Specialists*, Sussex, NJ, 1993.
2. Ben Lieberman, "What's So Bad About CFCs," *Machine Design Magazine* (October 22, 1993), p. 35.
3. Philip H. Abelson, "Unfunded Federal Environmental Mandates," *Science*, 262 (November 19, 1993), p. 1191.
4. Gordon Bishop, "Taking a Look at the Quality of Today's Life," *The Star Ledger*, October 27, 1993.

5. Richard Miniter, "Asset Forfeiture Laws Abused by Law Enforcement," *Intellectual Ammunition*, copyright the Heartland Institute, November/December 1993, p. 25.